MAY 28 2015

W9-CMZ-965

Praise for
Questions for Christians

"In a world where many people think they have to search on their own for an ultimate meaning of life, John Morreall offers a compelling alternative: remain Christian but understand Christianity through contemporary, postmodern eyes. The book insists it is not only legitimate but essential to ask questions, and faith without questions is not really faith. Students and questioning Christians of all ages need to read this book."

—Frederick J. Parrella, Santa Clara University

"John Morreall's new book is a reexamination of Christian doctrine from a critical, historical-political perspective that aims at revealing how Greek-speaking theologians and Roman rulers distorted the message of Jesus and how this distortion was continued, rather than corrected, by succeeding generations of Christians. We have a book that will provoke diverse intellectual and theological reactions and discussions, which is always much valued in theological scholarship."

**—Najib George Awad, Hartford Seminary;
author of *God Without a Face?***

"By the device of articulating apparently simple or even naive questions of the Christian tradition and then answering them in a way which is informed without being academic—and radical in the sense of getting back to basics—Morreall has written a lively book that will inform and challenge those seeking to discover whether Jesus has good news for today. While he offers many points of sharp critique, he also helps the reader find hope in traditional structures. He also offers, in his ten tenets, a metric for measuring spiritual authenticity which is both astringent and insightful. Thus he provides a prophetic critique for our time and invites his readers to the kind of new life that flows from truthful interpretation and simple response to Jesus' life and witness."

**—Stephen Cherry, director, Ministerial Development and
Parish Support, Diocese of Durham, UK**

QUESTIONS FOR CHRISTIANS

The Surprising Truths behind Basic Beliefs

John Morreall

ROWMAN & LITTLEFIELD
Lanham • Boulder • New York • Toronto • Plymouth, UK

Published by Rowman & Littlefield
4501 Forbes Boulevard, Suite 200, Lanham, Maryland 20706
www.rowman.com

10 Thornbury Road, Plymouth PL6 7PP, United Kingdom

Unless noted otherwise, quotations from the Bible are from the New Revised Standard Version.

British Library Cataloguing in Publication Information Available

Library of Congress Cataloging-in-Publication Data
Morreall, John, 1947–
Questions for Christians : the surprising truths behind basic beliefs / John Morreall.
pages cm.
Includes bibliographical references and index.
ISBN 978-1-4422-2317-2 (cloth : alk. paper) — ISBN 978-1-4422-2318-9 (electronic)
1. Theology, Doctrinal—Miscellanea. 2. Theology, Doctrinal—Popular works. I. Title.
BT77.M86 2014
230—dc23
2014003497

∞ ™ The paper used in this publication meets the minimum requirements of American National Standard for Information Sciences Permanence of Paper for Printed Library Materials, ANSI/NISO Z39.48-1992.

Printed in the United States of America

For Tamara, who's always got great questions

CONTENTS

1

WHY ASK QUESTIONS?

As children, most of us asked lots of questions. Some still do, but many ask fewer and fewer as we get older. In matters of religion, asking questions can make people feel uncomfortable. Some think that it shows a lack of commitment to one's religion, even a lack of faith.

Many Christians today think of their religion as including a complete set of truths provided by the scriptures and church traditions. So to determine the truth about any issue, all anyone has to do is check the Bible and church doctrines. These people assume there are no religious questions that haven't already been answered once and for all, so the only Christian who might need to ask a question is someone who hasn't looked up that bit of information in her Bible or creed. Like a geometry student who skipped the homework asking a question in class, she would already know the answer if she had read the book.

This simple way of thinking about Christianity as having a uniform set of truths started early. In the second and third centuries, church fathers such as Irenaeus, Origen, and Tertullian emphasized that the church was *catholic*, that is, universal. God had revealed one body of truths and so, Irenaeus wrote,

> No matter how different the languages of the world, the contents of tradition are the same everywhere, and neither the churches found in Germany have another faith or another tradition, nor those in Spain, Iberia, Gaul, nor those in the East, Egypt, and so forth; but as God's sun is one and the same for the whole world, so the preaching of the truth enlightens all men who are willing to see the truth.[1]

Vincent of Lérin (d. 434) said that the teaching of the church is what has been believed "everywhere, always, and by all."[2]

A. TWO SOURCES OF QUESTIONS: DISAGREEMENT AND CHANGE

If there really were such timeless, uniform teaching and belief among Christians, then there might be no need for them to ask questions, except for the geometry-class kind. The history of Christianity, however, shows that there has never been a uniform set of beliefs accepted "everywhere, always, and by all." From the beginning, Christian groups have disagreed with each other, and over the centuries groups have changed their own beliefs. Where two people have contrary beliefs, they can't both be right. And where a group changes from one belief to a contrary belief, the old belief and the new belief can't both be right. In both cases, it's reasonable to ask questions.

Most Christians know about the split between Roman Catholics and Protestants in the 1500s, but fewer are familiar with the split between Roman Catholics and the Greek Orthodox five centuries earlier. Around 1100, Anselm of Canterbury wrote *Cur Deus Homo* (*Why the God-Man*), a book in which he proposed a new explanation of salvation, the atonement theory. The death of Jesus on the cross, he said, was a payment to God for sin that allowed God to forgive humans and let them into heaven. Today many Christians think of the atonement theory as obviously correct, but before Anselm it hadn't been worked out. Most theologians before 1100 taught that the death of Jesus was a payment to Satan that got him to release the human race from bondage to him. We'll explore these ideas in chapter 5, but the point here is that starting around 1100, Roman Catholics changed their beliefs about salvation to the atonement theory. And by then the Greek Orthodox had already broken away from the Roman church, so they never adopted the atonement theory. That theory, then, is not something believed "everywhere, always, and by all."

The earliest disagreements between Christians go back a thousand years before the Catholic-Orthodox split, to the first Christians. They had contrary ideas about the movement they were starting. Some thought of themselves as a kind of Jews, and so required men joining the group to be circumcised. Paul and others thought of the movement as open to everyone and did not require circumcision. Right at the beginning of the movement, then, Christians faced the question "Do the followers of Jesus have to be Jews?"

In the second, third, and fourth centuries, questions and disagreements between Christians increased as the movement spread into what is today Syria, Turkey, Greece, and Western Europe, all of which were part of the Roman Empire. In those centuries, too, as we'll see, Greek philosophy and Roman politics changed Christianity in big ways, so that by the fifth century, Christians were teaching and doing things that Jesus would have questioned. To understand those changes, we need a basic understanding of what Jesus taught and did.

B. IN THE BEGINNING: JESUS AND THE KINGDOM OF GOD

In the Gospels, Jesus' preaching and actions are centered on the "Kingdom of God," which he also calls the "Kingdom of Heaven." The word "kingdom" here can be misleading because it sounds like a geographical place or the government of a place. The Greek word is *basilea*, which means rule or reign. The Kingdom of God doesn't mean a place or the government of a place. It means the rule or reign of God—a world in which people live the way God wants them to. As John Dominic Crossan says, "The Kingdom of God is what the world would be if God were directly and immediately in charge."[3] Jesus' primary teaching, from which most others flow, is that God expects two things of us—to love him and to love other people. We can call this the Love Ethic of Jesus. When he was asked which commandment was the greatest, he answered with two: "'You shall love the Lord your God with all your heart, with all your soul, and with all your mind.' . . . 'You shall love your neighbor as yourself.' On these two commandments hang all the law and the prophets" (Matthew 22:37–40).

"Love" has somewhat different meanings in these two commandments. To love God is to worship him and do his will. To love your neighbors is to show concern for their well-being and happiness.

Jesus did not invent these commandments—they can be found in Deuteronomy 6:5 and Leviticus 19:18, among other places. But he added to them new ways to understand "God" and "neighbor." While many Jews in the first century thought of God as an aloof, powerful lawgiver in the sky, Jesus called him Abba, "Father," and said that God loves us as his children. So we in turn should love God as "Our Father"—the first words of the Lord's Prayer. Neighbor, the literal meaning of which was the same as now, Jesus changed to mean people in general—the whole world.

In Jesus' preaching and in his life, there are several recurring themes. Had his disciples included a philosopher who could express his worldview and guidelines for living, they would have looked something like the following Ten Tenets.

Tenet 1. Love Ethic: Love God and Love All People

In criticizing the things that interfere with loving God and other persons, Jesus singled out material possessions. He preached against wealth, as in "It is easier for a camel to pass through the eye of a needle than for someone who is rich to enter the kingdom of God" (Matthew 19:24). He advised even poor people, "Do not worry, saying, 'What will we eat?' or 'What will we drink?' or 'What will we wear?' . . . But strive first for the kingdom of God and his righteousness, and all these things will be given to you as well" (Matthew 6:31–33). In other words, put your time and energy into helping people, and trust in God to provide for your daily needs. Jesus' own life shows this attitude. As far as we know, as an adult, he never had a job or home, and he spent most of his time helping people.

Tenet 2. God's Children: All Human Beings Are Brothers and Sisters, with God as Their Father

It is from mother, father, sisters, and brothers that most of us first learned about love. So Jesus uses the metaphor of family to explain the love he is talking about. He refers to God as Abba, Father, and speaks of all people as "children of your father in heaven" (Matthew 5:45) in order to evoke deep, early feelings of love.

Tenet 3. Equality: Each Person Counts the Same

Caring about everyone the way you care about your sisters and brothers was a surprising idea to Jesus' listeners. The hundreds of laws they had grown up with distinguished between how they should treat fellow Jews and how they should treat gentiles (non-Jews), and what was owed to men versus women and children. As in most ancient cultures, Jewish law was tribalistic—it favored fellow Jews and allowed harsh treatment of outsiders. The Amalek tribe, for example, attacked the Hebrews as they escaped from Egypt, and so even today, three thousand years later, some of the 613 laws followed by Orthodox Jews command the slaughter of not just every Amalek man, woman, and child, but all their oxen, sheep, camels, and donkeys (Deuteronomy 25:19; see Exodus 17:14; Numbers 24:20).

Jewish law was also patriarchal and sexist, giving men and women different rights and obligations. Young children had no rights, so infanticide was fairly common, especially with girls. In his reinterpretation of "Love your neighbor," Jesus transcends all such distinctions, counting each person—Jew or gentile, male or female, old or young—as equal to the others. His heart and hands go out to Samaritans (a group hated by most Jews) and Romans as well as Jews, and to women as well as men. He cures a Samaritan leper (Luke 17:16) and the servant of a Roman military officer (Matthew 8:5–13; Luke 7:1–10). In our child-centered culture, Jesus' attitude toward the little children being brought to him may seem merely "nice," but to the disciples pushing the children and their parents away, it was revolutionary:

> The disciples spoke sternly to them. But when Jesus saw this, he was indignant and said to them, "Let the little children come to me; do not stop them; for it is to such as these that the kingdom of God belongs. Truly I tell you, whoever does not receive the kingdom of God as a little child will never enter it" (Mark 10:14–15).

Tenet 4. Socialism: From Each According to Their Ability, to Each According to Their Needs

A family is not a merit-based system in which people receive benefits in proportion to their contributions. If that were the case, newborn babies, with nothing to contribute, would quickly starve. Instead, parents contribute most of the work and children receive most of the benefits. Eventually, most children will contribute, such as by doing chores or caring for younger ones, but a disabled child who cannot contribute should be loved just as much. And so, in Jesus' metaphor of God's family, we are supposed to distribute goods to those who need them without asking what they have contributed.

The Gospel of John refers twice to "the common purse" of Jesus and his apostles—the Greek word means bag—in which they pooled their money (12:6; 13:29). The Acts of the Apostles describes the first Christians as socialists.

> Now the whole group of those who believed were of one heart and soul, and no one claimed private ownership of any possessions, but everything they owned was held in common. . . . There was not a needy person among them, for as many as owned lands or houses sold them and brought the proceeds of what was sold. They laid it at the apostles' feet, and it was distributed to each as any had need (Acts 4:32, 34–35; see Acts 2:44–45).

Many people today, particularly in the United States, bristle at the very word "socialism" because they equate it with big government interfering in their lives. But early Christian socialism had nothing to do with the government. Jesus, in fact, was opposed to the kind of government resented today—leaders telling nonleaders what to do. Instead he preached the kind of leadership that you would expect in a loving family.

Tenet 5. Servant Leadership: Leading People Should Not Be Dominating Them, but Serving Them

The Gospel of Luke tells us that at the last Passover dinner he ate with his apostles,

> A dispute also arose among them as to which one of them was to be regarded as the greatest. But he said to them, "The kings of the Gentiles lord it over them . . . But not so with you; rather the greatest among you must become like the youngest, and the leader like one who serves. . . . But I am among you as one who serves" (Luke 22:24–27).

That night he showed what his new kind of leadership looked like, by washing the apostles' feet, even those of Judas, who was about to betray him (John 13:3–5).

Tenet 6. Festivity: Celebrate Your Loving Relationships

All of the concern for other people in Jesus' Love Ethic may sound like it would leave us unfulfilled personally, but think about it. Not only are you taking care of other people's needs, but they are taking care of yours at the same time. In a family or a circle of friends, this mutual care is more fulfilling than struggling to achieve some merely personal goal. Our caring about each other is something to celebrate, as at birthday parties and wedding banquets.

In ancient times, as now, sharing a meal was the basic way people showed that they cared about one another. In both Jesus' preaching and his life, when people want to enjoy each other's company, they have a feast. His Last Supper was a Passover meal with his friends.

The party or banquet is one of Jesus' images for the Kingdom of God, as in Matthew 8:11, Luke 14:15–24, and Luke 22:29–30. In the parable of the prodigal son, when the wayward young man came home after squandering his inheritance, his father "ran and put his arms around him and kissed him" and then told his servants to "get the fatted calf and kill it, and let us eat and celebrate" (Luke 15:20–23).

The Gospels describe Jesus as willing to eat with just about anyone of goodwill. His critics asked his disciples, "Why does your teacher eat with tax collectors and sinners?" (Matthew 9:11), and they called him "a glutton and a drunkard, a friend of tax collectors and sinners" (Matthew 11:19).

In the Gospel of John 2:1–11, Jesus' first miracle is at a wedding party where the wine had run out. He told the servants to fill six stone water jars, each holding twenty to thirty gallons. When they then took some to the chief steward, it had turned into superb wine. Six jars each holding twenty to thirty gallons—that's 120–180 gallons! To keep the math simple, suppose that there were 120–180 people celebrating at the wedding feast. That's a gallon of superb wine each for people who had already been drinking! Jesus was clearly not a sourpuss who didn't know how to have a good time. His Love Ethic was not some tedious mechanical law that interfered with human fulfillment—it was a recipe for human fulfillment.

Tenet 7. Antilegalism: Minimize the Number of Rules, and Apply Them Flexibly to Benefit People

As we have seen, the way of living Jesus preached was based on love of God and love of people. That Love Ethic doesn't eliminate traditional commandments like "Keep holy the Sabbath day" and "You shall not steal," but it treats them as guidelines for loving people, not as absolute laws to be obeyed no matter what. In first-century Palestine, the Mosaic law—the hundreds of laws in the Jewish scriptures—were often venerated as sacred in themselves, to be followed whether or not they benefited anyone. Jesus, however, saw laws as valuable only when they helped people.

So, for instance, when his followers were criticized for picking grain to eat on the Sabbath, he said, "The Sabbath was made for humankind, and not humankind for the Sabbath" (Mark 2:23–28). In a similar way, he ignored several purity laws because he saw no one benefiting from them. Jesus reduced the 613 traditional laws to: love God and love other people. And those two norms are so general that they are not laws to be enforced, but moral ideals. Paul Tillich wrote that "the law of love is the ultimate law because it is the negation of law." Joseph Fletcher was clearer when he said that in the Gospels "Love replaces law . . . We follow law, if at all, for love's sake."[4] Paul even wrote, in his Letter to the Romans 10:4, that "Christ is the end of the law."

Tenet 8. Divine Judgment: God Alone Is Judge

While "The kings of the Gentiles lord it over them" (Luke 22:25), creating laws and judging and punishing them when they disobey, Jesus told his followers not to judge and punish each other. At the end of the world, he said, God will judge and punish or reward everyone. Until then, the parable of the wheat and the weeds applies. God is like the master of the estate who told his servants not to uproot the weeds, but instead "Let both of them grow together until the harvest; and at harvest time I will tell the reapers, Collect the weeds first and bind them in bundles to be burned, but gather the wheat into my barn" (See Matthew 13:24–30, 36–43). This lesson is reinforced by Luke 6:37: "Do not judge, and you will not be judged; do not condemn, and you will not be condemned. Forgive, and you will be forgiven" (see Matthew 7:1–2).

Tenet 9. Forgiveness: Be Ready to Forgive Anyone for Anything

Instead of judging and punishing people, Jesus said to forgive them. When Peter asks how many times he should forgive—"as many as seven times?"—Jesus tells him, "Seventy-seven times," or in some ancient manuscripts, "seventy times seven times." As with the love of enemies, he ties forgiveness to the way God acts. The line in the Lord's Prayer is "Forgive us our debts, as we also have forgiven our debtors" (Matthew 6:12). A striking example in Jesus' life was when he was hanging on the cross and said, "Father forgive them; for they do not know what they are doing" (Luke 23:34).

Tenet 10. Pacifism: "Do Not Resist an Evildoer" (Matthew 5:39)

If you're familiar with the Sermon on the Mount, you know the next line: "But if anyone strikes you on the right cheek, turn the other also." In the violent ancient world, this pacifism seemed absurd to Jews and Romans alike. They believed in retaliation. Jewish and Roman legal systems treated justice for wrongdoing as tit for tat: "fracture for fracture, eye for eye, tooth for tooth; the injury inflicted is the injury to be suffered" (Leviticus 24:20). This is called the law of talion.

A few verses after saying "Do not resist an evildoer," Jesus goes even further with his pacifism: "Love your enemies and pray for those who persecute you, so that you may be children of your Father in heaven; for he makes his sun rise on the evil and on the good, and sends rain on the righteous and on the unrighteous" (Matthew 5:44–45).

A good example of pacifism in Jesus' own life was the way he did not resist arrest by the Romans, telling Peter to "Put your sword back into its place; for all who take the sword will perish by the sword" (Matthew 26:52). The first three centuries of Christians followed Jesus' example, becoming famous in the Roman Empire for not fighting back and not allowing soldiers to join their group. As John Driver notes in his book *How Christians Made Peace with War*, "Between [CE] 100 and 312 no Christian writers, to our knowledge, approved of Christian participation in warfare. In fact, all those who wrote on the subject disapproved of the practice."5

Analyzing what Jesus said and did by formulating these tenets is more precise than he was, because, as we'll see, he expressed himself in oral patterns rather than written patterns. He didn't define the words he used, and often he spoke in metaphors, parables, hyperbole (exaggeration), and other figures of speech, rather than literally. Nonetheless, I think that Jesus would agree that these guidelines capture what he was doing and what he was preaching.

Among the Ten Tenets, the first, the Love Ethic, is central. A good place to see its importance to Jesus is in his description of how everyone will be judged at the end of the world:

> Then the king [Jesus Christ] will say to those at his right hand, "Come, you that are blessed by my Father, inherit the kingdom prepared for you from the foundation of the world; for I was hungry and you gave me food, I was thirsty and you gave me something to drink, I was a stranger and you welcomed me, I was naked and you gave me clothing, I was sick and you took care of me, I was in prison and you visited me (Matthew 25:34–36).

Jesus says that when these people ask, "Lord, when was it that we saw you hungry and gave you food, or thirsty and gave you something to drink?" the king will tell them, "Just as you did it to one of the least of these who are members of my family, you did it to me" (Matthew 25:40). His treatment of the human race as one family, and identification of himself with the poorest among them, emphasize the supreme value of loving concern for other people.

The first generations of Christians took Jesus' words and example to heart. He had told them, "By this everyone will know that you are my disciples, if you have love for one another" (John 13:35), and that was how Christians came to be known in the Roman Empire. Women had prominent roles, gentiles soon outnumbered Jews, and the basic ritual was a celebratory meal, the Eucharist. One document that shows what early Christians thought of as important in their new movement is the *Didache*, also called *The Teachings of the Twelve Apostles*. Written around the year 100, it was used to instruct people who were going to be baptized. The first section quotes extensively from Jesus' Sermon on the Mount:

> There are two ways: one of life and one of death; and the difference between the two ways is great. The way of life is this: first, you should love God, who made you; secondly, love your neighbor as yourself; and whatever things you do not desire to be done to you, do not do them to someone else. Now the words of this teaching are this: Bless those who curse you and pray for your enemies, and fast for those who are persecuting you. For what credit is it if you love those who love you? Do not the Gentiles do the same thing? But love those hating you, and you will not have an enemy. Keep yourself from fleshly and bodily cravings. If anyone hits you on the right cheek, turn the other one to him also. And you will be acting maturely. If someone should force you to go one mile, go with him two. If someone takes your coat, give him your shirt also. If anyone should take from you what is yours, do not demand that he give it back, for you cannot. Give to everyone asking you and do not refuse.[6]

After this first section outlining "the Way of Life," the *Didache* has two other main sections, on rituals and church organization, but there is no section on theological doctrines such as the Trinity and the atonement. Doctrines, and the enforcement of their acceptance, would come centuries later. For the first Christians, as for Jesus, what was essential was loving God and loving people. To follow Jesus was to live a certain way— "the way of life," the *Didache* calls it.

C. TURNING CHRISTIANITY INTO A SET OF DOCTRINES

Thanks to the missionary work of Paul and others, more and more non-Jews joined the group, until in the second century it became distinct from Judaism. Then non-Jewish Christians trained in Greek philosophy began speculating on who Jesus was and how he was related to God, using Greek philosophical concepts that were not found in the Hebrew tradition of Jesus. Their writings about Jesus and God became the first Christian theology. The documents they produced were written to look like the philosophical tracts of the day. Using the vocabulary of popular Greek philosophies, these theologians presented their versions of Christianity as philosophies that could compete with Stoicism, Neo-Platonism, and Epicureanism. Justin Martyr (100–65), the first well-known Christian theologian, was fond of comparing Christian ideas to those of Greek philosophers, especially Socrates.

An important center of early Christian theology was Alexandria, Egypt, where the study of Greek philosophy flourished. Around 185 Christians there started a school for catechumens (teachers who prepared people for baptism). The first head of that school, Pantaenus, had been a Stoic philosopher. His successor, Clement (150–215), had been a pagan trained in the thought of Plato, Aristotle, Pythagoras, and Zeno the Stoic. Clement tried to bring together Platonic ideas about God and human beings with ideas in the New Testament. Christianity and Platonism were in essential agreement, he said, adding that Greek philosophers had been inspired by God. Just as God had given the law to the Hebrews to bring them to Christ, so God had given philosophy to the Greeks.

Clement's combining Christianity with Greek philosophy produced some ideas that Jesus and the first Christians would have questioned. Clement taught, for example, that matter and thought are eternal, and thus did not originate from God. He also accepted an idea of the philosopher Heraclitus that there were cosmic cycles *before* the creation of the world.

Origen (185–254), a student of Clement, succeeded him as head of the school in Alexandria in the early third century. Even more than Clement, he taught that Christianity was a philosophy superior to Greek philosophy, and that biblical revelation and Greek learning were compatible. Origen was especially fond of neo-Platonism, the last major movement in Greek philosophy. Its leading exponent at the time was Plotinus (204–269), who taught that God transcends all things and so is inaccessible to creatures. God generates a son, called the Logos, who is God's perfect image. Through the Logos, God creates an infinite world of pure spirits free to love and be loved. Some of them love less than they should, however, and so they "fall"—they are imprisoned in bodies of varying degrees of physicality. Least fallen are the good angels: they have the lightest bodies. Furthest fallen are the demons: they have heavy, ugly bodies. In between the good angels and the devils are humans. We return to God, Plotinus said, by liberating ourselves from our bodies.

As with his teacher Clement, Origen's combining of Greek philosophy with Christianity led to ideas that Jesus would have questioned.

Origen's idea that the souls of human beings existed before they were born, for example, is contrary to Jesus' teaching about the resurrection at the end of the world, and to the biblical understanding of human life.

Already by 254, the year Origen died, some theologians had made major changes to Jesus' teachings about God and human beings. Following Plato and Plotinus, they said that God transcends the world—he is infinitely above it and so is unknowable to creatures. Christian thinkers were also beginning to accept Plato's *dualism*. Dualism is the belief that a human being is two things: a physical body that can die, and a nonphysical soul/mind/spirit that is naturally immune from death. Dualism ranks the body as the inferior and more evil part of a human being that pulls down the soul/mind/spirit. None of these ideas were taught by Jesus, but within a few centuries, they became standard Christian teaching. By the early fifth century, Augustine of Hippo (354–430), who influenced virtually every Western theologian after him, would define a human being as "a rational soul using a mortal and earthly body."[7] That definition would have puzzled Jesus, who saw a human being as one thing, not two.

Once Christians accepted dualistic thinking, thinking of the body as evil and in need of discipline by the soul, many were attracted to asceticism—withdrawing from society to live as hermits or monks. Jesus never recommended that way of living, but it became popular starting in the fourth century. A century earlier Origen had so absorbed this rejection of the body that he castrated himself.

Jesus would have questioned all these Greek ideas being taught by people claiming to be his followers. So did Tertullian (160–225), a Christian thinker from Carthage in North Africa, in the western part of the Roman Empire. His famous question was "What has Athens to do with Jerusalem?" By that he meant, "What does Greek philosophy have to do with the biblical tradition of Christianity?" Tertullian's answer was that philosophy is not of use to Christians. He argued that Saint Paul

> expressly names *philosophy* as that which he would have us be on our guard against. Writing to the Colossians, he says, "See that no one beguile you through philosophy and vain deceit, after the tradition of men, and contrary to the wisdom of the Holy Ghost." He had been at Athens, and had in his interviews [with its philosophers] become acquainted with that human wisdom which pretends to know the truth, while it only corrupts it, and is itself divided into its

own manifold heresies, by the variety of its mutually repugnant sects. What indeed has Athens to do with Jerusalem? What concord is there between the Academy and the Church? What between heretics and Christians?"[8]

D. TURNING CHRISTIANITY INTO THE STATE RELIGION OF THE ROMAN EMPIRE

In the second through fourth centuries, as we said, two things changed Christianity in big ways: Greek philosophy and Roman politics. Having seen how Greek philosophy was the foundation for Christian theology, we can now consider how Roman emperors manipulated Christian leaders for their own political ends, using theological beliefs as a test for membership in the church and then for Roman citizenship. As bishops and popes submitted to Roman political authority, too, they came to model themselves on governors and emperors. That way of thinking can still be seen in the last absolute monarchy in the West: the Vatican State, ruled by the pope. Today the land over which the pope rules is small, but before 1870 the Papal States were double the size of Massachusetts.

Early in the 300s, a time of widespread social disorder, the Roman emperor Constantine was attracted by the cooperation and discipline he saw in Christian communities. In 313 he reversed centuries of persecution by making Christianity legal. In 319 he issued an edict exempting Christian clergy from taxation, and in 321 he proclaimed Sunday a holiday throughout the empire. He paid Christian clergy salaries and exempted them from military service; he gave lay Christians preference for government jobs.

These and other favors were not mere altruism on the emperor's part. Constantine hoped that this religion could bring new life and unity to his failing empire. If Christianity was going to unify the Roman Empire, though, it had to be unified itself. For Constantine that meant it had to have a uniform set of beliefs. So in 325 he summoned Christian leaders to the town of Nicaea, just south of his imperial capital Constantinople (City of Constantine), in what is now northwestern Turkey. His charge to them was to produce an official set of answers to questions like these: Was Jesus a man? Was he the Son of God? Was he

God? At the Council of Nicaea and at three more after that—Constantinople in 381, Ephesus in 431, and Chalcedon in 451—Christian leaders formulated answers.

The most important questions the bishops at Nicaea asked were about the relation between Jesus Christ and God. The view that received the most votes was that Jesus Christ and God the Father are *homoousios*, "of the same substance." But there were other views, most famously that of Arius (256–336) of Alexandria, Egypt, who said that Jesus Christ was created by God the Father and so was not equal to him. That idea can be supported by Jesus' saying in the Gospel of John 14:28, "the Father is greater than I." In the decades after the council, the minority view was often expressed by saying that Jesus Christ and God the Father are *homoiousios*, "of a similar substance," rather than *homoousios*, "of the same substance."

The majority view at Nicaea—that Jesus Christ and God the Father are *homoousios*—became part of the Nicene Creed, and was promulgated by Emperor Constantine. From then on, anyone claiming to be a Christian was required to believe that Jesus Christ and God the Father are *homoousios*, and believe all the other claims in the creed. Anyone who didn't, such as Arius, was a heretic deserving of punishment. Being a Christian was now defined not by the way people *live*, but by the theological doctrines they *believe*.

This new definition of Christianity was quite different from Jesus' preaching about the Kingdom of God, which was based on love. There is nothing in the Nicene Creed about love of God or love of neighbor. Making the creed even more different from Jesus' teaching was its political motivation. It was Emperor Constantine who announced that Christians had to have an official list of beliefs, and he did that because he wanted Christianity to unite his failing empire. It was he who called the bishops together and officially announced their documents. It was he who determined which people were heretics, and he who exiled them.

Decisions about which beliefs would be included in the creeds were political, too, since only the leaders who came to the councils could vote on what went into the creeds. In his book *Voting about God in Early Church Councils*, Yale historian Ramsay MacMullen explains how political that voting process was.[9] Of the first eight church councils, between 325 and 870, four were held in the imperial capital Constantinople (today's Istanbul, Turkey). That city is 850 miles from Rome, and farther from the more western parts of the Western Roman Empire. Two more church councils were held in Nicaea, just south of Constantinople, and one in Chalcedon, just north of Constantinople. At the first meeting in Nicaea, there were three hundred delegates, but only six from the western part of the empire.[10] One hundred bishops came from Asia Minor, where Nicaea was located, seventy from nearby Syria and Phoenicia, and twenty from Palestine and Egypt. At the second council in Constantinople in 381, no bishops at all from the western part of the empire attended.

Not only were delegates from farther away less likely to travel to the councils, but the whole activity of analyzing Christian beliefs philosophically to create doctrines was largely a Greek passion not shared by Latin-speaking Christians in Rome and the western part of the empire. One eastern theologian, Gregory of Nyssa, described how everyone around Constantinople seemed to be caught up in theological debates:

> The whole city is full of it, the squares, the market places, the crossroads, the alleyways; old-clothes men, money changers, food sellers: they are all busy arguing. If you ask someone to give you change, he philosophizes about the Begotten and the Unbegotten; if you inquire about the price of a loaf, you are told by way of reply that the Father is greater and the Son inferior; if you ask "Is my bath ready?" the attendant answers that the Son was made out of nothing.[11]

This kind of theological debating was not popular in Rome or the Western part of the Roman Empire. Early Christian theology was created largely by Greek-speakers familiar with Greek philosophy living in the eastern part of the empire.

As with other political decisions, the emperor's approval of a creed didn't have to be permanent. Three years after Constantine proclaimed the Nicene Creed, he changed his mind, called Arius back from exile, and from then on supported bishops who opposed the Nicene Creed he had commissioned. Arius was cleared of the conviction of heresy in 335 at the First Synod of Tyre, but was recondemned after his death by the First Council of Constantinople in 381. In 336 Emperor Constantine exiled Athanasius, the leader of the majority at the council of Nicaea, and in 337 Constantine was finally baptized—as an Arian Christian rather than a Nicene Christian. His sons were Arians, too, and several succeeding emperors were sympathetic to Arianism.

In the five decades after Constantine's Council of Nicaea, Roman emperors appointed Christians to political positions, gave bishops money and favors, provided basilicas (Roman public buildings) for use as churches, and generally integrated Christianity into the political structure of the empire. In 380 Emperor Theodosius declared Christianity to be the state religion of the empire. Then in 392 he decreed:

> From now on no one . . . shall anywhere or in any city sacrifice an innocent [animal] victim to a senseless image. He shall not venerate with fire the household deity by a more private offering, as it were the spirit of the house of the Penates [family gods of the household], and burn lights, place incense, or hang up garlands. If anyone undertakes by way of sacrifice to slay a victim or to consult with smoking entrails, let him, as guilty of treason, receive the appropriate sentence. [12]

Anyone caught venerating one of the old Roman deities with incense or garlands, Theodosius said, "shall be punished by the loss of that house or possession in which he worshipped according to the heathen superstition. All places that smoke with incense, if they are proved to belong to those who burn the incense, shall be confiscated." Someone who worships a non-Christian god on someone else's property or on public property will "be compelled to pay a fine of twenty-five pounds of gold." [13]

Christianity was now the required religion in the Roman Empire, and the defining feature of a Christian was not whether a person loved God and loved other people—Jesus' criterion—but whether they agreed with the theological claims in the Nicene Creed. Emperor Theodosius outlawed Arian Christianity and other nonapproved beliefs as heresy, a crime equivalent to treason. The first heresy trial to end in execution was just five years later, when the Roman authorities beheaded Priscillian, a Christian bishop from Ávila, in what is now Spain, and six of his followers.

E. WHAT WOULD JESUS DO?

A great deal had changed in the 350 years between Jesus' preaching the Kingdom of God and the beheading of Bishop Priscillian. Jesus' message of loving God and neighbor had been largely replaced by a philosophy that was then made the state religion of a brutal empire. What might Jesus have done had he appeared in the Roman Empire in 385? If he were at the beheading of Bishop Priscillian, it's reasonable to think he would have stopped it, as he blocked the trial and execution of the woman taken in adultery (John 7:53–8:11).

Jesus would probably also have had questions for the bishops who had married Christianity to the Roman Empire, questions such as: What were you *thinking*? It was the Roman Empire that had tortured him to death on a cross. He was hailed as the Messiah, and the Messiah was supposed to liberate the people of Israel from their oppressors—in his time, that was the Roman army occupying Palestine. After Jesus was gone, the Roman Empire continued to oppress his friends and relatives, and others living in Judea and Galilee. In the year 70, Roman armies destroyed the temple in Jerusalem and a good part of the city, dispersing the people who lived there. In 130, Emperor Hadrian drove the Jews out of Jerusalem and built a Roman colony in its place, naming it after himself. In the first through early fourth centuries, Roman emperors executed thousands of Christians, starting with leaders like Peter and Paul. Nero was the first to execute Christians, in 64 to 68, blaming Christians for the Great Fire in Rome. The Roman historian Tacitus described Nero's cruelty: "Besides being put to death they [the Christians] were made to serve as objects of amusement; they were clad in the hides of beast and torn to death by dogs; others were crucified, others set on fire to serve to illuminate the night when daylight failed."[14] Starting with Emperor Nero, being a Christian was a crime punishable by death in the Roman Empire.

The time when Emperor Constantine began favoring Christians was just a few years after the reign of Emperor Diocletian, who had killed at least three thousand Christians. So it's not surprising that the survivors were pleased with the change of leaders. But, as we said, Constantine's motives were political rather than religious. That's obvious in the traditional story about how he came to favor Christians, told in *The Life of Constantine*, written by Bishop Eusebius of Caesarea. In 312, as Constantine was preparing for battle against his coemperor Maxentius, he had a vision of the Greek letters chi and rho (the first two letters of "Christ"), with the words "In this sign you will conquer." At first the emperor didn't understand the vision, but then in a dream Christ advised him to use the power of the chi-rho symbol against his enemies. So Constantine made the symbol of Christ into a military banner, and he won the battle. Now the sole emperor, Constantine ordered that the head of the dead Maxentius be chopped off and paraded through the streets on a pike to celebrate this victory.

Jesus would have been surprised to hear that he had helped Constantine defeat and slaughter his coemperor. He would have been astounded to read Bishop Eusebius's praise of Constantine as a hero blessed by God in his many military campaigns. According to Eusebius, God had held

> him up to the human race as an instructive example of godliness. Accordingly, by the manifold blessings he has conferred on him, he has distinguished him alone of all the sovereigns of whom we have ever heard as at once a mighty luminary and most clear-voiced herald of genuine piety . . . So dear was he to God, and so blessed, so pious and so fortunate in all that he undertook, that with the greatest facility he obtained the authority over more nations than any who had preceded him. [15]

For Christians like Eusebius, God had ordained Constantine to become emperor, and had helped him conquer people after people for the empire! In Eastern Orthodox Christianity even today, Emperor Constantine is revered as a saint, as are nine emperors who came after him.

Declaring that an emperor who fought dozens of battles and killed thousands of people (including his own wife and son the year after the Council of Nicaea) was a saint had important effects on Christianity from the fourth century on. Treating Constantine as someone sent by God put a stamp of approval on violence and warfare, in opposition to the pacifism of Jesus and the first three centuries of Christians. As we saw, early Christians took Jesus seriously and did not fight back when attacked. They also refused to let soldiers join them. But if "Saint Constantine"—the ultimate soldier—was sent by God, and God blessed him with victory after victory, then violence and war must be acceptable, and so Jesus was wrong to preach pacifism. Early in the fifth century, Augustine of Hippo created his just war theory, which Christians have been using ever since to justify wars, including wars against other Christians.

Thinking of Constantine and other emperors as saints sent by God also led Christians to think of absolute rule by one man—what today we call dictators—as the ideal form of government. That quite naturally led to thinking of Christ himself as an emperor. If the Roman emperor gets his power from God, then Christ is an even greater emperor. Following this reasoning, Christians in the fourth century began worshipping Christ as "Pantokrator," which is Greek for "Ruler over All," and paintings and mosaics of Christ Pantokrator became some of the earliest Christian art.

Soon the bishops of Rome began thinking of themselves as Pantokrators of the church, with absolute authority similar to the emperor's and to Christ's. Pope Leo I (440–461) claimed that he was not just the bishop of Rome but ruler over all other bishops and all other Christians. Modeling himself on Roman emperors, he gave himself one of their titles, *Pontifex Maximus*, "Greatest Bridge Builder," which is why we still call the pope "pontiff."

As the church mapped out dioceses—territories ruled by bishops— their boundaries followed those of provinces in the Roman Empire. Like that empire, too, the church structured itself as a male-dominated hierarchy, with laypeople at the bottom, deacons and priests above them, bishops above them, all the way up to the pope. Modeling Christianity on the Roman Empire was helped by influential bishops like Ambrose of Milan, who had been imperial governor of northern Italy. As theologian Hans Küng says,

> The Church ministerial structure came to resemble the structure of the Roman civil service class, with its *ordines*: ministries as offices divided into several stages. The bishop became the civil agent at the head of a district, with presbyters, deacons and other church ministers as civil officials of lower rank; while he himself was subordinate to the metropolitan at the head of the province and the patriarch at the head of a division of the empire.[16]

As with the overturning of Jesus' pacifism, all this concern with power and hierarchy was quite contrary to the ethos of early Christians,

who treated each other as equals, following Jesus' advice in Luke
22:24–26:

> A dispute also arose among them as to which of them was considered
> to be greatest. Jesus said to them, "The kings of the Gentiles lord it
> over them; and those who exercise authority over them call them-
> selves Benefactors. But you are not to be like that. Instead, the
> greatest among you should be like the youngest, and the one who
> rules like the one who serves."

If Jesus had appeared in the late Roman Empire, then, some of his
questions might have been about why Christian leaders had cooperated
with and modeled themselves on brutal, power-hungry emperors. In
many ways the Roman Empire was the opposite of the Kingdom of God
that Jesus preached. It was sexist and racist. It was built on militarism,
slavery, economic exploitation, and terrorizing subdued peoples
through public torture such as crucifixion.

F. IS BELIEVING DOCTRINES THE ESSENCE OF CHRISTIANITY?

Another question Jesus might have asked the bishops in 385 is: Why
have you defined Christians as people who believe a set of doctrines,
rather than as people who pursue the Kingdom of God? What does
agreeing with certain philosophical claims about me have to do with
following me? Consider the burning issue of *homoousios* versus *homoiousios*—fought between people who said the Father and the Son are of
the same substance, and their opponents, who said the Father and the
Son are of a similar substance. In this debate, it's not at all clear that
Jesus would have voted with the majority. Nothing in the Gospels indicates that he would have even been interested in this philosophical
controversy, nor in later ones such as whether Jesus has one *physis*
(nature) or two, one *nous* (mind) or two, one *energeia* (motivating energy) or two, and one *thelesis* (will) or two. Like *ousia* (substance), these
abstract Greek philosophical terms were not part of Jesus' teaching or
even his vocabulary. In the fifth and sixth centuries, however, Christians
killed each other by the thousands over these and other philosophical
abstractions.

Had Jesus wanted his followers to accept a set of theological doctrines, it seems that he would have said so, and he would have had someone write down those doctrines in clear, precise language so that everyone would know just what they had to believe. According to the Gospels, however, he preached and taught mostly through metaphors, parables, analogies, hyperbole (exaggeration), and other figures of speech, not in theological doctrines, which require using well-defined terms literally. Jesus did ask people to believe in *him*, of course, but that meant trusting him as a person, not agreeing with philosophical assertions about him.

The very idea of what a follower of Jesus is, then, underwent a huge change in just four hundred years. By the middle of the fifth century, most people in the Roman Empire were "Christians" in the sense that they accepted official doctrines and were baptized. After all, the law said that they had to. Even the Vandals and the Visigoths, who plundered what is now France and Spain, and the city of Rome, had been converted (mostly to Arian Christianity). But who among all these "Christians" followed the way of life Jesus preached by loving God and loving their neighbors? Who was "Christian" in a way that Jesus would have recognized? And why do we today still call Christians "believers," as if that's what makes people Christians?

G. ASKING QUESTIONS IS PART OF BEING A CHRISTIAN

The answer to "Why ask questions?" should now be obvious. In just their first four centuries, Christians took contrary positions on essential issues. They also changed the message of Jesus in major ways. We could make this chapter into a whole book by examining the sixteen centuries that followed, as the diversity of Christians' thinking and practice grew exponentially. That would involve a look at the Great Schism of 1054 between the Eastern and Western churches, and the Protestant Reformation, with the thousands of churches it led to. According to the *World Christian Encyclopedia*, the result of all this splitting was that by the year 2000 there were thirty-four thousand Christian denominations.[17] In the chapters that follow, we will explore some of the disagreements that led to this splitting, but we don't have to go into historical detail to see that where several people have contrary ideas, they can't all be right. To be a thoughtful Christian, then, requires asking questions.

Unfortunately, most contemporary Christians are unaware of all the diversity in Christian belief because they haven't studied the history of Christianity. Many simply grow up within one tradition, become familiar with its teachings and rituals, and then keep going. They may switch churches for practical reasons, such as to please a new spouse, but they don't look carefully into the differences between the various Christian traditions, compare their pros and cons, and choose the one that seems closest to what Jesus intended. And it's unusual for pastors to encourage people to do historical study of the thousands of Christian denominations and their diverse theologies. This problem is made worse by the hundreds of pastors who themselves have little theological training. The most famous contemporary evangelist, Rev. Billy Graham, has preached to over 215 million people in 185 countries, but did not even attend a seminary. Joel Osteen currently leads the largest megachurch in the United States, drawing forty-three thousand people each Sunday and hosting the most popular Christian show on television, but he admits that he didn't even finish college, much less study in a seminary.[18] Typically, such preachers present their own positions as obviously correct and treat historical and critical discussion as unnecessary. As we've seen, however, asking questions, thinking carefully, making distinctions, and arguing for and against various positions have been part of Christianity from the days of Peter and Paul.

We are going to be thinking about nine topics: thoughtful faith, the Bible, Jesus Christ, the Trinity, the fall, heaven and hell, angels and demons, the good life, and churches. Under each topic, we'll ask five yes/no questions and explore answers from the history of Christian thought. Some answers you've probably heard often, but others may surprise you. When we discuss Jesus' ideas about life after death, for instance, we'll see that he didn't teach that our souls go to heaven when we die. When he talked about dying, in fact, he didn't even mention souls. We'll explore the view of many scholars that Jesus thought of death as the destruction of the person, so that people who have died are not in heaven, but "asleep in the dust," as the Bible politely puts it. What Jesus taught about death is that the dead will be resurrected—brought back to life—by God at the end of the world. That means that the common belief that dead people are now living with God in heaven is questionable, as are praying to saints, the existence of purgatory (a place where souls are purged of the effects of their sins so they can enter heaven), and other Christian practices and beliefs that assume that dead people are now alive somewhere.

Besides asking questions about Christianity over the centuries, we'll ask about the ways Christians live today in relation to what Jesus preached. Millions serve in armed forces around the world, for example, and thousands of clergy are military chaplains. Jesus, however, preached pacifism, and the first Christian groups did not admit soldiers.

Should we be surprised that things widely accepted by today's Christians don't match what Jesus says in the Gospels? Not if we consider the history of Christianity. Many ideas that were once common among Christians were later rejected by most of them. Before the sixteenth century, for example, it was standard teaching that loaning money at interest is sinful. John Calvin was the first major Christian thinker to say otherwise. Today it would be hard to find a Christian who believes that it's wrong to charge interest on a loan.

In the fifth century, many Christians thought that if you wanted to be really religious, you should live apart from society and all its pleasures. You should leave your home, move to the desert, live alone, stop bathing, and eat just enough to keep from starving. One of the most famous saints of that time, Saint Simeon Stylites, lived for thirty-seven years on a meter-square platform atop a pillar, forbidding any woman, even his mother, to come near the pillar. In the third century, as mentioned earlier, the church father Origen (185–254) had taken this anti-sex attitude to the extreme by castrating himself. While such practices were considered by some to be the highest form of Christian life, Jesus, like most Christians today, would probably have been shocked by them.

The critical method in this book, of asking questions and weighing the pros and cons of various answers, was once common in Christian thinking. In the twelfth century, Peter Abelard wrote a handbook for students called *Yes and No* in which he listed 158 questions with opposing answers from various Christian authorities. Two of his questions were: "Must human faith be completed by reason, or not?" and "Is God a single unitary being, or not?" In the thirteenth century, Thomas Aquinas wrote his *Summa Theologiae*, a handbook of theology, which then became a standard text in Catholic seminaries and universities. Thomas presents each issue not as a statement, but as a question. The section on the existence of God, for example, begins, "Does God exist?"[19] Thomas's way of discussing theological questions is to start with the position opposite to his own. The first answer he gives to "Does God exist?" is "It seems that God does not exist." That is followed by the strongest arguments Thomas could find *against* the existence of God. One is that if there were an infinite, all-good being, such a being would not allow evil in the world. But there is plenty of evil in the world, so an infinite, all-good being does not exist. Another argument Thomas gives against the existence of God is that if you can explain something by appealing to a few facts or appealing to more facts, it's better to use the simpler explanation. We can explain the existence of everything in the universe by appealing to scientific facts, Thomas continues, so there is no need to appeal to the existence of a supernatural God.

After Thomas presents his arguments *against* the existence of God, he counters with his famous five ways to argue *for* the existence of God. Then at the end he gives responses to the arguments he began with: that God does not exist. We need not go into those arguments and responses here, but it's important to realize that these come *after* the arguments against the existence of God. Thomas's method is to get Christians to ask questions and think about all the possible answers, not just the answers they were already familiar with.

Today millions of Christians are unfamiliar with this way of doing theology because for decades popular Christian leaders have avoided careful thinking about beliefs. Some of them would not be able to think carefully about theology because, as mentioned, they have little theological training.

The fact that many Christians do not think carefully is apparent in the number who accept beliefs that are contrary to standard Christian teachings. According to a 2009 survey by the Pew Forum on Religion and Public Life, 20 percent of Protestants and 28 percent of Catholics in the United States believe in reincarnation, and about the same number believe in astrology. Both beliefs are rejected by all major Christian churches, and so the millions of Christians who believe in reincarnation and astrology could benefit from some careful thinking.

H. PAYING CAREFUL ATTENTION TO WORDS

One way in which we will think carefully in this book is by paying close attention to the language used in scriptures and in theology. We will show how the creators of doctrines such as the Trinity did not distinguish between literal statements and figures of speech, especially metaphors. These Christians were mostly literate thinkers familiar with Greek philosophy, trying to understand the words of people whose style of thinking was oral rather than literate. The most influential of those oral thinkers were the writers of the Bible. At the time the Bible was written, writing with a full alphabet was only a few centuries old, and so the Bible retains many features of oral expression. When people *say* something orally rather than *write* it, for example, they tend to repeat themselves. That makes the message clear to their listeners and increases the probability that it will be remembered. The Bible has hundreds of verses in which something is said and is then repeated in slightly different words. In Genesis 1:26, for instance, "God said, 'Let us make man in our image, according to our likeness.'" The phrases "in our image" and "according to our likeness" are equivalent, so in writing, the second phrase isn't necessary. But the writers of Genesis lived in a mostly oral culture, and they thought in oral patterns. In an oral culture, repetition is valued because it helps listeners remember the message, and it gives the speaker time to think of what to say next.

Another feature of oral language found in the Bible is hyperbole (exaggeration). Like a redundant statement, an exaggerated one tends to be remembered. When Acts of the Apostles 5:42 describes how hard Peter and others worked at spreading the message of Jesus, for example, it says "Daily in the temple, and in every house, they did not cease teaching and preaching Jesus as the Christ." Did Peter preach *every* day in *every* house without once taking a break? Probably not. But nobody faults this line, because we are used to exaggeration in the Bible.

Yet another feature of oral thinking is comparison of one thing to another. Two basic forms are simile and metaphor. In a simile like "fierce as a lion" the comparison is explicit. In a metaphor like "On the football field, Tom is a lion" the comparison is implicit.

Not only the writers of the Bible, but the people in the Bible, were mostly oral thinkers. The most important for Christians is Jesus, who expresses himself in the Gospels through similes, metaphors, parables, allegories, and other oral patterns of thought. Consider his preaching about "Love your neighbor" in Matthew 10:27–37. That phrase itself is not a literal statement but a figure of speech, since by "neighbor" he doesn't mean "someone who lives near your house," but people in general. When someone asks "Who is my neighbor?" Jesus does not answer in a literate style by saying, "Everyone," but instead tells the parable of the good Samaritan—a story about a man helping a stranger in need. Here and throughout the Gospels, Jesus, like the overwhelming majority of the writers of the Bible, shows an oral style of thinking and expression rather than a literate style.

The first Christians were Jews and mostly oral thinkers, and they understood the oral style of the Hebrew Scriptures. But as Christianity spread to areas influenced by Greek philosophy, literate thinkers who were used to written texts using words precisely and logically, such as the books of Plato and Aristotle, began to read the Hebrew and Christian scriptures looking for the precise and logical use of words they were used to in philosophy books. In reading the scriptures that way, they often failed to appreciate the metaphors, allegories, analogies, and other oral patterns of expression in them.

As we have seen, the first Christian theologians were people trained in Greek philosophy who presented their scriptures as offering a new philosophy that could compete with Platonism, Stoicism, and other popular philosophies. But writing philosophy is a literate activity that requires using words literally, with precise meanings, and following the rules of logic. So in philosophy books, nonliteral figures of speech such as metaphors and parables are of little use. The scriptures, however, are full of nonliteral figures of speech. As early Christian theologians read those figures of speech, they often treated them as if they were literal statements in a philosophy book, and that led to trouble.

In thinking about the phrases "the Father" and "the Son of God," for example, they didn't respect the metaphorical language involved. Speaking literally, "father" names one of the two roles in sexual reproduction. It means a male human being whose sperm fertilizes an egg to produce a new human being. God is not a male human being and does not reproduce sexually, so God is not literally a father. Similarly, speaking literally, "son" means a male offspring of human sexual reproduction. God is not a human and does not reproduce sexually, so whatever the relation of Jesus to God is, it is not literally "son." But when Christian theologians created the theory of the Trinity, they thought of these metaphors as literal uses of language. As a result they mistakenly treated statements like "The Father begot the Son" as literal assertions. And not just any old literal assertions, but *doctrines*—assertions that must be believed on pain of eternal damnation and sometimes execution by the state!

The problem here is that it doesn't make sense to require people to *believe* a metaphor. They may understand its point, like it, use it frequently, and so on. But a metaphor is not something to be believed or disbelieved. Try to answer these three questions with either a yes or a no:

Is life a journey?
Was George Washington the father of his country?
Is all the world a stage, and are all the men and women merely
    players?

These don't work as yes/no questions because they treat metaphors as if they were literal descriptions that are true or false, to be believed or disbelieved.

In chapter 4, section D we'll examine the "son of God" metaphor in detail, but here we can point out that while metaphors can be effective in preaching, the writing of doctrines—official church teachings—is a different matter. When you tell people they have to believe a statement, you must use words literally, and they must have clear definitions. A metaphor won't do, because it's not literally true. (We'll say more about doctrines in chapter 4, section E.)

When you use a metaphor, you talk about one thing as if it were another thing, something to which it is similar in an unspecified way. "Joe is a bear," for instance, could suggest that Joe is big and strong, that he is not very smart, or that he'll eat anything. Even if the person who says "Joe is a bear" specifies a similarity—by adding, say, "He's so big and strong"—they don't ask their listeners to *believe* that Joe is *literally* a bear—a member of the biological family *Ursidae*. Similarly, Jesus' preaching about God as "father," and himself and other people as God's "sons" and "children," suggests many similarities between God and fathers—that he created humans, loves them, provides for them, gives them commands, and so on. But that only suggests that God is *like* a father, not that God *is* a father. The same applies to all the other metaphors applied to God in the Bible—rock, fortress, sun, living water, warrior, vine grower, and so on.[20]

In the formation of Christian theology, the problem of treating metaphors as literal statements was compounded by treating poetic verses as if they were sentences in a philosophy book. Some of the most troublesome are at the opening of the Gospel of John. "In the beginning was the Word, and the Word was with God, and the Word was God. He was in the beginning with God. All things came into being through him, and without him not one thing came into being." The author of these lines was obviously more poet than philosopher. What literal meaning can be given to "The Word was with God, and the Word was God"? How can A *be with* B and at the same time *be* B? Poetry is fine, of course, as long as we appreciate it as poetry. But early Greek theologians tried to interpret this poetry as philosophical assertions about God, Jesus Christ, and the creation of the world.

One indication that John's writing about "the Word" was poetic and not a literal description of Jesus is that John mentions "the Word" in just the first few lines of the gospel and never again, and none of the other New Testament writers ever call Jesus "the Word." Jesus, too, never called himself "the Word." In describing the creation of the world, furthermore, the Book of Genesis makes no mention of "the Word" or of the idea that "All things came into being through him, and without him not one thing came into being."

As we examine Christian beliefs, then, we will be sensitive to the kind of language being used, especially to the difference between literal and nonliteral uses of words.

We will spend seven chapters thinking carefully about traditional theological issues like the nature of Jesus Christ and his relation to God, original sin, life after death, and angels and demons. Then in chapter 9 we will turn to moral issues, asking about the morality preached by Jesus and its relation to the morality of Christians today. Was Jesus opposed to gays and lesbians? Would he join the Marines? Would he be a gung-ho consumer? Here, as earlier, we'll find major differences between what many Christians believe and do and what Jesus taught. In chapter 10 we'll ask about churches and their relation to Jesus' preaching about the Kingdom of God.

We will be discussing forty-five yes/no questions. As we go through them, you will probably agree or disagree with many of the answers you read. That's good—it shows you're thinking. When you have a different answer, you may want to write it down, along with your reasons for it. As the author of this book, I will often be arguing that one answer to a question is more credible than others, but nothing I write should be accepted as the final word. Like anyone else, I could be wrong about anything. So check the suggestions marked "For Further Reading," in which I have tried to include a wide range of positions.

In thinking about our forty-five questions, too, you may come up with questions of your own. And they don't have to be yes/no. They might be "what" questions, such as "What is redemption?" They might be "why" questions, such as "Why is monasticism no longer popular?" Write down your questions and do some research when you get time. You'll find with your own questions, as with the ones in this book, that Christianity is far richer and more complicated than most people think. It's not at all like geometry, with the correct answers listed in the back of the book.

For further reading:

John Dear, S. J. *The Questions of Jesus: Challenging Ourselves to Discover Life's Great Answers*. New York: Doubleday, 2004.

2

THOUGHTFUL FAITH

Most of us have heard faith praised so often that we think of it as intrinsically good, like freedom or patriotism. The three great Christian virtues are faith, hope, and love. Most theologians have said that faith is a gift from God. Martin Luther taught that faith is the only thing necessary for salvation; his motto *sola fides* is Latin for "faith alone." If faith is a virtue, a gift from God, and the one thing Christians need, then isn't it always good? And if faith is always good, isn't anything that might challenge it, such as asking questions, bad? Many Christians have answered yes to these questions, but, as we'll see, that way of thinking is simplistic and not true to the history of Christianity.

A. IS IT ALL RIGHT TO THINK CAREFULLY ABOUT THE RELIGION YOU GREW UP IN?

Many Christians today think of their religion as something they have accepted once and for all, completely and finally. It's a fixed set of beliefs, values, and rituals that is permanently theirs in the way their native language is theirs. With it they are saved and will go to heaven when they die.

If that's what Christianity is, why would anyone analyze their beliefs or ask questions about them? How could that help? And couldn't thinking carefully about your religion be dangerous, even lead you away from it?

Countless Christian pastors promote this complacent acceptance of their group's beliefs, values, and rituals. They don't encourage people to look into the history of Christianity or even the history of their own group, nor to contrast how they think and act with how other Christian groups think and act. They never mention in the pulpit that there are thirty-four thousand Christian denominations. When they preach about salvation or about heaven and hell, they simply present their group's ideas as if they were obviously true, rather than as ideas that have a history and that differ from the ideas of other Christians. Why trouble people in the pews with theology and history that might confuse or trouble them? It's much easier to give them one set of ideas as the unquestioned truth and leave it at that.

The pastors with the very largest congregations tend to minimize theology, history, and careful thinking in their sermons and maximize "feel-good" messages that assure people they are on the right track. That's the pattern in "megachurches"—congregations with weekly attendance of at least two thousand. The most successful of all feel-good preachers is Joel Osteen of Lakewood Church in Houston, Texas, who has over forty-three thousand attend weekly, with another million watching on television. To accommodate the huge numbers, Osteen bought a building that seats 16,800 from the Compaq computer corporation. His version of Christianity is not just "nondenominational" but so vague that the vast majority of his sermons sound like self-help seminars. Even if he wanted to add theology and history to his sermons, it wouldn't be easy, since he didn't even finish college and never attended a seminary.

If we look at the history of Christianity, we can see what's questionable about feel-good megachurches and their avoidance of careful thinking. The fact is that thinking carefully is not only acceptable for Christians, it's how Christianity got started. Jesus was a Jew who challenged the tradition he was raised in. It had over six hundred laws, but he broke dozens—maybe hundreds—of them, such as rules about preparing and eating food and rules about what you should not do on the Sabbath. He also opposed the vengeance built into its religious laws. As we saw in chapter 1, in the Sermon on the Mount, Jesus replaced "An eye for an eye and a tooth for a tooth" with "Turn the other cheek" and "Love your enemies." (Matthew 5:38–39, 43–45). If Jesus had not thought carefully about his religion, he would have lived and died as an anonymous Jewish peasant, and Christianity would have never existed.

All of Jesus' apostles, too, were Jews. They came to be his followers by challenging the religion they had grown up in. Paul of Tarsus (c. 10–c. 66) started out as Saul, a Pharisee who persecuted the followers of Jesus. But he became their most enthusiastic missionary, writing almost half of the New Testament. As Christianity spread beyond Palestine, it attracted many non-Jews, who also joined the movement by changing their worldviews. Justin Martyr (100–165), one of the earliest Christian theologians, was first a Stoic, then an Aristotelian, then a Pythagorean, and then a Platonist. Before coming to Christianity, Augustine of Hippo (354–430) was a Manichean, then a Platonist. If these people had simply stuck to the beliefs they were taught as children, we would have never heard of any of them, and the history of Christianity would be vastly different.

Even Christian leaders who were baptized as babies often became leaders by challenging the tradition they grew up in. Martin Luther began life as a Roman Catholic and became a monk, priest, and theology professor within Catholicism. He started what we now call Protestantism by protesting against certain practices and beliefs in the Catholic Church, such as the idea that some dead people are in a state of suffering called purgatory which can be shortened by buying indulgences. John Calvin grew up Roman Catholic, too, and for a while considered the priesthood. The Reformed tradition he started was also based on criticisms of Catholicism. If these men had not thought carefully about the religion they were raised in, they would have remained Catholics all their lives, and the history of Christianity would have been very different.

Christians who think carefully about the religion they were brought up in, of course, don't always start new churches. Anselm of Canterbury (1033–1109), for example, remained a Catholic his whole life and became a saint, but he rejected a teaching of the church that had been standard for seven centuries, a core teaching about how Jesus saved the human race. As we'll see in chapter 4, section C, it was that after Adam sinned, the human race became the property of Satan. Jesus' death on the cross, according to this teaching, was a ransom paid by God to Satan to liberate the human race from bondage to Satan. Anselm wrote solid objections to that teaching and replaced it with what is now called the atonement theory—that Jesus' death on the cross was a payment to *God*—not to *Satan*—that cancelled the debt owed by the human race to God for Adam's sin. Today the vast majority of Catholics and Protestants accept some version of the atonement theory, and it's hard to find one who has even heard of the older theory that God paid off Satan. But if Anselm had not thought about the religion he grew up in, all Christians might still believe that older theory.

If it was all right for these and other Christian leaders to think carefully about the religion they grew up in, then, clearly, it's all right for the rest of us. As we do, we need to think about their ideas, too, since some of them had questionable views. Paul, for example, taught that slavery was a legitimate social institution. In his Letter to the Ephesians 6:5, he wrote, "Slaves, obey your earthly masters with fear and trembling, in singleness of heart, as you obey Christ." In his First Letter to Timothy 6:1, Paul says, "Let all who are under the yoke of slavery regard their masters as worthy of all honor, so that the name of God and the teaching may not be blasphemed." This was not a trivial issue, since half of the thirty-three million people in the Roman Empire were slaves.[1] If at the beginning of Christianity, Paul had insisted on the equality of all human beings and advocated the abolition of slavery, that might have ended the immoral practice eighteen centuries before it actually ended. Instead, Christians kept slavery going until just a century and a half ago.

Paul also taught that all political leaders have been appointed by God, so that rebelling against any political leader is rebelling against God:

> Let every soul be subject to the governing authorities. For there is no authority except from God, and the authorities that exist are appointed by God. Therefore whoever resists the authority resists the ordinance of God, and those who resist will bring judgment on themselves (Romans 13:1–2).

If Paul was right, then the Christians who worked to end slavery were acting immorally, and so were those who fought against Hitler and Mussolini. But no thinking Christian today believes that slavery is moral or that dictators are appointed by God, so no thinking Christian believes that Paul was always right. Since his teachings about slavery and government are found in the Bible, that means that we have to ask questions even about what is said in the Bible.

Another issue on which hundreds of Christian leaders and theologians have been wrong is the responsibility of "the Jews"—all Jewish people around the world and across all the centuries—for the crucifixion of Jesus. Fourth-century Christians created a new kind of document called *Adversus Judaeos* (Against the Jews). Among leading bishops of the time, John Chrysostom (347–407) wrote the largest number of these diatribes. In eight sermons designed to persuade Christians not to associate with Jews, he says that Jews are lecherous, rapacious, and greedy; that they worship Satan and sacrifice their own children to demons.[2] Their synagogues are houses of prostitution. God always hated the Jews, and because they murdered Christ, Christians must hate them too.

This vicious anti-Semitism continued into modern times, when it led to systematic persecutions such as Hitler's attempt to kill all Jews. His "Final Solution" was foreshadowed in the writings of Martin Luther, whose book *On the Jews and Their Lies* (1543) piles up dozens of charges against the "blind, venomous Jews" who "are surely possessed by all devils."[3] In their synagogues "nothing is found but a den of devils in which sheer self-glory, conceit, lies, blasphemy, and defaming of God and men are practiced most maliciously."[4] What Christians should do about the Jews, Luther said, is burn their synagogues and schools, ban their rabbis from preaching, destroy their prayer books, prohibit Jewish prayer and teaching, forbid them from uttering the name of God publicly, demolish their homes, seize their property, force them into slavery, or banish them from Europe forever.[5] No reasonable Christian today believes what Luther said about the Jews, and so there is no guarantee that what he said about other issues is true, either. Like Paul, Luther is not to be simply believed without carefully examining his ideas.

Thinking about one's religion doesn't necessarily lead to switching to another religion, of course. Depending on what one discovers, careful thinking may deepen one's understanding of and commitment to one's religion. The point is that Christianity at its best has always allowed for careful and critical thinking.

As we think further about faith in this chapter, and about other topics in chapters to come, keep in mind that the questions we're asking, and the answers we discuss, are far from the only ones that are possible. As mentioned at the end of chapter 1, you may well have your own answers to the questions posed here, and may have your own questions, too. If you write them down, they will probably become clearer to you, and you will probably see ways to improve them. If you then share them with other people and get feedback, that's even better. In this process, as we said, nothing in this book should be treated as the last word. Instead of being the end of a discussion, each of our forty-five questions is meant to be a beginning.

For further reading:

Richard Swinburne. *Faith and Reason*. Oxford: Oxford University Press, 1981.

B. IS CAREFUL THINKING OPPOSED TO FAITH?

When Christians contrast faith with something, a standard choice is "reason." Reason is a broad concept, but essentially, to reason about something is to think carefully about it. Reasoning is asking questions, looking for hidden assumptions, searching for evidence, spotting logical fallacies, and so on. The noun "reason" is revealing here: when we *reason* about a belief, one thing we do is consider *reasons* for accepting it.

There is a long tradition in Christianity of saying that looking for reasons to accept a belief, and critical thinking in general, is opposed to faith. Martin Luther (1483–1546) had one of the strongest positions. In *Table Talk*, he said, "Reason is the greatest enemy that faith has; it never comes to the aid of spiritual things, but—more frequently than not—struggles against the divine Word, treating with contempt all that emanates from God."[6] Luther's last sermon in Wittenberg in 1546 includes these lines: "Since the devil's bride, Reason, that pretty whore, comes in and thinks she's wise, and what she says, what she thinks, is from the Holy Spirit, who can help us, then? Not judges, not doctors, no king or emperor, because [reason] is the Devil's greatest whore."[7] And so Luther's advice is "Whoever wishes to be a Christian, let him pluck out the eyes of his reason."[8]

Many theologians have agreed with Luther about the opposition between reason and faith. In the twentieth century one of the most famous was Karl Barth, whose *Church Dogmatics* is considered one of the great theological works of the twentieth century. According to Barth, our only access to God is through faith. God is totally different from creatures, Barth said, and so humans cannot figure out anything about God by reasoning from what they know about the world. So-called "natural theology," such as proving the existence of God, is impossible, according to Barth. The only way for people to know anything about God is for God to reveal himself to them. For that revelation to happen, people must receive the communication from God. They do not first understand what has been revealed, and then believe that it is true. They have to believe it in order for it to be revealed. So unless you already believe in God, you cannot receive God's revelation. And when you receive God's revelation directly from God, there is no reasoning to be done. Christian faith, then, is immune to critical questions and immune to careful thinking in general.

Are faith and careful thinking really pitted against each other, as Luther, Barth, and many others have claimed? Are Christians supposed to "pluck out the eyes" of their reason and simply have faith? One obvious question to ask here is why God would give us the ability to think but not want us to use it to understand the most important issues in our lives. Luther himself devoted most of his adult life to careful thinking about religion. Even his belief that reason is the enemy of faith is the conclusion of an argument involving a lot of reasoning!

If faith and careful thinking were really opposed to each other, too, we would expect that Jesus would have said so. But he never asked people to reject thinking or to believe in him for no reason. Instead, the Gospels say, he showed them "signs"—that he was no ordinary man and that he had power from God. The Gospel of John uses the word "sign" seventeen times and describes seven miracles performed by Jesus to convince people of his divine authority. The first was changing over a hundred gallons of water into superb wine at a wedding party. The second was healing a nobleman's son—while the boy was far away. Third, he healed a man at Bethesda. Fourth, he fed five thousand people with just five loaves of bread and two fish. Fifth, he walked on water. Sixth, he gave sight to a man born blind. And seventh, he raised his friend Lazarus from the dead. For anyone who was there and thought carefully about what they had seen, these actions of Jesus would provide strong reasons to trust him and have confidence in what he preached.

There is another problem with Luther's claim that Christians should not think about religion but just have faith: this claim doesn't tell us *what* we should have faith in. Among the thirty-four thousand Christian denominations, there are hundreds of teachings that contradict other teachings. Roman Catholics, for example, believe that Jesus Christ wants all Christians to submit to the pope, but Protestants reject that belief. Some churches teach that God predestines all events, and other churches say there is no predestination. Some Christians believe in free will; others reject that belief. Where two people contradict each other, I can't believe both of them, because by agreeing with one, I am automatically disagreeing with the other. Luther's saying that we should have faith doesn't tell us which side of these contradictions we should have faith in.

Two claims don't even have to *contradict* each other in order for it to be impossible to accept both. They may simply be *contrary* to each other. In a contradiction, either the first statement is correct or the second statement is correct. If I say, "Pat is twenty-five years old," you contradict me if you say, "Pat is not twenty-five years old." Either I am right or you are right. But suppose I say, "Pat is twenty-five years old," and you say, "Pat is twenty-six years old." These statements are contrary rather than contradictory. While both can't be right, both could be wrong.

To take an example of contrary beliefs from the fourth-century church councils, some theologians said that Jesus is "of the same substance as" God the Father, while other theologians said that Jesus Christ was only "similar in substance" to God the Father. Here both can't be right, but both could be wrong.

The lesson with both contradictory beliefs and contrary beliefs is that whenever one Christian believed something that is incompatible with what another Christian believed, we can't agree with both of them. With which one—if either—should we put our faith? As Luther's own theology shows, figuring that out involves reasoning, including critical thinking.

There is another way in which faith requires reason. Sermons about faith often cite Jesus' saying to his disciples that they should have faith in him. But for Jesus' disciples, faith in him was pretty simple. They *saw* what he did and *heard* what he said, and so they had confidence in him and what he told them. For Christians born in later centuries, however, faith can't be so easy. We haven't even met Jesus, and so our confidence in him can't be based on anything we have seen him do or heard him say. What we know about Jesus comes from what people have told us, such as our parents, teachers, and clergy. And they never met Jesus, either. They heard about him from people who heard about him from people who heard about him—and so on, going back two thousand years. The chain of communication here raises questions, and answering them requires thinking.

For most Christians, of course, the foundation for what should be believed about Jesus is the New Testament. As the old song says, "How do I know? The Bible tells me so." As we'll see in chapter 3, section A, the books that were put together to form the Bible in the fourth century were originally separate documents. Christians in the second century had the Gospels of Matthew, Mark, Luke, and John, but also another twenty, including the Gospels of Thomas, Peter, Judas, Nicodemus, Barnabas, Mary, the Nazareans, the Hebrews, the Egyptians, and the Ebionites.[9] How did church authorities eventually choose just the four Gospels we have now, and reject the others? They did it by carefully comparing and contrasting them, looking for evidence that the information came from Jesus' apostles and disciples. In other words, the four Gospels were judged to be reliable descriptions of Jesus by careful thinking about them and the other Gospels. If we reject reason in matters of religion, as Luther advocated, we have to reject the rational analysis that went into choosing the books that make up the Bible, and then we can no longer appeal to the Bible.

There is a related problem with Luther's claim that we should pluck out the eyes of our reason and simply have faith in what the Bible says about Jesus Christ. At one time it was widely believed that the four Gospels were written by eyewitnesses to the events they describe. Today, however, Bible scholars agree that none of the Gospel writers knew Jesus personally. The books of Matthew, Mark, Luke, and John were written from forty to seventy years after Jesus was gone, by people who had heard about him from others. For us to base our faith in Jesus on the Four Gospels, then, we have to trust that the people who wrote those Gospels were reliable. Jesus' friends could have faith in him based on direct experience. But for us to have faith in him, we need an additional kind of faith—in what the Gospel writers have told us about him. And deciding that the Gospels are reliable requires reasoning.

Not everything that Christians believe comes directly from the Bible, of course. The doctrines of the Trinity and the atonement, for example, were developed after the Bible was written, as Christians tried to make sense of what it said. This, of course, also involves reasoning. Reflecting on Jesus talking about "the Father," "the Son," and "the Spirit," for example, theologians produced the doctrine of the Trinity. Thinking about how the death of Jesus on the cross could benefit us, they reached the conclusion that it paid a debt humans owed to God because of sin. For us to have faith in conclusions like these, obviously, we have to think that those theologians were reasoning carefully. To make those judgments, we have to think carefully ourselves.

Regardless of Luther's comment that "Reason is the greatest enemy that faith has," then, any faith worth having will involve considerable thinking.

For further reading:

Terence Penelhum. *Reason and Religious Faith*. Boulder, CO: Westview, 1995.
Avery Dulles. *The Assurance of Things Hoped for: A Theology of Christian Faith*. Oxford: Oxford University Press, 1994.
Pope John Paul II. Encyclical *Fides et Ratio*, 1998.

C. IS FAITH A KIND OF KNOWLEDGE?

Many Christians think of faith as a special channel of information that adds to what we know from history, science, and other sources, or even makes other kinds of knowledge unnecessary. It's common to hear such people say that they are as certain of their religious beliefs as they are of anything else. So, for example, millions say that their certainty that the Book of Genesis is literally true outweighs any scientific evidence for the theory of evolution.

A prime example of someone who thought of faith as a kind of knowledge was the great Protestant reformer John Calvin: "We shall now have a full definition of faith if we say that it is a firm and sure knowledge of the divine favor toward us, founded on the truth of a free promise in Christ, and revealed to our minds, and sealed on our hearts, by the Holy Spirit." [10]

Calvin's definition, and similar definitions, of faith as a kind of knowledge don't apply to all faith, however, because many people have had faith in teachings that were false, and no one can know what is false. Knowledge, by definition, is of what is true. In the first several decades of Christianity, for example, almost everyone believed that the world would soon end, as Jesus returned to judge the human race. That faith was understandable, since in three of the Gospels Jesus predicts his return within the lifetimes of some of his listeners:

> For the Son of Man is to come with his angels in the glory of his Father, and then he will repay everyone for what has been done. Truly, I tell you, there are some standing here who will not taste death before they see the Son of Man coming in his kingdom (Matthew 16:27–28; see Luke 9:26–27 and Mark 9:1).

While we can say that early Christians *believed* that the world would end within a few decades, however, we can't say that they *knew* it would, because knowledge can only be of what is true, and it was not true that the world would end within a few decades.

Another problem with thinking of faith as knowledge arises from something we discussed in the last question: from the beginning of Christianity, people have had contrary and contradictory beliefs. Some of the first Christians believed that to be a Christian, a person first had to be a Jew: Paul believed that was false. They cannot both have been right, so either Paul was wrong or his opponents were wrong. Since knowledge cannot be of what is false, at least one of them did not *know* what they believed. So their faith was not a form of knowledge.

Today's Christians also have contrary and contradictory beliefs, as we have seen. On the issue of whether Jesus wants all Christians to follow the pope, either Roman Catholics' faith is incorrect or Protestants' faith is incorrect. Either way, millions of Christians have faith in what is false, so their faith cannot be knowledge.

If faith is not a kind of knowledge, what is it? A careful reading of the Gospels shows that Jesus thought of faith as an attitude—its basic form is confidence and trust in a person. Jesus speaks of faith most often as trust in him, and he criticizes his followers for having "little faith" after they have seen his miracles. Later Christians would emphasize faith in doctrines such as the Trinity and the atonement, but, as we'll see in chapter 4, section E, Jesus didn't teach doctrines or talk about faith in doctrines. When you trust a person, you trust what they tell you, of course, and so faith in Jesus includes faith in what he said, but, as we'll see, several Christian doctrines, including the Trinity and the atonement, were not taught by Jesus.

The word "faith" can be used to mean simply confidence, as in "I lost my faith in the mayor when he ran off with his secretary." But in religious discussions, faith usually has a more specific meaning. It means complete confidence in something for which the person does not have conclusive evidence. Though people have confidence that robins are birds, for example, no one would say they have faith that robins are birds. That's because it's perfectly obvious to everyone that robins are birds—they have wings and fly, lay eggs, and have all the other features of birds. When we know something, such as that robins are birds, there is no need for faith. We talk about faith when someone's belief is not shared by everybody and there is not conclusive evidence for it—in other words, when it is not something known.

The link between having faith that something is true and not having conclusive evidence for it is obvious in people's disagreements about matters of faith. Some Christians believe that hell is a place of unending suffering, for example, but others believe that God would not punish anyone forever. There isn't conclusive evidence for either of these contrary beliefs. If there were conclusive evidence for one, then those who have that evidence would present it to the world, and all reasonable people would accept it. That's how science works. In the 1950s, for example, the idea that we inherit features from our parents through DNA was at first just a hypothesis, but then, with many confirming experiments, it became a well-accepted theory. Today there is so much conclusive evidence that we can say we *know* that we inherit features from our parents through DNA. But the existence of hell, or the nonexistence of hell, isn't known because there isn't conclusive evidence for either position.

Here we can see that despite all the praise Christians have had for faith, it is not an ideal state in relation to something we believe. Knowledge would be better. Saint Paul suggested the inferiority of faith to knowledge when he contrasted our indirect and incomplete awareness of God in this life with the direct awareness of God in the next: "For now we see in a mirror, dimly, but then we will see face to face. Now I know only in part. Then I will know fully, even as I have been fully known" (1 Corinthians 13:12).

Though Jesus wanted his followers to have faith in him, he never said that faith in general is always well founded. Indeed, he warned, "Beware of false prophets, who come to you in sheep's clothing but inwardly are ravenous wolves" (Matthew 7:15). Even Luther, the great champion of faith, pointed out that having faith doesn't guarantee truth. As he wrote near the beginning of his *Large Catechism*, "If your faith and trust be right, then is your god also true; and, on the other hand, if your trust be false and wrong, then you have not the true God."[11]

An example of faith that was not well founded was the faith of the followers of the Rev. Jim Jones, infamous for ordering the largest civilian massacre in American history in 1978. Jones began his career in 1952 as a student pastor in a Methodist church in Indianapolis, and then started his own Community Unity Church in 1954. He was ordained by the Disciples of Christ in 1964, and in 1965 he moved his church to California, operating as the People's Temple in several cities. In the mid-1970s, under pressure from investigating journalists, he moved to Guyana, South America, where his community was informally known as Jonestown. When Congressman Leo Ryan received letters about abuses at Jonestown from unhappy relatives of its residents in 1978, he decided to investigate for himself. At first Rev. Jones welcomed Ryan and his aides, but then he ordered his followers to murder them, and then to kill their own children and themselves by drinking cyanide. The next day over nine hundred corpses lay on the ground. The faith that followers of Rev. Jim Jones had in him was clearly not well founded. They would have been better off if they had asked questions before turning their lives over to him.

If faith is trust in a person and what that person says, and if faith does not guarantee that either the person or what they say is worthy of trust, then faith is not an attitude to take toward just anyone or toward just anyone's teachings. As Jesus warned, there are false prophets. To avoid putting our faith in the wrong things, we have to think carefully. When we read or hear something that isn't obviously true, for instance, it's helpful to ask three *C* questions: Is it clear? Is it coherent? Is it credible? Let's consider these one at a time.

First, clarity. No matter how much we trust someone, we need to understand just what they are saying before we can believe it. Most of the time, I have confidence in what my wife tells me. But suppose that tonight she comes home with an old book by Lewis Carroll, opens it, and reads the poem "Jabberwocky": "'Twas brillig, and the slithy toves did gyre and gimble in the wabe. All mimsy were the borogoves, and the mome raths outgrabe." I can't have faith in what she is saying because it doesn't have any clear meaning for me.

The second *C* question we can ask about what someone tells us is "Is it coherent?" That is, do the parts of what they're saying fit together? If my wife were to say "It's noon on the sun," for example, she would be using familiar words arranged in the form of a sentence. Unlike in the Lewis Carroll poem, I know what the individual words "It's" "noon" "on" "the" and "sun" mean. But there's a big problem in putting these words together to form a meaningful sentence. "Noon" means when the sun is directly overhead. So we can talk about noon in London and noon in Tokyo. But it doesn't make sense to talk about "noon on the sun," because the sun cannot be directly over the sun. No matter how much trust I have in my wife and what she says, I can't believe "It's noon on the sun," because that's not a coherent statement.

The third *C* question to ask about something we hear is "Is it credible?"—do we have good reason to believe it? We don't need anything as strong as scientific proof, of course. But we need *some* reason to believe. No intelligent person believes everything that everyone says, or even everything that every religious person says. As mentioned in the last question, Jesus never asked his followers to trust him based on *blind* faith. As the Gospels say, he showed them that he was wise, powerful, and good, so that they had solid reasons to trust him. The First Letter of Peter 3:15 extends this idea that Christians are supposed to have reasons for their confidence: "Be ready always to give an answer to every man that asks you a reason of the hope that is in you."

In matters of religion, there are thousands of things that people have said over the centuries. It would be impossible to believe all of them, since many of them are incompatible with others. To simply believe what anyone said, even someone from your church, without asking if it's credible would not be thoughtful faith, but foolishness.

For further reading:

Terence Penelhum, ed. *Faith*. New York: Macmillan, 1989.
Terence Penelhum. *Reason and Religious Faith*. Boulder, CO: Westview, 1995.

D. COULD SOME OF MY RELIGIOUS BELIEFS BE FALSE?

When you believe in people, you have confidence in them, you trust them. Similarly, when you believe some religious teaching, you have confidence in it, you trust that it is true. Like other beliefs, however, religious beliefs sometimes turn out to be false. As we saw in the last question, early Christians believed that the world would end soon. But it didn't. Similarly, William Miller, a Baptist preacher, taught that Jesus Christ would return to earth in 1844. The Rev. Samuel S. Snow was more precise, preaching that it would happen on October 22, 1844. Thousands of believers awaited that day; to get ready, some gave away all their possessions. After October 22 and then December 31 came and went, this came to be known as "the Great Disappointment." Later, Ellen White, founder of the Seventh-Day Adventists, preached that the world would end in 1850.

Besides incorrect beliefs about the future, Christians have also had beliefs that were incompatible with the beliefs of other Christians. As we saw in chapter 1, the first Christians had contrary beliefs about whether a person first had to be a Jew to join the group. In later centuries, as we'll see in chapters to come, Christians had contradictory and contrary beliefs about the nature of Jesus and his relationship to God, about whether human beings have free will, and about moral issues such as war and homosexuality.

Over the centuries, too, popular beliefs changed about major issues such as how Jesus saved the human race. As mentioned in question A of this chapter, before 1100, the standard belief was that after Adam sinned, the whole human race was under the dominion of Satan. The death of Jesus was a ransom payment God made to Satan—like the money people pay to kidnappers—that got Satan to release the human race from its bondage to him. Virtually all Christians believed that, because it was taught by most theologians and church authorities. It is still believed by some Eastern Orthodox Christians, but virtually all Roman Catholics and Protestants today would say that it is not true.

When one person makes a claim like "Jesus' death was a payment to Satan" and another person says, "No, it wasn't," they can't both be right: one of them must have a false belief. So on any question to which some Christians have answered yes and other Christians have answered no, some of those people must have had false beliefs. Most of the forty-five questions in this book are like that, and there are hundreds more when you count the finer points of theology. On hundreds of issues, then, millions of Christians have had false beliefs.

When I think about my own beliefs, of course, I usually don't think about them in this big picture. Instead, I think of my own beliefs as the way things really are. In my mind, it's the people who disagree with me who have false beliefs. But if I'm honest with myself, I have to ask: What makes *me* so special? If millions of Christians have false beliefs, how do I know that I'm not among them? Is there some guarantee that all my beliefs must be true?

My own certainty—my confidence that I'm right—is not enough, because people can be absolutely certain about something and completely wrong at the same time. Think of the loyal followers of Rev. Jim Jones, for example. As he ordered the community to commit mass suicide, some of them stuck by him, certain that their faith in him was solid. But that faith didn't guarantee anything—except their death.

If we look at famous religious leaders in history, many of them came to see some of their beliefs as false, and so they changed their minds. As we've seen, Saint Paul started out as Saul, a Pharisee who thought that the followers of Jesus should be suppressed. Augustine went through several phases before coming to Christianity. He was a Manichee for a while, then a Platonist. Justin Martyr was a Stoic, then an Aristotelian, then a Pythagorean, then a Platonist, then a Christian.

If you've had just one set of religious beliefs all your life, you probably think of them as the naturally right ones, in the same way that if you grew up with just one language, you think of it as the perfect language. But a little thought experiment might show you how you could have had very different religious beliefs. Suppose that in the hospital where you were born, there was a mix-up between two babies, so that instead of your parents taking you home, another couple took you home, and your parents took home the other child. And suppose that the religions of the two families were very different, say Hindu and Christian. Do you think that you would have the religion you have now? If you are now a Christian, then if this mix-up had occurred, you would have been raised a Hindu. If that happened, do you think that you would have rejected Hinduism and insisted on being baptized as a Christian?

If millions of Christians have had false beliefs, and there's nothing special about me that makes me immune from error, then I may be one of the millions of Christians with false beliefs. That makes it important for me to think carefully about what I believe.

For further reading:

Kent Bendall and Frederick Ferré. *Exploring the Logic of Faith: A Dialogue on the Relation of Modern Philosophy to Christian Faith.* New York: Association Press, 1962.

E. IS FAITH ALWAYS GOOD?

Once we realize that having a belief doesn't guarantee its truth, we can see that faith has limitations. As we said above, the word "faith" is used so often with a positive meaning that we might think faith is always a virtue. But careful thinking will show that it isn't.

The way Christians look upon the beliefs of opposing Christian groups shows that they don't believe that faith is always a virtue. Baptists don't praise Roman Catholics for their faith in the pope or faith in the saints, for instance. In fact, because of what Catholics believe, some Baptists deny that Catholics are Christians. The same attitude of condemning the faith of other Christians goes back to the early centuries of Christianity. Augustine didn't value the faith of the Donatists, a group of fellow Christians who disagreed with him on minor theological issues. In fact, he advocated launching a war against them because of their faith.

If we look at faith outside of religion, too, we see that believing something for which you don't have solid evidence is usually objectionable rather than praiseworthy. Normally, we expect people to adjust the level of their confidence in a belief to the evidence they have for it. If they have conclusive evidence, that justifies great confidence, but if they have only weak evidence, we expect them not to have great confidence. Someone who watched a cable TV program on the Loch Ness monster, for example, and then said, "Now I'm 100 percent convinced that there really is a dinosaur-like creature living in Loch Ness" would be considered less than rational.

Similarly, a chemist, lawyer, banker, engineer, surveyor, or accountant who accepted people's claims "on faith" instead of checking them would not last long in her profession. In general, whenever we have responsibility for other people's welfare, believing in something for which you have only weak evidence is blameworthy, even criminal. If an engineer assigned to inspect a bridge after an earthquake did not carefully examine the hundreds of joints in the structure but simply looked at the bridge from a distance and concluded, "I believe it's as strong as ever," he could go to prison if the bridge later collapsed.

In religion, too, there are cases of objectionable faith. Muhammad Atta and his eighteen colleagues on September 11, 2001, were men of deepest faith. Right up to the morning of the attacks, they were praying to God to increase their faith. Just think of the confidence it would take to fly a jet into the World Trade Center so that it explodes in a fireball. But does anyone think that the faith of these men was a virtue? Similarly, the 909 men, women, and children who died in the mass suicide at Jonestown had faith in Rev. Jim Jones. Imagine the faith it would take to obey Jones's order to give your child a cup of poison and, as the child lay dying, to drink poison yourself. But that faith was hardly a virtue.

Another example of harmful faith emerged in 1997 at Rancho Santa Fe, California, when Marshall Herff Applewhite engineered the largest mass suicide on American soil. Applewhite was the son of a Presbyterian minister. Very religious from a young age, he enrolled in Union Presbyterian Seminary after college to become a minister. Then he left the study of theology to pursue a musical career, starting as music director of a Presbyterian church in North Carolina. After earning a master's degree in music, he taught first at the University of Alabama and then at the University of Saint Thomas in Houston, Texas, where he was also choral director of an Episcopal church.

After several personal crises, Applewhite became friends with Bonnie Nettles, a nurse who was interested in biblical prophecy. Together they opened a bookstore called the Christian Arts Center and began to develop their own religion. When the bookstore failed, they traveled around the southwest working out their belief system by studying the King James Bible, the life of Saint Francis of Assisi, mystics like Helena Blavatsky, and science fiction writers such as Robert Heinlein and Arthur Clarke. By mid-1974 they had formulated their own worldview, for which they tried to recruit followers. They told audiences that they were the two witnesses mentioned in the Book of Revelation and that they had been chosen to fulfill biblical prophecies. One of their pamphlets described a reincarnation of Jesus that closely matched the features of Applewhite. Starting in 1975 they began to persuade audiences. Part of their message was the idea that in ancient times, space aliens had visited earth and left a few of their own here; eventually they would come back to collect these visitors. Using language from the popular *Star Trek* television show, Applewhite promised young people that they would be biologically transformed into a new, higher species. Calling themselves "Bo" and "Peep," Applewhite and Nettles soon had a flock of about seventy. Over the next two decades they would reorganize their followers several times and teach them different things to believe. Nettles's death from cancer in 1985 left Applewhite despondent, but he said that she had gone to the "next level." Referring to her as "the Father," he told followers to think of him as Christ. Jesus, he said, was an extraterrestrial who came to earth, was killed, rose from the dead, and then traveled on a spaceship to the next level. Every two thousand years, there was a new opportunity for humans to travel to the next level, and the next one would be in the 1990s.

In the early 1990s Applewhite began to talk about suicide as a way of ascending to the next level. Everything "human" had to be left behind to reach the next level, he said, including the body. At this point he gave his cult a new name: Heaven's Gate. Like some early Christian ascetics, Applewhite preached about the need to suppress sexual urges. Sexuality chains us to our bodies, he said, and so keeps us from rising to the next level. Here he cited Jesus' saying that there would be no marriage in heaven (Matthew 22:30; Mark 12:25; Luke 20:35). With seven followers, Applewhite hired a Mexican surgeon to castrate them. He also had his followers wear unisex clothing and haircuts. In 1996, Heaven's Gate rented a mansion in Rancho Santa Fe, California, and prepared to "evacuate Earth." At that time the Hale-Bopp comet was approaching earth, and Applewhite said that Nettles was in a spaceship behind the comet coming back to take him and his followers to the next level. In March 1997, the group recorded some farewell statements and prepared for the "final exit." The suicides were spread over three days: wearing identical black uniforms with "Heaven's Gate Away Team" patches, they consumed alcohol and barbiturates and then put bags over their heads. The thirty-nine corpses were found with bags next to them containing IDs and a little money, presumably for use in the next level.

I have gone into detail about the Heaven's Gate group because, although it wasn't a mainstream church, it had many similarities to thousands of Christian groups over the centuries. Among those similarities, it had a charismatic savior leader who told his followers what to believe, it taught that we need to escape this evil world to reach a higher plane of existence, and it offered a way to achieve that escape.

Here someone might object that while the followers of Marshall Herff Applewhite and Rev. Jim Jones had faith, it was faith in the wrong kind of leader and the wrong kind of teaching. These were not good and truthful men, and their teachings were not true, so they did not deserve the faith that their followers had in them. That's certainly right, but it concedes the point that faith is not always good. And it doesn't tell us how to make sure the person or teaching we have faith in is the right kind, except by saying that the person should be good and truthful, and the teaching should be true. That's hardly useful advice, because it merely tells us that in order to know that our faith is good, we have to know that the person we have faith in is good and truthful and the beliefs we have faith in are true. But if we already *know* that the person is good and truthful, and *know* that our beliefs are true, then we already have *knowledge*, and so *faith* is unnecessary. To use Luther's language, the only way to tell whether "your faith and trust be right" or "your trust be false and wrong," is to already *know* what you are accepting on faith. But if you *know* something, there is no need for *faith*.

For further reading:

Sam Harris. *The End of Faith: Religion, Terror, and the Future of Reason.* New York: W. W. Norton, 2005.

3

THE BIBLE

Many Christians think of the Bible as God's direct communication to the human race, as "the word of God" given to us as an instruction manual for life. It's common to hear that we need the Bible in order to live a good life, and many evangelicals say it's all we need to live a good life. When we look into what the Bible is, however, and how it was written, edited, copied, and translated through the centuries, things are not so simple.

A. IS THE BIBLE A BOOK?

This may seem like a stupid question. It's bound in one volume and called "the Good Book." People often say it's the best-selling book of all time. The fact that something is called a "book," however, doesn't prove that it's a standard book—a single text composed of certain sentences, written by one or more authors. A telephone book, for example, isn't a standard book. To see how different the Bible is from a standard book, imagine walking into a bookstore and buying two items—a volume titled *Why We Can't Wait*, by Martin Luther King Jr., and another volume titled *The Bible*. The first one is clearly a book, but how much is the second one like it?

One person, Dr. King, wrote *Why We Can't Wait* over a few years, so his name is on the cover. By contrast, at least forty people, over many centuries, wrote the documents that were eventually grouped together and called "The Bible." The canon—the official list of writings included in the Bible—was not determined until the late fourth century, long after the writers of those documents were dead. It consisted of older documents called the Old Testament, or Hebrew Bible, and documents written by early Christians called the New Testament. Most of the writers of these documents didn't know any of the other writers, and none knew that what they were writing would later become part of "The Bible."

Why We Can't Wait also has a central theme—the struggle for civil rights in the United States—and one kind of writing—history mixed with the author's personal experiences and reflections. The Bible, by contrast, has dozens of themes and many diverse kinds of writing. In Genesis, there are stories, in fact conflicting stories, about how all things were created. Chapter 1 says that God created trees and plants on the third day, birds on the fifth day, and land animals on the sixth day. At the very end, on the sixth day, it says, God made human beings. Chapter 2 says that God made trees, birds, and land animals *after* he made human beings.

Besides creation stories, the Bible has accounts of the lives and preaching of Ezekiel, Jeremiah, Isaiah, and a dozen more prophets. It also has historical accounts in books like Joshua and Kings. Books such as Leviticus and Deuteronomy present hundreds of laws given by God to the people of Israel. There is also a collection of psalms and a collection of proverbs. The book called Ecclesiastes is a philosophical reflection on how life is pointless and empty, and the Book of Job is the story of a man who was God's favorite, but whose life was ruined when God let Satan destroy all his possessions, kill his children, and cover his body with painful sores. The Song of Solomon is a poem in which two lovers express their passion for each other and don't even mention God.

The writings Christians added to the Hebrew Bible are called the New Testament. It consists of the four Gospels, stories about the life and teachings of Jesus Christ; the Acts of the Apostles, stories about Jesus' followers after he was gone; letters (epistles) written by Paul, James, Peter, John, and Jude; and the Book of Revelation, a vision of how the world will end.

The diversity of all these documents makes the Bible quite different from standard books. It is more like a small library. This is acknowledged in the tradition of calling the major parts of the Bible "books."

Another difference is that a standard book has a certain number of chapters—*Why We Can't Wait* has eight—while there is no agreed-upon number of books in the Bible. Different churches have different canons—lists of the books in the Bible. The Bibles used by most Protestants are sixty-six books, the ones used by most Catholics are seventy-two or seventy-three books, and the ones used by most Orthodox Christians are seventy-six books. The Wisdom of Solomon, for example, is a book in Roman Catholic and most Orthodox Bibles that is found in no Protestant Bibles.

It's misleading, therefore, to talk about "*the* Bible"—there are only *Bibles*. We will follow tradition and continue talking about "the Bible," but we have to acknowledge that we're not talking about a single text.

Not only do different groups of Christians have different books in their Bibles, but those books themselves come in different versions—different sets of words. That variation requires some explanation for people who haven't studied handwritten manuscripts. All the copies of King's *Why We Can't Wait* were made on printing presses, so they are all the same text—the same words in the same order. When the writings that later became the Bible were composed, on the other hand, there were no printing presses, only people writing words on scrolls and codices (groups of flat-bound pages: the singular is *codex*). Those texts are called manuscripts, from the Latin *manus* (hand) and *scribere* (write), and the people who wrote them are called scribes. After a text was written by hand, if people wanted another copy, they had a scribe look at the first manuscript and write the words on a new scroll or codex. In that copying, scribes often made changes, accidentally or on purpose. If you've ever copied part of a book yourself by writing it on paper, you know what happens: you unintentionally skip a word or phrase here and there, or you change a word to one that sounds better to you.

Consider, for example, the biblical story of the leper who came to Jesus and asked to be cured. Most of today's Bibles say that Jesus felt sorry for him. *The New Revised Standard Version* says, "Moved with pity, Jesus stretched out his hand and touched him." But some authoritative ancient manuscripts say that Jesus felt anger rather than pity for the man. What may have happened here is that two Aramaic words got confused—*ethraham* (he had pity) and *ethra'em* (he was enraged). A scribe may have looked at *ethra'em* and, knowing that in the story Jesus heals the man, read it as *ethraham*. A scribe may also have deliberately changed "he was enraged" to "he had pity" to make Jesus look kinder in the story.

Over centuries, scribes created manuscripts by copying not the original manuscripts, but copies that were themselves made from copies that were themselves made from copies and so on, back to the original manuscripts, which may well have been lost or destroyed. In the process, changes multiplied. Even if we assume that there was a single original manuscript for Genesis or the Gospel of Mark, it was lost or destroyed many centuries ago. All we have today of Genesis or Mark is not the exact words that the author wrote, but hundreds of manuscripts whose words differ from each other. If we looked through the more than 5,400 ancient manuscripts of the New Testament in Greek that have survived, we wouldn't find a single verse that was the same in all of them. Indeed, as the *New Oxford Annotated Bible* says, "There is no phrase in the New Testament for which there is not some variant."[1] Imagine reading through 5,000 copies of King's *Why We Can't Wait* and finding that not a single phrase was the same in all of them!

To appreciate the diversity of versions of the New Testament, consider two parts of the Gospel of Mark, the beginning and the end. Many Bibles today have this opening for Mark: "The beginning of the good news of Jesus Christ, the Son of God." But there are authoritative ancient manuscripts of Mark that read simply "The beginning of the good news of Jesus Christ."

More complicated is the end of Mark's Gospel, in chapter 16.[2] In all authoritative versions, this chapter says that three women went to the tomb of Jesus early on the first day of the week. They were concerned about who would roll away the stone at the entrance, but when they got there, "they saw that the stone, which was very large, had already been rolled back." (16:4). Going in, they saw a young man in a white robe, who reassured them that Jesus "has been raised; he is not here . . . But go, tell his disciples and Peter that he is going ahead of you to Galilee; there you will see him, just as he told you." Then verse 8 says, "So they went out and fled from the tomb, for terror and amazement had seized them; and they said nothing to anyone, for they were afraid."

The oldest manuscripts of the Gospel of Mark end here, but today's Bibles usually add twelve more verses, verses 9–20, which describe Jesus appearing to Mary Magdalene, to two other followers, and then to the eleven remaining apostles. Verses 15–20 are translated something like this:

> And he said to them, "Go into all the world and proclaim the good news to the whole creation. The one who believes and is baptized will be saved; but the one who does not believe will be condemned. And these signs will accompany those who believe: by using my name they will cast out demons; they will speak in new tongues; they will pick up snakes in their hands, and if they drink any deadly thing, it will not hurt them; they will lay their hands on the sick, and they will recover." So then the Lord Jesus, after he had spoken to them, was taken up into heaven and sat down at the right hand of God. And they went out and proclaimed the good news everywhere, while the Lord worked with them and confirmed the message by the signs that accompanied it (16:15–20).

Most New Testament scholars say that verses 9–20 were not part of the original Gospel of Mark, but were added later to strengthen the message that Jesus had been resurrected. As evidence, they point out that the oldest and most reliable manuscripts of Mark do not have verses 9–20, and that the fourth-century church leaders Ambrose and Eusebius said that most of the versions of Mark they had seen did not have those verses.[3] Also, scholars say, the writing style in verses 9–20 is quite different from the rest of Mark's Gospel, with many words and expressions that occur nowhere else in Mark. Even some early manuscripts that do include verses 9–20 mark them with asterisks to indicate that they are an addition to the original text.

Besides the manuscripts that end with verse 8 and those that add the passages above after verse 8, two more versions of Mark's Gospel were already circulating by the fifth century. Some have this "shorter ending" after verse 8: "And all that had been commanded them they told briefly to those around Peter. And afterward Jesus himself sent out through them, from east to west, the sacred and imperishable proclamation of eternal salvation." Still other manuscripts include verses 9–20 and add some or all of these words after verse 14:

> And they excused themselves, saying, "This age of lawlessness and unbelief is under Satan, who does not allow the truth and power of God to prevail over the unclean things of the spirits. Therefore reveal your righteousness now"—thus they spoke to Christ. And Christ

replied to them, "The term of years of Satan's power has been fulfilled, but other terrible things draw near. And for those who have
sinned I was handed over to death, that they may return to the truth
and sin no more, that they may inherit the spiritual and imperishable
glory of righteousness that is in heaven."

Earlier we cited several dissimilarities between the Bible and standard books to argue that the Bible is not a book. Here we can see that at
least some of the "books" of the Bible are not books, either. A standard
book is composed of certain sentences, but there is no single Gospel of
Mark composed of certain sentences. There are only many manuscripts
composed of different sentences. So, just as we said there is no such
thing as the Bible—there are only Bibles, we can say there is no such
thing as the Gospel of Mark—there are only Gospels of Mark.

What the many variations in manuscripts calling themselves the Gospel of Mark show is that early Christians did not understand the scriptures to be determinate texts that had to be copied word for word. In
other words, they did not understand the "books" that became the Bible
to be what we now call "books." The grand collection of them into "The
Bible," as we have seen, is even less like what we now call "a book."

For further reading:

The New Oxford Annotated Bible. 4th ed. Oxford: Oxford University Press, 2010, 2185–2253.
Bart D. Ehrman. Misquoting Jesus: The Story behind Who Changed the Bible and Why.
    New York: HarperCollins, 2007.
Richard Friedman. Who Wrote the Bible? San Francisco: HarperOne, 1997.

B. IS THE BIBLE THE WORD OF GOD?

Every religion that uses writing has documents they consider sacred.
Jews have the Hebrew Bible, Christians the Christian Bible, Muslims
the Qur'an, and Hindus the Vedas. We call these "scriptures," a word
coming from the Latin verb scribere, to write. Some religions make a
further claim that their sacred writings were revealed by God—God
spoke certain words to human beings, who wrote them down, or he
inspired human beings to write down certain words. That's how the
Hebrew Bible, the Christian Bible, and the Qur'an are often described.
This claim is easiest to understand with the Qur'an, which, Muhammad

said, was recited to him by the angel Gabriel over a period of years. Throughout the Qur'an, the speaker is God. Muhammad memorized what he had heard, and later it was written in Arabic, the language in which Gabriel recited it. If that message is changed in any way, many Muslims say, as by translating it, then what results is not the Qur'an because it is not the words that God revealed to Muhammad. For Muslims who understand the Qur'an this way, it makes sense to say that the Qur'an is the word of God.

Many Christians talk about the Bible in the same way as the word of God. In books like Norman Geisler's *From God to Us: How We Got Our Bible*, the words of the Bible are described as sent to us by God. Evangelical Christians think this way, and so the Bible is at the center of their lives.

Despite the popularity of the idea that the Bible is God's word, things are not as simple with the Bible as with the Qur'an. As we have seen, it was composed over many centuries, of variant versions, of dozens of documents, in many kinds of writing, by at least forty writers. That process seems hard to reconcile with the claim that the Bible is messages God sends us. After we read the four endings of the Gospel of Mark, for instance, we might ask why God would have four endings for a story he tells us. A more basic question is why he would communicate the Gospel, the good news of Jesus Christ, four times with four stories that have inconsistencies. The Gospel of Mark 15:25, for example, says that "It was nine o'clock in the morning when they crucified him." The Gospel of John 19:13–16 says that "it was about noon" when Pilate presented Jesus to the crowd, and they cried out "Crucify him." So sometime after noon "he handed him over to them to be crucified."

Another problem with the claim that the Bible is the word of God is that while many passages in the Bible describe God's communicating with people, many others do not. Several passages in Exodus and Leviticus begin "The Lord said to Moses: Tell the Israelites . . . " The Gospels tell how after Jesus was baptized by John, a voice from a cloud said, "This is my beloved son, with whom I am well pleased" (Matthew 3:17; Mark 1:11; Luke 9:35). It makes sense to think of passages like these, in which God talks to people, as "the word of God." But how about the many books of the Bible that do not seem to be God's speaking to human beings or revealing anything to them? The Psalms, for instance, are words addressed *to* God *by* people, not the other way around. Psalm

141 begins, "I call upon you, O Lord; come quickly to me; give ear to my voice when I call to you." *The New Oxford Annotated Bible* subtitles this prayer "A Psalm of David" because it was supposedly composed by King David. But what would it mean to say that it is "the word of God"? Why would *God* say, "I call upon you, O Lord; come quickly to me"? And what would it mean to say that this calling upon God is God's *revelation*?

One response here might be that while God didn't *say*, "I call upon you, O Lord; come quickly to me," he *inspired David to say it*. If that's right, then we may still want to say that Psalm 141 is "God's word." There are other books of the Bible, however, where it's much less plausible to say that God inspired the person writing them. The Song of Solomon, for example, consists of erotic poetry spoken by two lovers. There is nothing said by God and nothing said about God. As *The New Oxford Annotated Bible* says, "The Song is about how glorious it is to be in love."[4] The whole book consists of lines like these:

> (the woman speaks}
> I slept, but my heart was awake,
> Listen! My beloved is knocking. . .
> I had put off my garment;
> How could I put it on again?
> My beloved thrust his hand into the opening,
> and my inmost being yearned for him.
> I arose to open to my beloved.
> (the man speaks)
> Your rounded thighs are like jewels, the work of a master hand.
> Your navel is a rounded bowl that never lacks mixed wine.
> Your belly is a heap of wheat, encircled with lilies
> Your two breasts are like two fawns, twins of a gazelle . . .
> You are stately as a palm tree, and your breasts are like its clusters.
> I say I will climb the palm tree and lay hold of its branches.

These lines don't sound like the words of God, or like words inspired by God. They sound like the words of two passionate lovers.

Another kind of writing in the Bible for which it seems implausible to say that God inspired humans to write the words is the many historical passages describing events that anyone who was there at the time could have simply recorded. Here, for example, is part of the account in the Book of Numbers, chapter 33, of the Hebrews' travels after they left Egypt. Moses, the book says, kept records of all these trips.

> They departed from Kibroth Hattaavah and camped at Hazeroth. They departed from Hazeroth and camped at Rithmah. They departed from Rithmah and camped at Rimmon Perez. They departed from Rimmon Perez and camped at Libnah. They departed from Libnah and camped at Rissah. They departed from Rissah and camped at Kehelathah. They departed from Kehelathah and camped at Mount Shepher. They moved from Mount Shepher and camped at Haradah. They moved from Haradah and camped at Makheloth. They moved from Makheloth and camped at Tahath. They departed from Tahath and camped at Terah. They moved from Terah and camped at Mithkah.

After this passage there are nine more moves recorded, and before this passage there were another twelve. Let's assume that this account has all the details exactly right. Still, why would anyone claim that this passage is God's words, inspiration, or revelation? Why would God reveal to anyone that the Israelites "departed from Kibroth Hattaavah and camped at Hazeroth," and made dozens of other moves? Why not just say that Moses recorded this information and it was later written in the Book of Numbers?

Two more books of the Bible—Job and Ecclesiastes—also seem to be poor candidates for writings revealed by God. That is not because they don't mention God or because they record events people could have seen for themselves, but because they protest against how God has set up the world and how he treats people.

In the Book of Job, Job is described as "blameless and upright," and God is so pleased with him that he boasts to his angel Satan (not the devil of Christianity), "There is no one like him on the earth" (1:8). Satan answers that it's easy for Job to be so good—he is rich and prosperous and has a loving family. "But stretch out your hand now and touch all that he has, and he will curse you to your face" (1:11). God accepts this challenge, betting that Job will stay faithful to him even when his possessions and family are wiped out. When that happens, Job does not curse God, so God wins that bet. But Satan challenges God again. Job is still healthy and not in pain, he says, but if you inflict great suffering on him, Job will "curse you to your face" (2:5). God accepts this second bet. When Job is covered in sores from head to foot, he starts to protest. First he curses the day he was born, saying that his life is pointless. Then, as three of his friends advise him that he or his children must have sinned to deserve so much suffering, he insists that they are wrong and that God is torturing him for no reason. As Job and his friends argue, he looks beyond his own pointless suffering to that of the human race, arguing that life in general is full of undeserved suffering. "A mortal, born of woman, few of days and full of trouble, comes up like a flower and withers, flees like a shadow and does not last" (14:1–2). And after all the suffering comes death, which throughout the Old Testament is understood as the destruction of the person.

At the end of the story, God says to one of Job's friends, "My wrath is kindled against you and against your two friends, for you have not spoken of me what is right, as my servant Job has" (42:7). God tells the three men to ask Job to pray to him to spare them, which Job does. Then "the Lord restored the fortunes of Job . . . and the Lord gave Job twice as much as he had before" (42:10).

In this story God is described as at least unjust and perhaps cruel. On two bets with Satan, he has Satan inflict horrible, undeserved suffering on his favorite servant. After Job protests that God is cruel and unfair, God says that Job has spoken the truth. What would it mean to say that this story is God's word, his revelation to the human race? Is God supposed to be saying to the human race that he *is* cruel and unfair?

The speaker in the Book of Ecclesiastes has even stronger complaints about the way God runs the world. Not just lives like Job's that are full of suffering but *all* human lives are pointless, empty, like "chasing after wind," the speaker says. And since his voice is the only voice throughout the book, if God is revealing something in Ecclesiastes, it is what the narrator is saying. "All is vanity. What do people gain from all the toil at which they toil under the sun?" (1:2–3). In chapter 3, the narrator complains that "the fate of humans and the fate of animals is the same; as one dies, so dies the other . . . All go to one place; all are from the dust, and all turn to dust again" (3:19–20). Those who say that the Bible is the word of God, his revelation, have to say that Ecclesiastes is God's revelation. But the central messages in this book are that all endeavors are futile, all things are wearisome, and humans die like dogs, decomposing into the dust from which they came. Do any Christians believe these messages? And if these messages are false, then they cannot have been revealed by God.

The biblical writer cited most often by people who say the Bible is the word of God is Paul. They often quote his Second Letter to Timothy 3:16 as "All scripture is inspired by God and is useful for teaching, for reproof, for correction, and for training in righteousness." But, as with many passages in the Bible, there is more than one way to translate the Greek words here. *The New Oxford Annotated Bible* uses the translation above but notes that the passage could also mean "Every scripture inspired by God is also useful for teaching, for reproof . . . " In other words, *some* scripture is inspired by God, but *some* isn't, and the scripture that is inspired by God is useful for teaching and other purposes.

We must remember, too, that when Paul was writing, scripture meant only "religious writing," not "The Bible." None of the Gospels had been written yet, and no collection of books had been designated the Old Testament or the Hebrew Bible. Though several of Paul's letters became part of the Christian Bible three centuries after he died, he did not think of them as the Bible. He felt guided by God, but he also distinguished between his own opinions and what God might say about various issues. In his First Letter to the Corinthians, he says this about divorce: "I say—I and not the Lord—that if any believer has a wife who is an unbeliever, and she consents to live with him, he should not divorce her" (7:12). Later in that letter, he has this advice for virgins: "Now concerning virgins, I have no command of the Lord, but I give my opinion as one who by the Lord's mercy is trustworthy. I think that, in view of the impending crisis, it is well for you to remain as you are" (7:25–26). In his Second Letter to the Corinthians, Paul says, "Let no one think that I am a fool, but if you do, then accept me as a fool, so that I too may boast a little. What I am saying in regard to this boastful confidence, I am saying not with the Lord's authority, but as a fool; since many boast according to human standards, I will also boast" (11:16–18). Clearly, these words are *the words of Paul*, not *the word of God*.

Calling the whole Bible "the word of God," then, is inaccurate.

For further reading:

Norman Geisler. *From God to Us: How We Got Our Bible*. Chicago: Moody Press, 1974.
The Jesus Seminar. *The Five Gospels: What Did Jesus Really Say?* New York: Macmillan, 1993.

C. DOES THE BIBLE TELL US ALL WE NEED TO KNOW TO LIVE A GOOD LIFE?

Linked to the claim that the Bible is God's word is the idea popular among evangelicals that in the Bible God tells us all we need to know to live a good life. In the fourth century, Athanasius, the bishop of Alexandria who dominated the Council of Nicaea, said that "The holy and inspired scriptures are fully sufficient for the proclamation of truth."[5] Today, the website of the Billy Graham Evangelistic Association says, "For almost two thousand years, Christians have agreed that the Bible alone is God's Word, and that it tells us everything we need to know about Him."[6]

In this way of thinking, the Bible is an instruction manual for living. Christian bookstores have dozens of examples of this way of thinking, in books that apply Bible verses to issues such as marriage, family life, money matters, health, and nutrition. Among the books of recipes derived from the Bible, for example, one is the inspiration for the Ezekiel 4:9 bread sold in American supermarkets.

Despite its popularity, the idea that the Bible is a complete guide to life is questionable. On issues related to marriage, for instance, many books of the Bible seem to be not just incomplete guides, but false guides. Dozens of passages in the Old Testament speak approvingly of men having several wives and concubines (sexual partners to whom one is not married). Among the laws given by God to Moses is this one for bigamists:

> If a man has two wives, one of them loved and the other disliked, and if both the loved and the disliked have borne him sons, the firstborn being the son of the one who is disliked, then on the day when he wills his possessions to his sons, he is not permitted to treat the son of the loved as the firstborn in preference to the son of the disliked, who is the firstborn (Deuteronomy 21:15–16).

Abraham, the founder of the whole Judeo-Christian tradition, had two wives, Sarah and Keturah, as well as concubines. When Sarah could not conceive a child, she gave her servant Hagar to him to have sex with and produce a child (Genesis 16:3; 21:1–13; 25:1). Abraham's grandson Jacob, who was renamed Israel and after whom the whole Jewish tradition is named, had four wives. Genesis 29 describes his marriages to the sisters Leah and Rachel, and Genesis 30 describes his marriages to Bilhah and Zilpah. No Christian today reading these chapters would take them to be a guidebook for marriage. Even less would Christians reading the First Book of Kings emulate the celebrated kings of Israel. King David, from whom the Bible says Jesus was descended, had seven wives (1 Chronicles 3). Of King Solomon, the Bible says, "Among his wives were seven hundred princesses and three hundred concubines" (1 Kings 11:3). Most of these women were not Israelites but followers of gods such as Astarte, Milcom, Chemosh, and Molech. Solomon built shrines "for all his foreign wives, who offered incense and sacrificed to their gods" (1 Kings 11:5–8). While the Bible makes it clear that Solomon displeased God, it says that the issue was his worshipping foreign gods, not his having a thousand wives and concubines (1 Kings 11:9–10).

Christians are often surprised to learn that the New Testament does not forbid polygamy, either. In First Timothy 3:2, First Timothy 3:12, and Titus 1:6, Paul says that bishops, deacons, and elders should be "husbands of one wife." That requirement would be pointless if no early Christian men had ever married more than one wife.

The Bible is unreliable as a guidebook not only for marriage, but for family life. For decades in the United States, Christian broadcasters such as Dr. James C. Dobson of the Focus on the Family radio ministry, and programs on the Family Life Radio network, have promoted the idea that the Bible teaches "family values" that should govern our families today. But if we read the Bible, we see that life in ancient Palestine was so different from life today that it would be dangerous to impose ancient practices on our families. Consider, for instance, this law given by God in Exodus 21:7, shortly after the Ten Commandments in Exodus 20: "When a man sells his daughter as a slave, she shall not go out [be freed in the seventh year] as the male slaves do." Or this law given by God in Leviticus 20:9: "All who curse father or mother shall be put to death." Or the law right after that: "If a man commits adultery with the wife of his neighbor, both the adulterer and the adulteress shall be put to death" (Leviticus 20:10). Immediately following are more laws stipulating the death penalty for a man having sex with his father's wife, or his daughter-in-law, or another man, or his mother-in-law, or an animal (Leviticus 20:11–15).

What if we lived by those biblical laws today? A man selling his daughter as a slave would violate not only civil laws but the moral laws of all Christian churches. Christian parents who executed their child for cursing them would not be praised but charged with murder. So would a person who killed a couple for adultery, or killed someone for any of the other forbidden actions mentioned above.

If the Old Testament does not offer reliable principles for today's family living, how about the Gospels? The most obvious thing to say here is that Jesus did not get married and have a family. Choosing to remain single is accepted today, but in first-century Palestine, it was highly questionable, since a person's descendants and ancestors determined his very identity. A man like Jesus, still unmarried at age thirty, was not living up to the "family values" of that time.

Jesus also preached a way of life quite opposed to the modern nuclear family. Today the ideal family consists of a mother and a father, one or both working, and several children, living in a stable home. But the Gospels do not say that as an adult Jesus ever had a job or lived in a home. Indeed, when a man promised to follow him wherever he went, Jesus said, "Foxes have holes, and birds of the air have nests, but the Son of Man has nowhere to lay his head" (Matthew 8:19–20).

Those who say the Bible guides us in managing money would be hard put to give examples from the life of Jesus. He preached a life of radical poverty completely contrary to today's ideal of financial security. When he said, "Blessed are you who are poor, for yours is the kingdom of God" (Luke 6:20), his word for "poor" was not *penēs*, the Greek word for poor peasants, but *ptōchoi*, the word for destitute beggars.

Further distinguishing Jesus' preaching from today's "family values" are his warnings that following him will require breaking with one's family.

> I have come to set a man against his father, and a daughter against her mother, and a daughter-in-law against her mother-in-law, and one's foes will be members of one's own household. Whoever loves father or mother more than me is not worthy of me; and whoever

loves son or daughter more than me is not worthy of me (Matthew 10:35–37).

Even stronger is Jesus' preaching that "Whoever comes to me and does not hate father and mother, wife and children, brothers and sisters, yes, even life itself, cannot be my disciple" (Luke 14:26).

If the Bible doesn't tell us all we need to know about family life, it's not surprising that it isn't a guide to good citizenship, either. Today we take for granted the idea that political power comes from the people. But throughout the Bible, the standard form of government is rule by an all-powerful king. No one in the Bible ever votes. Saint Paul says, "Let everyone be subject to the governing authorities, for there is no authority except from God, and those authorities that exist have been instituted by God. Therefore, whoever resists authority resists what God has appointed, and those who resist will incur judgment" (Romans 13:1–2). If that's correct, then no Christian should ever protest against any political leader, for they have all been appointed by God. Christians who have resisted dictators such as Adolf Hitler, then, were rebelling against God and should be condemned. Do you or anyone you know believe that?

The political ideas in the Bible are contrary not just to democracy but to the Universal Declaration of Human Rights proclaimed by the United Nations in 1948. That document says, "All human beings are born free and equal in dignity and rights" (article 1), "Everyone has the right to life, liberty and security of person" (article 3), and "No one shall be held in slavery or servitude" (article 4). Nowhere in the Bible is there approval for the idea that people are born free and equal, or that they have a right to life and liberty. Millions of people were slaves through- out the period in which the Bible was written, and no biblical writer complained that slavery was immoral. In the Bible, God even regulates slavery, as we saw in his law about female slaves not going free after seven years (Exodus 21:7). Saint Paul, as mentioned earlier, encouraged slaves to be subservient to their masters: "Slaves, obey your earthly masters in everything, not only while being watched in order to please them, but with a sincere heart, fearing the Lord" (Colossians 3:22). His Letter to the Ephesians 6:5 says, "Slaves, obey your earthly masters with respect and fear, just as you would obey Christ."

Beyond the inadequacy of the Bible as a guide to marriage, family life, and politics, it doesn't even mention hundreds of issues we face today. In global affairs, consider the threat of nuclear war and the need to control carbon emissions. In medicine, there are debates about stem-cell research, in vitro fertilization, and treating patients with terminal cancer. None of these were issues in ancient Palestine, and so they understandably are not covered in the Bible. Even simpler questions like whether children should be educated in schools or at home, and how best to protect them from sexual predators, are not even mentioned in the Bible.

However valuable the Bible is, then, and whatever good advice it has on certain topics, it does not tell us all we need to know to live a good life.

For further reading:

Deirdre Good. *Jesus' Family Values*. New York: Church Publishing, 2006.

D. IS THE BIBLE NECESSARY FOR LIVING A GOOD LIFE?

Challenging the idea that the Bible is a complete guide to life may not seem revolutionary once you consider the details, but many Christians are still committed to a related idea that seems harder to question. It is that the Bible is *necessary* for living a good life. Even if the Bible doesn't tell us everything we need, doesn't it at least tell us certain essential things that we couldn't get any other way? That has been the view of many Christians, especially those who follow Martin Luther's motto *sola scriptura*, "by the Bible alone."

One problem with saying that the Bible is necessary for living a good life is that, as we've seen, there is no single text called the Bible. There are only thousands of texts with different words. Someone who claims that "the Bible is necessary for living a good life" would need to specify which version is necessary. Is it one of the Bibles used in Protestant churches, which have sixty-six books? If so, which one, and which translation? Or is the necessary Bible one of those used by Catholics, which have seventy-two or seventy-three books? If so, which of those, and which translation? Or perhaps the Bible that everyone needs is one of the Orthodox Bibles, which have seventy-six books. Notice that if the version of the Bible necessary for living a good life is one with more than sixty-six books, then no Protestant book is the Bible, and so no Protestant can live a good life, at least if people need *the whole Bible* to live a good life.

If they don't need the whole Bible, then, of course, it's misleading to say that *the Bible* is necessary for living a good life. What they should say is that *certain parts of the Bible* are necessary for living a good life. Then they need to tell us which parts those are. It seems we could get along fine, for example, without that long passage from Numbers 33 cited in the last section, listing the dozens of places the Israelites camped in the Sinai Desert. There are also dozens of laws in the Old Testament that Christians do not consider themselves bound by, such as the one in Leviticus 19:19 and Deuteronomy 22:11 that forbids wearing clothing made of different fibers woven together.

What parts of the New Testament, if any, might also be unnecessary for living a good life? Perhaps the story of Jesus cursing the fig tree in Matthew 21:18–22 and Mark 11:12–14, 20–25? The passages in Paul's letters where he tells slaves to submit to their masters do not seem necessary for living a good life.

Even if there were a way to choose one of the versions of the Bible as the "right" one, and specify the necessary parts of that version, there is a simple historical fact that calls into question the idea that any version of the Bible or part of the Bible could be necessary to live a good life. It is that none of the texts included in the Bible were written before 3,000 years ago, but our species, *Homo sapiens*, goes back 150,000 years. If only people who have read the Bible can live good lives, then everyone who lived and died before the Bible was written did not live good lives. That time period—between 150,000 years ago and 3,000 years ago—is 98 percent of human history! Could the all-good Creator set up the world so that all people born before the Bible was written were automatically condemned to live bad lives?

Even when the first texts that would eventually be part of the Bible were written, there was no Bible—there were only scrolls with a few hundred to a few thousand words on them. If living a good life became possible only after church authorities decided which scrolls and codices would be included in the canon, then no one lived a good life before 382, when Pope Damasus at the Council of Rome declared an official list of books in the Bible. Even that list is controversial, since Protestants reject seven of the books it includes. If they are right and Pope Damasus was wrong, then the first time there was an authentic "Bible" was in the 1500s when Protestants changed the Catholic canon.

The idea that no one could live a good life before 1500, or before 382, seems highly questionable. Abraham, Moses, the prophets, Jesus, and Mary all lived before the books that now comprise the Old Testament were decided upon, and before any book of the New Testament was written. Paul, who wrote almost half of the New Testament, died before any of the Gospels were written. If the Bible is necessary for living a good life, then none of these people lived a good life.

Even if we look at the period after the first canon was announced by Pope Damasus, there have been millions of people who never heard of the Bible. Do we want to say that none of those millions in China, Africa, the Americas, and Australia could have lived good lives over all those centuries? Would an all-good God condemn people for not reading something that did not exist where they lived?

That brings up a related question about Christians in the West. For the vast majority of the time versions of the Bible have been available, most Christians have been illiterate and so could not read them. Through the Middle Ages—roughly 500–1500—books of any kind were rare, and only men in holy orders were taught to read and write. Most men and virtually all women were illiterate. If they knew anything from the Bible, it was not because they read it, but because some cleric had read it to them or told them about it. If someone claims that the Bible is necessary for living a good life, does he or she mean that a person has to *read* the Bible, or is it enough to hear about some of it from someone who can read?

When Luther preached his message of *sola scriptura*, making the Bible seem necessary for salvation, Thomas Müntzer was enthusiastic at first. But as Müntzer thought more about how people could achieve salvation and live good lives, he came to see that the Bible could not be the only way. After all, he reasoned, Jesus' apostles and disciples didn't have the Christian Bible, and yet they lived good lives. "If a man in his whole life had neither heard nor seen the Bible, he could nevertheless have an undeceivable Christian faith through the teaching of the Spirit—like those who wrote the Scripture without any books."[7]

Even before the time when the scriptures were written, it seems that we can imagine someone living a good life. In that 98 percent of human history, people organized themselves socially, had moral rules, and re-warded good actions while punishing bad ones. Then, as after the Bible was written, all cultures told people that they should respect their parents, care for their children, tell the truth, and not steal or murder. Those who followed the moral rules of their communities, helping others while harming no one, would certainly seem to please God. One such person, in fact, is described in the Book of Job. Though not an Israelite—he was from "the land of Uz"—and living long before the Bible was written, Job so pleased God that God bragged about him to Satan, "There is no one like him on the earth, a blameless and upright man who fears God and turns away from evil" (Job 1:8).

To explain how someone like Job could live a life pleasing to God even before the Bible existed, Christian thinkers like Thomas Aquinas have appealed to the idea of natural law. Aquinas knew that the Bible's Ten Commandments forbid lying, theft, and murder, for example, and that they command respect for one's parents, but he also knew that cultures that had never heard of the Bible had similar moral rules. So, he reasoned, the Bible cannot be the only way to find out what is right and wrong. Within human nature, he said, there are certain patterns of what works and what doesn't work that form a system of natural law. When babies are born, for instance, they are the most helpless animals on the planet: if no one cared for them, they would die within hours. So part of natural law is that parents nurture their children. As they grow up, children contribute to the family by helping the parents, and so it is also part of natural law that children obey and respect their parents. Cultures in which these rules are followed flourish, and any culture that did not follow them would die out within a few generations.

We can give a similar explanation of the rules against lying found in cultures around the world. Lying violates the nature of human communication, and so it is part of natural law that people tell the truth. As a species, we have always depended on the information we get from other people. We get a phone call or e-mail from a friend, for instance, saying that they will pick us up at a certain time in a certain place. From a medical lab we get a report on the results of our cancer screening. We deposit a two-hundred-dollar check at the bank and get a receipt saying we now have two hundred dollars more in our account. In these and dozens of other interactions each day, we count on the information other people give us to be true. If other people told us the truth only half the time, and lied to us the rest of the time, all communication and record keeping would break down. For anything we wanted to know, it would be as useful to toss a coin as to ask someone. Communication and so human culture would come to an end. Lying, then, is naturally wrong.

There is much more that could be said about natural law, but the basic idea is clear: human beings flourish when they act in certain ways, and they decline when they act in other ways. When we all take care of our children, respect our parents, tell the truth, respect people's property, and so on, we tend to live happy, fulfilled lives. When we act contrary to these natural patterns, we suffer. For Christians in the tradition of natural law, intelligent people anywhere should be able to figure out what is right and wrong, and that is why cultures around the world have created similar moral rules.

None of this plays down the value of the Ten Commandments and all the other valuable guidelines for living in the Bible. It just shows that the Bible is not the only way to get those guidelines, and so the Bible is not necessary for living a good life.

For further reading:

Jacqueline A. Laing and Russell Wilcox, eds. *The Natural Law Reader*. Malden, MA: Wiley Blackwell, 2013.

E. IS THE BIBLE SCIENTIFICALLY AND HISTORICALLY ACCURATE?

Closely linked to the traditional idea that the Bible is revealed by God is the claim that all of the Bible is true. Today most evangelical Protestants and many Catholics say that the Bible is "inerrant"—without error. If God is the author of the Bible, they say, everything in the Bible must be true. The Chicago Statement on Biblical Inerrancy of 1978, signed by over three hundred evangelical scholars, puts it this way:

> Being wholly and verbally God-given, Scripture is without error or fault in all its teaching, no less in what it states about God's acts in creation, about the events of world history, and about its own literary origins under God, than in its witness to God's saving grace in individual lives.

From the early centuries of Christianity, most theologians and church leaders have agreed that the original manuscript for each book of the Bible was without error. But, as we've seen, none of those manuscripts exist today—all we have are copies of copies of copies, with significant variations between them. When the original texts were translated into other languages, too, there was no guarantee that the inerrancy of the original manuscripts was preserved. These issues haven't bothered many Christians over the centuries, however. Most have been confident that their very own Bibles were utterly reliable.

In the nineteenth century, though, there were two challenges to the idea of Biblical inerrancy that seemed much more threatening and that pushed some Christians to adopt a stronger position. The first of those challenges was new scholarly research on the Bible suggesting that it was a collection of humanly written documents shaped by the historical circumstances of their authors. This shocked Christians used to thinking of the biblical writers as writing down words dictated by God. Scholars such as William Robertson Smith and Julius Wellhausen, for example, challenged the traditional belief that Moses wrote the first five books of the Bible. Instead, they said, those books were compiled from four sources long after Moses was dead. The second challenge was Charles Darwin's new theory of evolution, which said that living things evolved over millions of years. The clash here was with the Book of Genesis, which says that God created everything in six days.

In response to these challenges, some Christians insisted that the entire Bible is not only without error but *literally true*, just as a good science book or history book is literally true. The first "fundamental" of the new Christian fundamentalists in the early twentieth century was "The inerrancy, infallibility, and literal truth of the Bible in every detail."

Now, as we noted, from Christianity's early centuries, the scriptures have been thought to be without error. But that did not mean that all the scriptures must be literally true. In the third and fourth centuries, as Christian leaders were deciding on the books that would comprise the Bible, they agreed that those books were inerrant. But they did not say that everything in the Bible is literally true in the way science books and history books are literally true. For one thing, science books and history books as we know them today did not exist yet. Nothing written before 1500, in fact, was held to modern standards of scientific and historical accuracy.

For another thing, the church fathers recognized that there are different genres among the biblical books—different kinds of writing—including poetry, metaphor, allegory, personification, hyperbole, and other nonliteral uses of language. While there is truth throughout the Bible, they said, the verses that use language nonliterally need not be literally true. Origen, for example, noted that in Genesis the name of the first man is "Adam," a Hebrew word meaning "man." Those who know that "Adam" means "man," he said, will be able to read the story of Adam as an allegory of what happens to all human beings.[8]

Another example of a figure of speech in the Bible is the personification of wisdom in the first nine chapters of the Book of Proverbs. There wisdom is described as a woman who helped God create the world:

> The Lord created me at the beginning of his work, the first of his acts of long ago. Ages ago I was set up, at the first, before the beginning of the earth. . . . when he marked out the foundations of the earth, then I was beside him, like a master worker, and I was daily his delight. . . . Wisdom has built her house, she has hewn her seven pillars. She has slaughtered her animals, she has mixed her wine, she has also set her table (Proverbs 8:22–23, 29–30; 9:1–2).

If the whole Bible is literally true, then these words are literally true, and there was a female figure named Wisdom whom God created first to help him create the world. She also built a house, shaped its pillars herself, and did many other jobs around that house. No Christians today believe that such a female figure existed, and that shows that the truth in the Book of Proverbs does not consist in all its sentences being literally true.

Similarly, in the Gospels Jesus says many things about himself that are obviously metaphors, such as "I am the gate for the sheep" (John 10:6–7), "I am the bread of life" (John 6:35), and "I am the true vine, and my Father is the vinegrower" (John 15:1). Contrary to the fundamentalists' insistence on the "literal truth of the Bible in every detail," none of these figures of speech is literally true. Jesus is not actually a gate, bread, or a vine. If there were just one metaphor in the Bible, that would refute fundamentalism; in fact there are hundreds. (We'll say more about metaphors in Jesus' preaching in chapter 4, section E.)

One of the biggest controversies in recent years between those who insist on the literal truth of the whole Bible and those who say that the Bible has many nonliteral figures of speech is over the word "day" (*yom* in Hebrew) in Genesis. Chapter 1 of that book says that God created the world in six "days," which the literalists say must mean six periods of twenty-four hours. From the early centuries of Christianity, however, commentators have said that *day* could mean a longer period. They have pointed out that when God warns Adam in Genesis 2:17 not to eat of the tree of the knowledge of good and evil, he says, "For in the day that you eat of it you shall die." But Adam did not die within twenty-four hours of eating of that tree—Genesis 5:5 says that he lived centuries more, dying at the age of 930.

Both the Old and New Testaments, too, say that to God a thousand years are as a day is to us (Psalm 90:4; 2 Peter 3:8). Justin Martyr used that idea to explain his interpretation of the "days" in Genesis as being a thousand years long.[9] That would fit the story of Adam dying "in the day" he ate from the forbidden tree. Clement of Alexandria said that the writer of Genesis used the six "days" of creation to indicate the order of creation and God's priorities in it, not to claim that creation took place within 144 hours.[10] Augustine said that the first two chapters of Genesis were written to suit the simple understanding of the people of that time, so that the sentences need not be literally true. In fact, according to Augustine, God made everything simultaneously.[11] As for the six "days" of creation, he said, "At least we know that it [a day in Genesis 1] is different from the ordinary day with which we are familiar."[12]

In contrast to the nuanced way these church fathers understood Genesis, consider the people who built and operate the Creation Museum in Petersburg, Kentucky. It is designed to show visitors that the earth and all living things were created directly by God over six twenty-four-hour days about six thousand years ago. There are over eighty moving dinosaurs, many "living" among human beings. The Noah's ark exhibit features a triceratops and a stegosaurus, and to emphasize that dinosaurs were created at the same time as humans, there is Cera the saddled triceratops for children to ride. The museum staff know, of course, that biology books say that dinosaurs had been extinct for sixty million years when humans evolved, but they stick to their literal interpretation of Genesis. According to museum spokesman Mark Looy,

"There may not be any fossil evidence showing dinosaurs and people in the same place at the same time. But it is clearly written [in the Bible] that they were alive at the same time."[13]

The trouble with this literalist approach to the Bible is that it treats the Bible as comparable to modern science books, as if Genesis were written in the way Darwin's *Origin of Species* was—as a scientific explanation for the origin of plants and animals. But the books of the Bible are quite different from science books, so it is unreasonable to expect Genesis to provide the kind of scientific information a biology book provides.

It's not a criticism of the Bible to say that it doesn't adhere to modern standards of accuracy any more than it's a criticism of Roman chariots to say that they didn't have shock absorbers. Precise literal truth is a modern idea that arose out of advanced literacy. At the time Genesis was composed, alphabetic writing was only a few centuries old, and the people who could write still communicated in mostly oral styles rather than in the literate styles found today in science and history books. Modern writing, with its reliance on evidence and fact checking and its distinction between literal claims and figures of speech, came much later. To expect the writing in the Bible to conform to modern standards of scientific and historical accuracy is to misunderstand the kind of writing it is.

If we read carefully the account in Genesis of how God created everything in six days, for example, we can see that it is not intended to compete with our science books. Genesis 1:14–19 says that God made light on the first day of creation and made the sun, moon, and stars on the fourth day. For those to be literal, scientifically accurate statements, there must have been light for three days before the sun, moon, and stars existed! Already by 225, Origen had pointed out that since the sun was created on the "fourth day," the word "day" could not have had its ordinary literal meaning.[14]

Another way to see that we should not expect modern standards of accuracy in literal use of language when we read the Bible is to consider its inconsistent descriptions of events. As we saw in chapter 3, section A, chapter 1 of Genesis says that God created humans *after* plants and animals, while chapter 2 says that God made humans *before* plants and animals. If we treat these two accounts as literal, scientific claims, they are contrary: if the first is true, then the second is false; if the second is true, then the first is false. Either way, part of Genesis has to be false—again, if we are treating Genesis as making literal, scientific claims.

The New Testament also has contrary descriptions of the same events. Three examples are the two accounts of how Jesus was descended from King David, the two accounts of when Jesus was crucified, and the four accounts of what happened at the tomb of Jesus on Easter morning.

First, the Gospels of Luke and Matthew each trace Jesus' ancestry back through Joseph to King David, but they do it through different ancestors. Luke lists the father of Joseph as Heli, while Matthew says that Joseph's father was Jacob. From Heli, Luke continues with Matthat, Levi, Melchi, Jannai, Joseph, Mattathiah, Amos, Nahum, and so on. From Jacob, Matthew continues with Matthan, Eleazar, Eliud, Achim, Zadok, Azor, Eliakim, Abiud, and so on. At the beginning of the chain, Luke has King David, then Nathan, Mattatha, Menna, Melea, Eliakim, and so on. Matthew has King David, then Solomon, Rehoboam, Abijah, Asa, Jehosophat, and so on.

Secondly, as we saw in chapter 3, section B, Mark 15:25 says, "It was nine o'clock in the morning when they crucified him," while John 19:13–16 says, "it was about noon" when Pilate presented Jesus to the crowd and they cried out, "Crucify him."

Thirdly, while the four Gospels agree that Mary Magdalene found the tomb of Jesus empty on Easter morning, and that someone told her that he had been raised, they differ in many details. John mentions only Mary at the tomb; Matthew writes about "Mary Magdalene and the other Mary"; Mark writes about those two, along with Salome. In Mark 16:5, the one who tells them that Jesus has been raised is "a young man." In Matthew 28:2–3, it is "an angel of the Lord." In Luke 24:4, the message comes from "two men," and in John 20:12, from "two angels." Whomever the women saw in the tomb that day, it cannot have been exactly one man and exactly one angel and exactly two men and exactly two angels.

It's rare for Christians to even notice these discrepancies between the four Gospels because they all tell the same basic story: the women could not find the body of Jesus because he had been raised from the dead. Similarly, the Gospels say that Jesus was descended from David and that he was crucified by Pilate. Historical accuracy is simply not an issue in these cases—unless, that is, you insist that every line of the

Bible is historically accurate, which, as these examples show, cannot be the case.

While the idea that the Bible is inerrant is still alive and well, then, the idea that all the writings in the Bible are literally true is naive and untenable.

For further reading:

Richard White. *Bibles, Science and Sanity*. Boulder, CO: Westview, 2007.

4

JESUS CHRIST

Jesus Christ is at the center of Christian thought and practice. Most of the beliefs of Christians center on him. Jesus didn't write anything, as far as we know, and the four Gospels about him were written from forty years to seventy years after he was gone. So it's understandable that from the first century to now, questions and debates have arisen about who Jesus was and what he said and did.

One way to approach the questions asked about Jesus is to consider the many titles applied to him, especially Rabbi (Teacher), Son of David, Son of Man, Son of God, Messiah, Christ, and Savior. It would be helpful if each of these words and phrases were clearly defined in the Bible, and if it each time one of these titles appeared in the Bible, that definition applied. But, as we saw in the last chapter, the writers of the Bible, as well as the figures they wrote about, lived in a mostly oral culture where words were not defined, thinking was not logically precise, and language included many metaphors and other figures of speech.

To see how the Gospel writers were not careful, logical thinkers, consider how three of them report this conversation between Jesus and his followers:

> Once when Jesus was praying alone, with only the disciples near him, he asked them, "Who do the crowds say that I am?" They answered, "John the Baptist; but others, Elijah; and still others, that one of the ancient prophets has arisen." He said to them, "But who do you say that I am?" Peter answered, "The Messiah of God" (Luke 9:18–20).

The same story is told in slightly different words in Matthew 16:13–20 and Mark 8:27–30. All three Gospel writers present the common opinions about Jesus without critical comment, as if it made sense to say that Jesus was John the Baptist, that he was Elijah, and that he was one of the ancient prophets who had come back to life. The Gospel writers did not agree with those opinions, of course, but they present them as something conceivable, as clear ideas that people *could* think.

Anyone who thinks logically, however, would reject as inconceivable the claim that Jesus was John the Baptist, and they would seriously question the claim that Jesus was Elijah or a resurrected ancient prophet. The problem with saying "Jesus is John the Baptist" is that there is no possible way that it could be true. It's like saying that Angela Merkel (current chancellor of Germany) is Benazzir Bhutto (former prime minister of Pakistan, assassinated in 2007). One person cannot be another person alive at the same time. Jesus was in his early thirties at the time of this conversation. John the Baptist was born a little before him. When they were both around thirty years old, John baptized Jesus in the Jordan River. No one watching that baptism would have said, "Jesus is John." The idea must have arisen after John was executed by King Herod. But even after John died, it made no sense to identify him with Jesus. Perhaps some people confusedly said that John somehow "came back as" Jesus in a kind of resurrection or reincarnation, so that Jesus' life was a continuation of John's life. That is not a clear, conceivable idea, however, because Jesus and John were near contemporaries— their lives overlapped almost completely. Jesus lived almost his whole life while John was alive, so no kind of resurrection or reincarnation could make Jesus' life be a continuation of John's life. So it isn't just *false* that Jesus was John the Baptist. It is *inconceivable*—it is not even a clear idea.

Despite the absurdity of the claim that Jesus was John the Baptist, however, the three Gospel writers don't comment on it but simply report it as a common opinion. That shows that they, like the confused people they described, were not careful in their thinking about Jesus. What the Gospel writers say about him, then, cannot simply be taken at face value as clear, articulate descriptions.

The idea that "one of the ancient prophets had arisen" in the first century as Jesus of Nazareth may come closer to being conceivable, but it is still highly questionable. The resurrection of the dead was something that was supposed to happen to everyone (or at least all the people of Israel) at the end of the world—not something that would happen to this or that individual in first-century Palestine. But again, none of the Gospel writers has any comment about the highly questionable idea that Jesus was a resurrected ancient prophet.

As we explore the claims made about who Jesus is and what he did, then, we have to be ready for words and phrases that are not well defined being used without precision.

A. IS JESUS CHRIST THE MESSIAH?

This question may sound odd since the Greek word *Christos*, which became *Christ*, is the Greek equivalent of *messiah*. *Christos* and *messiah* mean "anointed one." From the first century, followers of Jesus called him "Christ," "Anointed One." Since those terms are equivalent to *messiah*, isn't Jesus Christ obviously the Messiah?

Here we need to understand that the term *messiah* is used in different ways in the Bible. At the time of Jesus, it had an older, general meaning and a newer, more specific meaning. In its general sense, *messiah* meant someone whom God has chosen and empowered to do something. In the Old Testament, the noun and its verb forms are applied to David, Saul, priests, and prophets, because they were "anointed" by God for various tasks. To be a messiah in this general sense, a person didn't even have to be an Israelite. In Isaiah 45:1, King Cyrus of Persia is called *messiah*, anointed one, because God chose him to liberate the people of Israel from captivity in Babylon: "Thus says the Lord to his anointed, to Cyrus, whose right hand I have grasped to subdue nations before him and strip kings of their robes."

In this general sense of someone chosen by God to do something, Jesus was *messiah*, of course, but so were kings, prophets, and others. When people called Jesus "the Messiah," they had in mind something more specific than that. At the time of Jesus, "the Messiah" usually meant a Jewish king who would liberate the Jews from foreign domination. For over half a century, the Jews of Palestine had lived under Roman occupation. Before the Romans, they had been part of Alexander the Great's empire. Before that, the Persians ruled Palestine, and before that the Babylonians. The Babylonians had not only destroyed the temple in Jerusalem in the early sixth century BCE, but had taken Jewish leaders back to Babylon with them, where they were captive for half a century. Two centuries before that, in 722 BCE, the Assyrians had attacked and dispersed the ten northern tribes of Israel, leaving only the two southern tribes of Judah.

All these centuries of occupation and oppression had left the people of Israel dreaming of a time when they would live on their own land and control their own destiny. So over time they developed the idea of a powerful liberator, a savior, a king anointed by God to defeat their oppressors and put them back on the map as an independent nation. Thinking fondly of a thousand years earlier when Israel had flourished as an independent state under King David, Jews at the time of Jesus spoke of the "Anointed One" as a powerful king descended from David who would make Israel a great nation once again.

In the first century CE, then, "the Messiah" had a more specific meaning than someone chosen by God to do something. It meant someone who was (1) a king, (2) a political liberator, and (3) a descendant of David. Now, according to the Gospels of Matthew and Luke, Jesus had that third feature: he was descended from David and was even born in David's hometown of Bethlehem. But what about the first two features? Was Jesus a king? Hardly. A king has political power, but Jesus had none. When the Romans tortured him to death, they mockingly put a sign on his cross—"King of the Jews"—to indicate how absurd it was to call him "king" of anything. What about the second feature of "the Messiah," then? Was Jesus a political liberator? Here, too, no. He did not liberate the Jewish people from the Romans; he didn't even protest Roman domination. After he was gone, the Romans still controlled Palestine, and forty years later their armies destroyed the Second Temple and scattered the Jewish people.

So if by "the Messiah" we mean what that phrase meant at the time of Jesus—a king descended from David who liberated the Jews from foreign domination—then Jesus does not come close to meeting the criteria. That's why most people at the time rejected the very idea that he might be the Messiah.

How, then, could Jesus' followers call him the Messiah? They seem to have done that by changing *the Messiah* from a phrase with a clear meaning—a king descended from David who liberated the Jews from foreign domination—to a phrase with one or more unclear meanings.

The Messiah was a term with strong heroic connotations, so they wanted to apply it to their leader, even if he lacked two essential features in the term's meaning. Had they been careful thinkers who prized clear meanings, they would have explained what *the Messiah* could mean without two of its essential features, but they didn't do that. They used the phrase in vague ways in order to keep its heroic connotations, even as they applied it to a politically powerless non-king who not only didn't defeat the Romans, but was tortured to death by them.

As the new Christian movement spread from Palestine, where most people were Jews, to Asia Minor, Greece, and Rome, where the majority were not Jews, this shift of meaning became less of a problem. *Christos* and *Messiah* weren't words used by non-Jews, so they didn't have any particular meaning in mind for them. As missionaries like Paul preached about Jesus being "the Christ," then, they could use "Christ" in new ways, unrestricted by the meaning it had for Jews—a king descended from David who would liberate the Jews from foreign domination. Paul, in fact, used "Christ" hundreds of times in his letters, without once explaining exactly what he meant by that word. Today many Christians say that Jesus is the Messiah without even knowing what the term meant at the time of Jesus.

For further reading:

Alfred Edersheim. *The Life and Times of Jesus Messiah*. Rev. ed. Peabody, MA: Hendrickson, 1993.

B. IS JESUS CHRIST THE SAVIOR?

In the first century, as we have seen, an essential part of the idea of the Messiah/the Anointed One/the Christ was that he would liberate people from political oppression. The followers of Jesus called him by those titles, but since he did not save people from political oppression, they thought of other ways in which he could be said to save them. Over the succeeding centuries, they came up with many ways to understand Jesus as "savior" and the process of "salvation." We will briefly describe seven, and then in the next question, we'll discuss the most popular of them, which are based on the idea that Jesus Christ died to pay a debt created by human sin.

One early idea of salvation was that Jesus' death on the cross was a sacrifice to God to atone for sin, like the sacrifice of doves, lambs, and other animals in the temple in ancient Israel. Infinitely greater than one of those sacrifices, Jesus' death pleased God so that he forgave humans' sins. That sacrificial understanding is captured in the traditional reference to Jesus as the "Lamb of God who takes away the sins of the world" from John 1:29 and the saying that we are "washed in the blood of the lamb." Augustine wrote that Jesus Christ was the "true and perfect sacrifice" who was also a high priest offering himself as the sacrificial victim.[1]

A second early idea of salvation was liberation from slavery or captivity. Half of the people in the Roman Empire were slaves, and, as in the Middle East and North Africa today, people were often kidnapped and held for ransom. So the idea of being freed from slavery or captivity was powerfully attractive. The greatest example in the Bible is God liberating the Israelites from slavery in Egypt, as described in Exodus. According to Origen, Irenaeus, Gregory of Nyssa, and Augustine, after Adam sinned, the whole human race was captive to Satan. Because they were under his control, they went to hell when they died. To liberate them, God made Satan an offer he couldn't refuse—in exchange for releasing the human race, he would give the life of his Son, Jesus Christ, to Satan. The devil agreed, but he had been tricked by God, because three days after Jesus died on the cross, God brought him back to life. This account of salvation is sometimes called the mousetrap theory, after Augustine's explanation:

> The devil jumped for joy when Christ died; and by the very death of Christ the devil was overcome: he took, as it were, the bait in the mousetrap. He rejoiced at the death, thinking himself death's commander. But that which caused his joy dangled the bait before him. The Lord's cross was the devil's mousetrap: the bait which caught him was the death of the Lord.[2]

Today, few Western Christians have even heard of the mousetrap theory, but for seven centuries it was the most popular explanation of how the death of Jesus saved the human race. Around 1100, however, Anselm of Canterbury worked out a third account of salvation, now called the atonement theory. Over the last nine centuries, it has been widely accepted and modified. According to Anselm, God is a king and deserves to be honored by all his subjects. When a king's honor is offended, the offending party incurs a debt. Justice requires that debt to be paid before the offense can be forgiven. By sinning, Adam incurred a debt that was then inherited by all human beings after him. Because the king was the infinite God, the offense was infinite and so could not be paid by the humans who owed it. The only person who could pay an infinite debt was God, but in doing that he had to act on behalf of the human race. That required that God become a member of the human race, which he did by being born as the God-man, Jesus. In Anselm's words, "it is necessary that a God-Man should pay" for sin, since, "no one can pay except God, and no one ought to pay except man."[3] By offering up his life on the cross, Jesus paid the debt humans owed, and thus saved them, allowing them to go to heaven when they die.

In the sixteenth century, Martin Luther and John Calvin modified Anselm's atonement theory to fit a different understanding of justice, one based on the punishing of crimes. That created a fourth explanation of how Jesus Christ saved the human race. Now called the penal substitution theory, it is based on the idea that sin, like crime, requires punishment. Enduring the punishment is a debt owed by the sinner, just as criminals must "pay their debt" by serving time in prison. As in Anselm's theory, however, the debt for the original sin of Adam could not be paid by him or his descendants. So God, in the form of the God-man Jesus, stood in for them and endured the punishment in their place by submitting to the crucifixion. Though Jesus was innocent, God imputed the guilt for original sin to him, and he endured the punishment that was due. That paid the debt owed by the human race to God and secured for them his forgiveness, thus saving them. Luther, commenting on Galatians 3:13, explained it this way:

> We are sinners and thieves, and therefore guilty of death and ever-lasting damnation. But Christ took all our sins upon him, and for them died upon the cross . . . all the prophets did foresee in spirit, that Christ should become the greatest transgressor, murderer, adulterer, thief, rebel, blasphemer, etc. that ever was . . . for he being made a sacrifice, for the sins of the whole world, is now an innocent person and without sins . . . our most merciful Father, seeing us to be oppressed, overwhelmed with the curse of the law, and so to be holden under the same that we could never be delivered from it by

our own power, sent his only Son into the world and laid upon him all the sins of all men. [4]

These four explanations of salvation have been the most popular ones through the centuries, and they share the monetary concept that Jesus made a payment that saved or redeemed the human race. The second, third, and fourth explanations also frequently incorporate the first explanation—that the death of Jesus Christ was a sacrifice.

The last three of our seven explanations do not include the idea of making a payment or the idea of sacrifice, and they have been less popular over the centuries in Western Christianity. But we include them to show that there is no single idea of salvation or the Savior among Christians.

Our fifth explanation of Jesus as savior is quite different from the first four and is not based on his crucifixion. Instead, in the words of the second-century theologian Clement of Alexandria: "The Word of God had become man so that you might learn from a man how a man may become God."[5] The God-man taught us, Clement said, what God is and how we can progressively become more like him. In the fourth century, Athanasius added, "By becoming man, he made us sons to the Father, and he deified men by himself becoming man."[6] This understanding of salvation is called *theosis*, Greek for "becoming God," and dominates Eastern Orthodox theology, which does not have Anselm's or Luther's or Calvin's atonement theories. In the twentieth century, Protestant theologian John Hick explored this alternative to atonement theories in his book *The Metaphor of God Incarnate*.[7]

The sixth explanation of salvation that we'll mention is found in the work of twelfth-century theologian Peter Abelard, who got parts of it from Augustine. According to Abelard, Jesus Christ saved us by serving as a moral exemplar of unselfish love for us to emulate. This is sometimes called the "moral influence theory."

> We have been justified by the blood of Christ and reconciled to God in this way: through this unique act of grace manifested to us—in that his Son has taken upon himself our nature and preserved therein in teaching us by word and example even unto death—he has more fully bound us to himself by love; with the result that our hearts should be enkindled by such a gift of divine grace, and true charity should not now shrink from enduring anything for him.[8]

Our seventh and last explanation of how Jesus saves people is the newest, dating from the late twentieth century. Called liberation theology, it returns to the idea of the Messiah as a political liberator. This theory arose in Latin America in the late 1960s as a response to social injustice and political repression, and its proponents urge Christians to see the saving work of Christ as, in part, political liberation of the poor and oppressed people of the earth. Liberation theologians such as Leonardo Boff and Gustavo Gutierrez say that God loves social justice and hates injustice; that's clear in his liberating the people of Israel from slavery in Egypt and in the preaching of the prophets. Jesus, too, told his followers to "seek first the kingdom of God and his justice" (Matthew 6:33; Luke 12:31), and his own saving work includes bringing about social justice.

"Is Jesus Christ the Savior?", then, isn't a simple question. Since there are many possible ways in which Jesus might be said to save us, the question can have many meanings. Answering it requires that we be more specific about the way in which Jesus might be said to save us. With that in mind, we'll focus on the two most popular ideas of salvation among Western Christians, the atonement theories of Anselm and of Luther and Calvin, and ask a more specific question: Did Jesus save us by dying for our sins?

For further reading:

Athanasius. *Discourses Against the Arians*. In Philip Schaff and Henry Wace, eds. *The Nicene and Post-Nicene Fathers*, second series, vol. 4, 100–48. Grand Rapids, MI: Wm. B. Eerdmans, 1968.

John of Damascus. *On the Orthodox Faith*, 2:12.

Peter Abelard. *Exposition of the Epistle to the Romans*. In *The Library of Christian Classics*, vol. 10, *A Scholastic Miscellany: Anselm to Ockham*, edited by Eugene R. Fairweather. Philadelphia: Westminster, 1956, 276–87.

John McQuarrie. *Principles of Christian Theology*. 2nd ed. London: SCM, 1977.

Gustav Aulén. *Christus Victor: An Historical Study of the Three Main Types of the Idea of Atonement*. London: Macmillan, 1977.

John Hick. "Salvation as Human Transformation." In *The Metaphor of God Incarnate: Christology in a Pluralistic Age*. London: SCM, 1993.

Leonardo Boff. *Jesus Christ Liberator: A Critical Christology for Our Time*. Maryknoll, NY: Orbis, 1978.

C. DID JESUS CHRIST DIE FOR OUR SINS?

If you ask most Western Christians today about how Jesus Christ saved human beings, they are unlikely to talk about liberation theology or Augustine's mousetrap theory. Instead you're likely to hear some version of either Anselm's atonement theory or the penal substitution theories of Martin Luther and John Calvin. In these three accounts, Jesus Christ died to pay the debt owed for human sins—Adam's original sin and the sins people commit themselves. That is called the atonement. Most atonement theories also include the idea from our first explanation that Jesus' death was a sacrifice that pleased God. Thousands of Christian books, sermons, and hymns have been based on the idea that the human race owed a debt they could not pay, so God became a man to pay the debt for them. As the sign in front of the Christian Church of Anchorage (Alaska) said in June 2013, "We Use Duct Tape to Fix Everything. God Uses Nails."

But not all Christian thinkers have accepted the family of explanations in which Jesus' suffering and death pleased God and thus atoned for human sins. One early critic of the whole atonement approach was Peter Abelard in the twelfth century. In his *Exposition of the Epistle to the Romans* (2:3, 5), he points out that in nailing Jesus to the cross, human beings tortured God's only son to death! Surely, Abelard said, God was not pleased by that horrific act.

> In what way does the apostle [Paul] declare that we are justified or reconciled to God through the death of his Son, when God ought to have been more angered against man, inasmuch as men acted more criminally by crucifying his Son than they ever did by transgressing his first command in paradise through the tasting of a single apple? . . . And if that sin of Adam was so great that it could be expiated only by the death of Christ, what expiation will avail for that act of murder committed against Christ? . . . How did the death of his innocent Son so please God the Father that through it he should be reconciled to us—to us who by our sinful acts have done the very things for which our innocent Lord was put to death? . . . Indeed, how cruel and wicked it seems that anyone should demand the blood of an innocent person as the price for anything, or that it should in any way please him that an innocent man should be slain—still less

that God should consider the death of his Son so agreeable that by it
he should be reconciled to the whole world![9]

If we examine atonement theories carefully, we will also find five
questionable assumptions they make about God and about sin. First,
they assume a monetary understanding of wrongdoing as creating a
debt which, like a parking ticket or a library fine on overdue books, can
be paid by someone other than the wrongdoer. Anselm's explanation
has many words associated with paying money: "He who does not ren-
der this honor which is *due* to God, *robs* God of what is *his own* and
dishonors him; and this is sin . . . So then, everyone who sins ought to
pay back the honor of which he has *robbed* God; and this is the *satisfac-
tion* which every sinner *owes* to God."[10] In Anselm's theory, it is humans who "owe the debt" but God "pays the debt" by sending his Son,
Jesus Christ, to die on the cross.

There is nothing about a monetary debt, of course, that requires that
only the debtor's money be used to pay it. If I'm broke this month, a
friend may pay my rent. But having one person pay another's debts is
not part of modern understandings of morality, where each person is
responsible for their own wrongdoing, and no one can "pay" for another's bad actions. If a man has been convicted of murder and has
been sentenced to life imprisonment, no legal system in the world will
let a friend of the murderer go to prison in his place. So the whole
monetary model of God "paying the debt" for humans is inappropriate.
Sinning is not the same as owing money.

A second questionable assumption in atonement theories is that persons can pay debts to themselves. In Anselm's atonement theory and in
Luther and Calvin's penal substitution theory, "the debt" is not only
paid *by* God, but paid *to* God. But "paying yourself" is a confused idea.
If you owe me twenty dollars but tell me that you can't pay me, I might
jokingly take a twenty-dollar bill out of my shirt pocket and put it into
my wallet. But that would just be a gracious way of canceling the debt—
it would not be paying the debt to myself. Debts are relations between
different persons, and so is paying. You can't pay yourself any more than
you can owe yourself. So the idea that God pays himself the debt owed
to him by human beings is not coherent.

Atonement theories make a third questionable assumption: that the
debt created by Adam's sin was infinitely great because the person who

was offended, God, is infinitely great. That assumption doesn't fit modern religious ethics. Stealing from a queen, say, is not a greater wrong than stealing from a homeless woman. If anything, we might judge it worse to steal from the homeless woman because she has suffered more harm.

Also, most Christian theologians say that God is perfect and unchanging, making God incapable of suffering at all. That casts further doubt on the idea that Adam's disobedience was *infinitely* offensive.

Nor does the idea that *any* offense against God creates an *infinite* debt fit with the biblical practice of sacrificing animals to atone for sins. In that system, a small offense required the sacrifice of a small animal such as a dove and a larger offense required the sacrifice of a lamb, or, for an even larger offense, an ox. But if all sins create *infinite* debts, then no sacrifice could even begin to atone for even the tiniest sin. And then the very practice of sacrifice for sin that is the basis for the atonement theory makes no sense.

In a talk I heard decades ago, John Hick had yet another objection to the claim that God had to demand the payment of an infinite debt in order to forgive the human race. Demanding the full payment of a debt, Hick said, is not *forgiving* that debt. When you forgive a debt, you *forgo* something to which you are entitled. You *don't* demand everything to which you are entitled. If I borrow a serving bowl from you for a party I'm having, and I accidentally chip the bowl, you're not *forgiving* me if you say, "That bowl cost $16.99 plus $1.36 tax. So pay me the $18.35 you owe me."

A fourth assumption of atonement theories is that the debt for Adam's sin was inherited by the human race. That idea is called original sin. In the ancient world, it was common to blame a person's descendants for their wrongdoing. The idea of inherited guilt appears in the Bible in the first commandment: "I the Lord your God am a jealous God, punishing children for the iniquity of their parents, to the third and the fourth generation of those who reject me." In modern religious ethics, however, no one would condone punishing a man's great-great-grandchildren for what he did long before they were born. We deserve punishment only for what we have done or have failed to do, so the idea of inherited guilt does not make sense. How could a just God blame billions of people, the whole human race, for what one person—their most distant ancestor—did?

Fifth is the assumption that paying the debt for Adam's sin, or for other human sin, has to take the form of a *sacrifice*—a ritual slaying that will please God. Except perhaps for the first Christians who continued their Jewish practices, sacrificing animals has never been part of Christian ritual. Nor has sacrificing human beings. The assumption that the atoning payment to God that allowed him to forgive Adam's sin had to be a killing puts major restrictions on how God can forgive people.

The Gospels say that Jesus forgave people's sins, and there was no such restriction on the way he forgave. He never once asked the person being forgiven to "pay their debt" by killing something, draining its blood, and burning the carcass on an altar. Is God bound by restrictions not binding on Jesus? And, to repeat Peter Abelard's question, what kind of person would God be if he were pleased by the slaughter of any innocent living thing?

To test your own intuitions about the atonement theory, try this thought experiment. Suppose that a Catholic family brought a lamb to Sunday Mass and asked the priest to slaughter it on the altar as a sacrifice to God. Do you think the priest and the congregation would join in, helping to bind the lamb's feet, slit its throat, drain its blood, and burn the body? Why or why not? And what would happen if, instead of a lamb, the family brought a man to the altar to be sacrificed? Once you've given your answer, figure out its implications for the atonement theory as found in "the sacrifice of the Mass"—that the killing of Jesus, "the Lamb of God," is a sacrifice pleasing to God?

For further reading:

Paul Van Buren. *Christ in Our Place: the Substitutionary Character of Calvin's Doctrine of Reconciliation*. Edinburgh: Oliver and Boyd, 1957.
Hastings Rashdall. *The Idea of Atonement in Christian Thought*. London: Macmillan, 1920.
Gustaf Aulen. *Christus Victor: An Historical Study of the Three Main Types of the Idea of Atonement*. Eugene, OR: Wipf & Stock, 2003.
Vincent Taylor. *The Atonement in New Testament Teaching*. London: Epworth, 1940.
John Hick. "Atonement by the Blood of Jesus." In *The Metaphor of God Incarnate: Christology in a Pluralistic Age*. London: SCM, 1993.

D. IS JESUS CHRIST THE SON OF GOD?

From the beginning, Christians have called Jesus Christ "the son of God," but as with "Messiah" and "Savior," we need to ask what this phrase could mean. "Son of" has a literal meaning—the male offspring of sexual reproduction—but it is also used in many metaphors and other figures of speech, such as "son of Ireland," "Sons of Liberty," and "son of a gun." In the Bible, Jesus is called "son of David" and "son of man," though his father was not David or man; and he nicknames his apostles James and John, who are literally sons of Zebedee, "sons of thunder."

When we ask if Jesus Christ is the son of God, we are not asking about nicknames, metaphors, or other figures of speech. Of course, "son of God" can apply to Jesus Christ as a figure of speech. All that's needed to create a metaphor is some similarity, and there is certainly a similarity between Jesus' loving relationship with God and a son's loving relationship with his father. But that metaphor can be applied to anyone whose relationship to God is anything like a son's relationship to his father—and that includes all human beings, since they all owe their existence to God. When Christians say that Jesus is the son of God, they don't think of that as a metaphor or other figure of speech, but as a literal statement. The trouble with that, as we mentioned in chapter 1, is that "son of God" doesn't have any literal meaning, since God does not reproduce sexually.

Here it's useful to consider how "son of God" is used in the Bible. The phrases "son of God" and "sons of God" occur dozens of times in the Old and New Testaments. The first is in Genesis 6:1–4:

> When people began to multiply on the face of the ground, and daughters were born to them, the sons of God saw that they were fair; and they took wives for themselves of all that they chose. . . . The Nephilim [giants] were on the earth in those days—and also afterward—when the sons of God went in to [had sex with] the daughters of humans, who bore children to them. These were the heroes that were of old, warriors of renown.

Here "the sons of God" seems to refer to physical beings who are enough like men that they can mate with women on earth to produce divine-human hybrids, "heroes . . . warriors of renown." Since the sons of God are man-like beings who reproduce sexually, their father would also be a man-like being who reproduces sexually. It would be from him that they inherited their sexual organs. "Son" means a male offspring of sexual reproduction, so they are literally "the sons of God" and he is literally their father, just as princes are "the sons of the king" and the king is literally their father.

Christians, of course, generally reject the idea of God reproducing sexually, since God is not a physical being, much less a being with sexual organs. And, rejecting the idea of God reproducing sexually, they would say that "the sons of God" in Genesis 6 cannot be a literal expression, but must be a metaphor or other figure of speech. The literal meaning of "son" is "male offspring of sexual reproduction," so, speaking literally, God cannot have sons, just as he cannot have daughters in the literal sense of "female offspring of sexual reproduction." The lesson here is that when Christians use "sons of God," it should be nonliterally, since a literal use implies that God reproduces sexually.

Fortunately, as we look through the rest of the Bible for "sons of God" and "son of God," we find these expressions being applied metaphorically rather than literally—to angels and humans who love God and serve him as sons serve their fathers. The Book of Job 1:6–7, for instance, says that "the sons of God came to present themselves before the Lord, and Satan also came among them." When God asks Satan (not the devil—that's a later idea) where he has come from, Satan says, "From going to and fro on the earth, and from walking up and down on it." Here "sons of God" refers to God's agents who travel around and report back to him about what people are doing. They are not literally God's sons but more like what we call angels. Calling them his sons is a metaphorical way of saying that they love him and serve him. Similarly, in Psalm 2:7, God says to a king, "You are my son: today I have begotten you."

No biblical writers announced that they were using metaphors, because they didn't have the distinction between literal and metaphorical uses of language. The books of the Bible didn't start out as books, as writing. They started out in oral form, as stories, prayers, proverbs, and so on. And even when they were written down after centuries of being handed down orally, they kept their oral patterns of thought and expression, including metaphors, parables, and other figures of speech.

When we get to the four Gospels, we find that the father-son metaphor is central in the preaching of Jesus. He calls God "Abba," "Father," and thinks of God as the father of everyone, not just him. He tells his followers to "love your enemies, bless those who curse you," so "that you may be sons of your father in heaven" (Matthew 5: 44–45).

When he composes a prayer for his followers to use, it begins "Our father."

If "son of God" is a metaphor applied to someone who loves and serves God, then what does adding "the" to this phrase do? What could it mean to call Jesus *"the* son of God"? I suggest that it makes the metaphor stronger. "The son of God" refers to someone who loves God completely and devotes his life to doing God's will. That, of course, applies perfectly to Jesus and his close relationship with God.

But, some might object, "the son of God" must mean more than that. While Jesus was in fact someone who loved God completely and devoted his life to serving him, *he was more than that—he was literally the Son of God*. But, as we saw in Genesis 6, that can't be right. The literal meaning of *son* is "a male offspring of sexual reproduction." For A to be *literally* the son of B means that B is a man or woman whose sperm or egg developed into A. God isn't even physical, much less a man, and God doesn't reproduce at all, much less sexually. So *"the* Son of God," like "son of God," has to be a metaphor, and so does "God the Father." In the Bible, only Genesis 6 uses an expression like "the Son of God" in a literal way, and it was written at an early time when people thought of God as a powerful man-like being who reproduced sexually to produce sons who could mate with women. If, as Christians believe, God is not physical and does not reproduce sexually, then, speaking literally, God cannot have sons (or daughters). That simple point was made long ago in the Qur'an (19:92).

Calling Jesus Christ the son of God is perfectly appropriate as a metaphor, then, just as calling God "Father" is. These expressions comparing God to a loving father and Jesus to a loving son are central to Jesus' message and so to Christianity. But both are metaphors, not literal descriptions. Speaking literally, neither Jesus nor anyone else could be "the son of God" because God does not reproduce sexually. This simple truth, unfortunately, has been ignored by the millions of Christians who have thought of "the son of God" as a literal description of Jesus. In the next chapter we'll see how treating God the Father and God the Son as literal expressions rather than metaphors has created great confusion in the doctrine of the Trinity.

For further reading:

Mogens Müller. "Son of God." In *The Oxford Companion to the Bible*, edited by Bruce M. Metzger and Michael D. Coogan. Oxford: Oxford University Press, 1993, 710–13.
John Hick. *The Metaphor of God Incarnate: Christology in a Pluralistic Age*. London: SCM, 1993.
Walter Ong. *Orality and Literacy*. London: Taylor and Francis, 2002.
James Dunn. *Did the First Christians Worship Jesus?* Louisville, KY: Westminster John Knox, 2010.
Ramsay MacMullen. *Voting about God in Early Church Councils*. New Haven, CT: Yale University Press, 2006.

E. DID JESUS CHRIST TEACH DOCTRINES?

When Christians think of what defines religions—their own and other people's—they often think of beliefs. Most religions don't define themselves that way, but starting in the fourth century, Christian leaders wrote official statements of beliefs such the Nicene Creed and used them to determine who was a Christian and who wasn't. As we saw in chapter 1, those with unorthodox beliefs were branded "heretics," and in the Roman Empire in the late 300s, heresy was an act of treason, punishable by death. Less than a century after the Nicene Creed, Augustine of Hippo worked out his theory of just war to justify attacking the Donatists, a Christian group who disagreed with him about whether notoriously sinful bishops should lose their church positions. (They said yes, he said no.) Yale historian Ramsay MacMullen estimates that between 325 and 550 fighting between Christians with different beliefs caused "not less than twenty-five thousand deaths."[11] And since then, tens of thousands more Christians have killed other Christians for having "the wrong" beliefs. From 1209 to 1220, Pope Innocent III conducted a "crusade" to wipe out the heretical Cathars in southern France. In the fighting at the Lastours castles, crusade leader Simon de Montfort ordered his troops to gouge out the eyes of one hundred prisoners, cut off their lips and noses, and have a prisoner with one remaining eye lead them back to the castles.[12] When those in the city of Béziers refused to surrender, they were slaughtered and their city burned to the ground. A report sent to the pope said that twenty thousand were killed, in what would today be called genocide.

To eliminate heretics like the Cathars, the Roman Catholic Church established the investigative institution called the Inquisition, which tried people suspected of having incorrect beliefs. Set up temporarily in southern France in 1184, the Inquisition became permanent in 1229. It was run by the new order of Dominican friars.

While issuing official lists of doctrines and punishing people who don't agree with them go back a long way in Christian history, they don't go back to Jesus. Creating and enforcing doctrines requires that leaders define exactly what has to be believed, and that requires writing things down. As far as we know, Jesus never wrote anything at all, much less official teachings. Scholars such as John Dominic Crossan, who have spent their careers studying what can be known about Jesus, say that as a landless first-century Mediterranean peasant, Jesus would not have been taught to read and write.[13] Nor did he tell his mostly illiterate followers to write anything.

The first of the four Gospels, Mark, wasn't written until about 70, forty years after Jesus was gone, and the other three were written in the 80s and 90s. Even a casual reading of the Gospels reveals a man whose ways of speaking and thinking are oral rather than literate.[14] Unlike a theologian or philosopher, Jesus doesn't define his terms, and he doesn't stick to using words literally. Throughout the Gospels, he expresses himself in parables (fictional stories), metaphors, hyperbole (exaggeration), and other figures of speech. One of his two great moral principles—"Love your neighbor"—uses "neighbor" nonliterally. And when he is asked to clarify what "neighbor" means, he doesn't answer as a philosopher might, by saying, "Every human being." Instead, he tells a story, the parable of the good Samaritan. Jesus often warned about the possibility of what we now call "hell," but he didn't call it that. He called it "Gehenna," the name of a smoldering garbage dump outside Jerusalem. That works as rhetoric, but not as theology.

Because Jesus' parables, and his preaching generally, are not literal assertions, he has often been misunderstood—by those he talked to, and by succeeding generations of Christians. When, for example, Jesus told Nicodemus that to see the Kingdom of God, a person has to be born again, Nicodemus was puzzled and said, "How can anyone be born after having grown old? Can one enter a second time into the mother's womb and be born?" (John 3:3–4). When Jesus told the Samaritan woman at the well, "Everyone who drinks of this water will be thirsty again, but those who drink of the water that I will give them will never be thirsty," she said, "Give me this water, so that I may never be thirsty or have to keep coming here to draw water" (John 4:13–15). If people like these, talking one-on-one with Jesus, could mistake his metaphors for literal assertions, is it any wonder that later Christians, who have only reports of his words, often misinterpreted them?

In the second century, as we saw, literate Christians trained in Greek philosophy began to interpret the sayings attributed to Jesus in the Gospels as if he had taught a clear, systematic philosophy that could compete with Stoicism, Platonism, and other popular philosophies. In doing that, they read many of Jesus' figures of speech as if they were literal statements, like those in a philosophy book. In the last question, we saw how "the son of God" could only be a metaphor, though the vast majority of theologians, even today, treat it as a literal description. From the idea that Jesus is the Son of God, theologians moved to the claim that Jesus is himself God, citing lines such as "The Father and I are one" (John 10:30). But Jesus often spoke of persons being "one" without implying that they were the same thing. Praying for his followers, he asked God to protect them "so that they may be one, as we are one" (John 17:11; also 17:20–21). What he appears to mean is solidarity, unity of spirit and purpose. Being one with God does not involve *being* God. And several things that Jesus said show that he did not think of himself as being God, the plainest being "The Father is greater than I" (John 14:28). If you've been paying attention to the Bible citations in parentheses, you've probably noticed that they are all from the Gospel of John. That Gospel is the one that most influenced theologians as they created and discussed doctrines such as the incarnation (the claim that God became man) and the Trinity (the claim that God is three persons in one substance). John is the Gospel which most emphasizes that Jesus is "the Son of God" and is himself God. What those who use this Gospel to create theological arguments usually overlook, however, is that it has dozens of metaphors, especially metaphors that Jesus applies to himself. He says, for instance, "I am the light of the world. Whoever follows me will never walk in darkness but will have the light of life" (John 8:12). "Light of life" has no literal meaning—it can only be a figure of speech. And "light of the world" is clearly a metaphor: used literally, it would mean sunlight, and Jesus is not sunlight.

Often, as we said, Jesus' figures of speech went over people's heads. In John 10, he begins by saying, "Anyone who does not enter the sheepfold by the gate but climbs in by another way is a thief and a bandit. The one who enters by the gate is the shepherd of the sheep" (10:1–2). The

Gospel writer explains that "Jesus used this figure of speech with them, but they did not understand what he was saying to them. So again Jesus said to them, 'Very truly, I tell you, I am the gate for the sheep'" (10:6–7).

Jesus applies more metaphors to himself in John's Gospel. He says, "I am the bread of life" (John 6:35) and "I am the true vine, and my Father is the vinegrower" (John 15:1). Comforting Martha after the death of her brother Lazarus, Jesus tells her, "I am the resurrection and the life. Those who believe in me, even though they die, will live" (John 11:25–26).

Now, early theologians did not use these metaphors of "the gate," "the bread," "the vine," "the resurrection," and "the life" from John's Gospel to create doctrines about Jesus. They did apply the metaphor of "light" to both Jesus and God in the Nicene Creed, making it obligatory for Christians to *say* that Jesus is "light" begotten from "light," though no one today *believes* that God is literally light. Early theologians also made the "Son of God" metaphor into a doctrine, and that in turn led to the doctrine that Jesus is himself God. Treating the Son of God metaphor and the God the Father metaphor as literal names, they then created the doctrine of the Trinity, which, as we'll see in the next chapter, adds even more confusion. With few exceptions, like John Hick and Sallie McFague, later theologians have not called attention to these misunderstood metaphors, and to their misuse in creating doctrines.[15]

Writing a doctrine requires the careful, literal use of words arranged into an assertion. Metaphors won't work in doctrines, because they violate the definitions of words and so are literal falsehoods. When Jesus said he was a gate, bread, and a vine, we shouldn't treat those as assertions. If we do, we have to say that Jesus was lying, because he is not a gate, bread, or a vine.

Since metaphors are not assertions and are not true, people don't believe them, or disbelieve them. As we said in chapter 1, I may like Shakespeare's line "All the world's a stage and all the men and women merely players," but that's not something I believe, because it's not an assertion. It would be silly, then, for someone to tell me that I must believe it, as church leaders and Roman emperors told Christians they must believe the Son of God metaphor, the God the Father metaphor, and the light metaphor. Requiring people to believe a metaphor makes no more sense than requiring them to believe a parable—the good Samaritan, say, or the prodigal son.

Jesus, of course, did ask people to *believe in him*, but that meant having personal trust in him, not agreeing with theological doctrines about him. With his oral ways of thinking and expressing himself, he had neither the vocabulary nor the political motivation to create and enforce doctrines. As we suggested in chapter 1, he would probably have been shocked had he returned in 385 to witness the beheading of Bishop Priscillian and his friends for heresy. Even if Jesus had agreed with the judge that these Christians had incorrect beliefs, the idea that they should die for that error would likely have repelled Jesus.

If you want more concrete evidence of how different Jesus' whole worldview was from the worldview of the early Christian theologians who created doctrines about him, read Jesus' Sermon on the Mount in Matthew 5–7, and then read these two parts of the creed produced by the Council of Chalcedon in 451:

> Our Lord Jesus Christ, the same perfect in divinity and also perfect in humanity; truly God and truly man, of a reasonable soul and body; of the same substance with the Father according to divinity, and of the same substance with us according to the humanity; in all things like unto us, without sin; begotten before all the ages of the Father according to the divinity, and in these latter days, for us and for our salvation, born of the Virgin Mary, the Mother of God, according to the Manhood; one and the same Christ, Son, Lord, Only-begotten, to be acknowledged in two natures, inconfusedly, unchangeably, indivisibly, inseparably; the distinction of natures being by no means taken away by the union, but rather the property of each nature being preserved, and concurring in one Person and one Subsistence, not parted or divided into two persons, but one and the same Son, and only-begotten, God the Word, the Lord Jesus Christ.
>
> . . .
>
> These things, therefore, having been expressed by us with the greatest accuracy and attention, the holy Ecumenical Synod defines that no one shall be permitted to bring forward a different faith, nor to write, nor to put together, nor to excogitate, nor to teach it to others. But some dare either to put together another faith, or to bring forward or to teach or to deliver a different Creed to such as wish to be converted to the knowledge of the truth from the Gentiles, the Jews, or any heresy whatever. If they are bishops or clerics, let them be

deposed, the bishops from the episcopate, and the clerics from the clergy; but if they are monks or laity, let them be anathematized [cursed by church authority]. [16]

While Jesus taught no metaphysical doctrines and preached love, tolerance, and forgiveness, the writers of this creed say nothing about love, tolerance, or forgiveness, but present a list of metaphysical claims "expressed by us with the greatest accuracy" that must be accepted by everyone, on pain of being banished.

For further reading:

John Dominic Crossan. *Jesus: A Revolutionary Biography*. San Francisco: Harper SanFrancisco, 1994.
Walter Ong. *Orality and Literacy*. London: Taylor and Francis, 2002.
T. A. Burkill. *The Evolution of Christian Thought*. Ithaca, NY: Cornell University Press, 1971.

5

THE TRINITY

For sixteen centuries the idea that there is only one God but God is three has been a distinctively Christian teaching. That doctrine is called "the Trinity," a word coming from the Latin *trinitas*, meaning "threeness." The three are usually called the Father, the Son, and the Holy Spirit. The other Abrahamic religions, Judaism and Islam, agree that there is only one God, but reject the idea of Trinity as incompatible with God's oneness. Jews and Muslims share much with Christians, including the Old Testament. The Qur'an describes Jesus as the Messiah and one of the greatest prophets, and Islamic teaching attributes to him miracles that are not reported in the Gospels. Chapter 19 of the Qur'an is titled "Mary" and says that Jesus was born of a virgin. Despite all this agreement with Christianity, however, Muslims, like Jews, reject the claim that Jesus *is God*. That, they say, is polytheism—belief in more than one God. Jews and Muslims also accept the Bible's descriptions of "the Spirit (of God)," but they reject the claim of many Christians that "the Spirit" names a person distinct from the God of the Bible.

There has never been just one teaching called "the Trinity" that was agreed upon by all Christians. There have been only diverse teachings over which Christians have argued. That by itself indicates that "the Trinity" does not name one clear doctrine. Among the many meanings given to "the Trinity," the most popular has been that God is three persons in one substance.

The word "persons" is not straightforward here, since the standard definition of "person" is "individual human being," and no Christian believes that God is three individual human beings. So saying "God is three persons" requires an extended meaning for "person." Though theologians seldom explain what that special meaning for "person" is as applied to God, the explanation would probably go something like this: a person is something that thinks, desires, makes choices, communicates, and acts. These are the main features of human beings we have in mind in calling them "persons," and they are what we attribute to nonhuman beings such as God, angels, and devils when we apply *persons* to them.

As with most theology, teachings about the Trinity were developed in order to explain certain passages in the Bible. The most important was Matthew 28:19, in which Jesus tells his followers, "Go therefore and make disciples of all the nations, baptizing them in the name of the Father and the Son and the Holy Spirit." Another was Paul's Second Letter to the Corinthians, which closes this way: "The grace of the Lord Jesus Christ, the love of God, and the communion of the Holy Spirit be with all of you" (13:13).

Theologians asked what the three terms "Father," "Son," and "Holy Spirit" mean in Matthew, and what "Lord Jesus Christ," "God," and "Holy Spirit" mean in Paul's letter. They reasoned that in both writings there must be a difference in meaning between the three expressions—otherwise, why would Jesus and Paul use three terms instead of just one? Then they went on to ask what the three terms might mean.

In the Greek-speaking world, this question was discussed using philosophical concepts like *activity*, *substance*, *aspect*, and *mode of being*. To keep things as simple as possible, we can deal with just the formula for baptism in Matthew 28:19. Are the Father, the Son, and the Holy Spirit different *activities*? they asked. Or are they different *substances*—different individual things? Or could they be different *aspects* or *modes* of a single thing? Over a period of centuries, the idea that was most widely accepted was that God is three *persons* in one *substance*. While that is what most Christians now mean when they talk about the Trinity, it was worked out in a confusing way, and it has questionable implications, as we'll see.

A. ARE JESUS CHRIST AND GOD "OF THE SAME SUBSTANCE"?

An early step toward the doctrine of the Trinity was saying that Jesus, the Son of God, is equal to God. That provided two of the three members of the Trinity, "the Son" and "the Father." The idea that the Son of God is equal to God may have arisen from the observation that in ancient times princes often acted in place of their fathers and then succeeded their fathers as kings. So the son of a king deserved the same respect as his father. That kind of equality seems to be what's behind Mark 16:19: "He ascended into heaven, and sat down at the right hand of God," which came into the Apostles' Creed as "He ascended into heaven, and sits on the right hand of God the Father Almighty."

To draw conclusions like these from facts about fathers and sons, God would have to literally be a "father" and Jesus would have to literally be his "son." But, as we saw in chapter 1, these are at best metaphors when applied to God and Jesus, since God does not reproduce sexually. Because God is not literally a father or a king, and Jesus Christ is not literally the son of God or a prince, we can't draw reliable conclusions about the relationship between God and Jesus Christ from observations about fathers and sons, kings and princes. Nor, as we saw in chapter 1, is it reasonable to make doctrines out of metaphors, though that is what the creeds do with "God the Father" and "God the Son."

In a similar mistaking of nonliteral language for literal language, theologians over the centuries have appealed to the opening lines of the Gospel of John to show that Jesus is equal to God:

> In the beginning was the Word, and the Word was with God, and the word was God. He was in the beginning with God. All things came into being through him, and without him not one thing came into being (1:1–2).

We don't know who wrote this, but it was obviously not a logic professor. If we try to interpret these words literally, as assertions, the individual concepts are unclear, and put together, they are confusing. What does it mean to say that "the Word" existed in the beginning? And how can we think of "the Word" as male ("him")? What would it mean for God to create things "through" the Word? If God created everything "through the Word," why doesn't the description of creation in Genesis even mention "the Word"? And how can "the Word" both *be with God* and *be God*? Try to make sense of a similar sentence: "Jane was with Alice, and Jane was Alice."

Greek philosophers like Plato had told stories about the Demiurge, a creator god who made things by using ideal "forms" as mental blueprints or templates. The author of John's Gospel seems to have something like that in mind. But the mental blueprints said to be used by the Demiurge were not a person, as Jesus Christ is supposed to be. And, anyway, the omnipotent Christian God certainly doesn't need mental blueprints, or anything else, to create. Despite all these problems, those opening words of John's Gospel have been used thousands of times to justify the claim that Jesus Christ *is* God.

At the Council of Nicaea in 325, the bishops discussed the relation of Jesus Christ to God, and the majority voted for the position defended by Athanasius that the Son and the Father are *homooúsios*. In Ancient Greek, *homós* means "same" and *ousía* means "being, substance." The bishops didn't explain their use of *oúsios*, but three meanings are possible in ancient Greek. First, it can refer to some individual being, such as the woman I just met. If "the same substance" applied to God the Father and Jesus Christ in that sense, then the claim would be that the Father and the Son are the very same individual being. But none of the bishops at Nicaea seemed to have that in mind, and it seems an incoherent idea, anyway. If A is the very same individual being as B, then any feature of A is a feature of B, and vice versa. There is only one thing, in fact, and A and B are just different words referring to it. Suppose that the woman I just met is the mayor. Then, since the woman I just met is fifty years old, the mayor must be fifty years old. The mayor drives a BMW, so the woman I just met must drive a BMW. Let's apply this logic to Jesus Christ and God. If Jesus Christ is the very same being as God, then whatever features Jesus Christ has God has, and vice versa. But Jesus Christ went to sleep at night; God doesn't sleep. Jesus Christ had arms and legs, but God doesn't. Going the other way, God is eternal, but Jesus Christ was born. God can't die, but Jesus Christ died on the cross. When the bishops said that Jesus Christ and God are "of the same substance," then, it was not reasonable for them to mean that Jesus Christ is the very same being as God.

A second possible meaning of *substance* in Greek is the type, class, or species to which individuals belong. Two human beings, for example, have in common the "substance" of humanity, so each of them can be said to be "of the same substance" as the other. This does not appear to be what the theologians at Nicaea meant by substance, either (though, as we'll see, later theologians would use this idea). A big problem with saying that Jesus Christ and God are individuals of the same type (divinity), as two humans are individuals of the same type (humanity), would be that it implies that Jesus Christ and God are two gods, as Mary and John, say, are two humans. That is polytheism, belief in several gods, and so unacceptable to Christians.

What the bishops at Nicaea seemed to mean by *substance* is a third possibility: the material, the stuff, out of which something is composed. We still use the word *substance* this way, as when we say that ice, water, and steam are the same substance—H_2O. When the bishops at Nicaea said that the Father and the Son are *homooúsios*, they seemed to mean that the Father and the Son are composed of the same material, the same stuff. Augustine was thinking this way when he compared the members of the Trinity to three statues made of the same substance, gold.[1] Athanasius, the lead proponent of the *homooúsios* idea at Nicaea, said that when a father begets a son, that boy comes out of the substance of the father.[2] That is, the boy's body is made of material that came from the father's body.

While it makes sense to say that three statues are made of the same material, and that a father and son are composed of the same material, however, it is not at all clear what this could mean applied to God the Father and God the Son (even if we overlook the problem that these phrases are metaphors). Physical objects like statues and human bodies are made of parts, which have smaller parts, which have still smaller parts, all the way down to the atomic level. All gold statues are ultimately composed of atoms of a common substance, the element gold. All human bodies are ultimately composed of atoms of the same substances—carbon, hydrogen, oxygen, and so on. But there aren't any parts, atoms, or elements in God, because God is not physical. There is nothing simpler than God out of which God is composed. A statue can be made of gold or wood, but there doesn't seem to be any God material, God stuff out of which the Father and the Son could be made. If by *homooúsios* those at Nicaea did mean that the Father and the Son are made of the same material, the same stuff, they didn't explain how the Father and the Son could be composed of any material or stuff at all, nor did they say what it might be. The idea of being composed of a substance seems limited to physical things.

The claim of the bishops at Nicaea that the Father and the Son are "of the same substance," then, was not clear. A likely meaning for the claim is that God and Jesus Christ are composed of the same stuff, but we have no good reason to think that God and Jesus Christ are composed of any stuff at all.

Whatever individual bishops thought *homooúsios* meant, historian William Placher tells us that after the Council was over, "it soon emerged that those who had signed the Nicene Creed could not agree on what it meant."[3] A majority then changed their minds. As historian Robert Barr says, "They withdrew their signatures. One by one most of the Eastern hierarchy let it be known that they no longer professed the Nicene *homooúsios*."[4] Even with this rejection of the most important phrase in the Nicene Creed, however, that creed became the standard statement of belief for Eastern and Western Christians—Orthodox, Catholic, and Protestant.

Besides the lack of clarity in the claim that the Son is of the same substance as the Father, there are other problems with the attempt of some of the bishops at Nicaea to put the Son and the Father on an equal footing. Jesus never claimed equality with God. He said that "The Father is greater than I" (John 14:28) and that he lived to do God's will. Throughout the Gospels and the rest of the New Testament, Jesus Christ is clearly subordinate to God. In his First Letter to the Corinthians, for example, Paul says, "God is the head of Christ" (11:3).

Even in the Greek philosophical reasoning about the Father and the Son, the Son is subordinate rather than equal. According to the Nicene Creed, the Father "begot" the Son. That's a metaphor, as we've seen. One way to express the idea literally is to say that the first person of the Trinity caused the second person of the Trinity to exist. The expanded Creed of Constantinople (381) says that Jesus Christ was "born of the Father before all ages," but that doesn't change the causal dependence of "the Son" on "the Father." The second person is and always has been an effect of the first person. The second person has always depended for his very existence on the first person. The first person, by contrast, is *not* an effect of the second person, or an effect of anything else, and has never depended on the second person at all. The relationship between a causally dependent being and the causally independent being on which it depends cannot be equality.

The claim that the second person of the Trinity is caused ("begotten") also contradicts one of the most basic features of God in Christian theology: unlike everything else, God is *agenetos*, uncaused. How could something that is caused, such as Jesus Christ, *be* God, when God is completely uncaused? The objection here is very simple:

> God is uncaused.
> Jesus Christ is caused.
> So Jesus Christ is not God.

This objection, by the way, also applies to the third person in the theory of the Trinity, the Holy Spirit, who is said to "proceed from the Father," that is, be caused by the Father.

> God is uncaused.
> The Holy Spirit is caused.
> So the Holy Spirit is not God.

The desire to present the Son as equal to the Father also led the bishops at Nicaea to say that both of them are "light." As we mentioned earlier, no one today would say that either God or Jesus is light in a literal sense and yet this metaphor, like the metaphors of son and father, were included in the Nicene Creed.

For further reading:

John 1:1; 1:18; 20:28.
Romans 9:5.
Titus 2:13.
Hebrews 1:8–9.
2 Peter 1:1.
1 John 5:20.
Karl Rahner. *The Trinity*. New York: Herder and Herder, 1970.
M. C. Steenburg. *A World Full of Arians: A Study of the Arian Debate and the Trinitarian Controversy from AD 360–380.* http://www.monachos.net/content/patristics/studies-themes/56-a-world-full-of-arians?title=A_World_Full_of_Arians.

B. DOES "THE HOLY SPIRIT" REFER TO SOMEONE OTHER THAN THE GOD OF THE BIBLE?

In the fourth century, after it was widely accepted that Jesus Christ is equal to God, some Christians began saying that the Holy Spirit is also equal to God. In later centuries the Holy Spirit was said to be *a person*. That led to the now standard version of the doctrine of the Trinity, the claim that God is three persons—the Father, the Son, and the Holy Spirit—who are one substance.

While there are difficulties with saying that Jesus Christ and God are equal, at least Jesus is clearly a person, and God can be understood to be a person in the extended sense we proposed—something that thinks, desires, makes choices, communicates, and acts. But it is not at all clear that "the Holy Spirit" refers to a person, even in that extended sense.

In the Bible, God has a name—"Yahweh"—and "Jesus" is a name. There is a lot of biographical information about both of them. Yahweh created the universe but then was so disgusted with the human race that he flooded the planet. He called Abraham to lead a special nation—the Hebrews. He liberated the Hebrews from slavery in Egypt and then led them to a promised land. He gave hundreds of laws to Moses. He chose kings and prophets. In describing all these actions, the Bible tells us what Yahweh thinks, wants, and says.

Similarly, the Gospels tell us that Jesus was born of the virgin Mary in Bethlehem and grew up in Nazareth as the son of the carpenter Joseph. At about age thirty, he was baptized by his cousin John in the Jordan River, and then he preached about the Kingdom of God. He chose twelve apostles and performed miracles, such as raising Lazarus from the dead. His preaching got him into trouble with the Romans occupying Palestine, and they crucified him around the year 30. As with Yahweh, we are told quite a lot about what Jesus thinks, wants, and says.

With these biographical details, it is natural to think of God and Jesus as persons. But the Bible gives us neither a name nor biographical information for "the Holy Spirit." We aren't told that the Holy Spirit thinks, wants, or says anything at all. The phrase "Holy Spirit" itself is not a name but a description—like "worthy cause" and "good idea." And spirit isn't even a special word coined for God. It's just a translation of the Latin word for breath, *spiritus*, which is a translation of the Hebrew *ruach* and the Greek *pneuma*, words for *breath* or *wind*.

A basic feature of persons is gender—Jesus is male and God is described as male. But the Holy Spirit has no gender.

Persons are remembered for the words they speak. Yahweh launched the creation of the world by saying, "Let there be light," and hundreds of times in the Bible he speaks, as with the commandment "I am the Lord your God, who brought you out of the land of Egypt, out of the house of slavery; you shall have no other gods before me" (Exodus 20:2–3). The sayings of Jesus have been quoted millions of times: "Blessed are the poor in spirit," "Love your enemies," "When you give alms, do not let your left hand know what your right hand is doing." If you were offered a thousand dollars for each quotation you could give from Jesus, you might get rich. But what if you were offered a million dollars for each quotation you could give from the Holy Spirit? Even if you were allowed to look in the Bible, you would come up empty-handed.

The words "holy" and "spirit," furthermore, often refer to things other than persons, so it's not at all clear that the Holy Spirit has to refer to a person. Indeed, before the fourth century, Christians did not think of the Holy Spirit as a person different from the God of the Bible. As Alan Richardson points out,

> The Holy Spirit was not generally held by the ancient church to have a personality distinct from the personality of God. The Spirit is not to be conceived of as a second personality (in the modern sense) over against the personality of God. He is rather God himself in action— God immanent in the world.[5]

Another way Richardson puts it is that "The Holy Spirit is not, according to the doctrine of the ancient Church, a Divine Individual."[6]

The phrases "Holy Spirit," "the Spirit," and "the Spirit of God" are based on the Greek *pneuma*, which means *wind, breath, air in motion*. Different biblical writers and different theologians used *spirit* in different, often confusing ways. In his Letter to the Galatians 4:6, for example, Paul says, "And because you are sons, God has sent forth the Spirit of his Son into your hearts, crying out, 'Abba,' Father!" Is Paul talking about a *person* when he says "the Spirit of his Son"? If so, is it the same person as the Holy Spirit? In *On the Trinity*, Augustine wrote, "The Trinity can be called also the Holy Spirit, because all three are God and

Spirit and Holy."[7] So, according to Augustine, we can say that the Holy Spirit *is a member of* the Trinity, and the Trinity *is* the Holy Spirit!

The New Testament writer who uses the word "spirit" the most is Paul, but it's often difficult to figure out what he might mean by it. Sometimes he identifies the Holy Spirit with the Word of God, that is, Jesus Christ, which makes it hard to reconcile the three-person theory of Trinity with Paul's teaching. Paul also makes things confusing by applying the word "spirit" to several different things in the same passage. Consider this section of his First Letter to the Corinthians, where he is talking about "the things which God has prepared for those who love Him":

> But God has revealed them to us through his spirit. For the spirit searches all things, yes, the deep things of God. For what man knows the things of a man except the spirit of the man which is in him? Even so no one knows the things of God except the Spirit of God. Now we have received, not the spirit of the world, but the spirit who is from God, that we might know the things that have been freely given us by God. These things we also speak, not in words which man's wisdom teaches but which the Holy Spirit teaches, comparing spiritual things with spiritual (2:10–13).

If you're not already confused, underline each of the seven occurrences of the word "spirit" above and try to explain what each one means. Whatever Paul is saying here, he is not at all clear on what "the Spirit of God" and "the Holy Spirit" refer to.

The references to "the Spirit of God" in the Old Testament are much clearer. In Genesis 1:2, the Spirit of God hovers over the waters before God says, "Let there be light." The Spirit of God inspires prophets to speak, as if God had breathed the words into them. In Joel 2:28, God says, "I will pour out my spirit upon all flesh. Your sons and your daughters shall prophesy." In Numbers 11:29 Moses says, "Oh, that all the Lord's people were prophets and that the Lord would put his spirit upon them." What passages like these describe is not two persons but one person—God: God creating the world, God moving prophets to speak, God changing people's lives. "The Spirit of God" means God in action, especially God inspiring people. It does not mean some additional person.

As an analogy for the Spirit of God, consider the spirit of a football team. Their team spirit is not some person, like an extra player or extra coach. It is simply the team insofar as they support each other and show enthusiasm.

In the New Testament, as in the Old Testament, people are said to be moved by the Spirit of God or the Holy Spirit, usually to speak for God. The Second Letter of Peter says that "prophesy never came by the will of men, but holy men of God spoke as they were moved by the Holy Spirit" (1:21). In Luke 12:11–12, Jesus tells his friends that "when they bring you to the synagogues and magistrates and authorities, do not worry about how or what you should answer, or what you will say. For the Holy Spirit will tell you in that very hour what you ought to say." At Pentecost, Acts 2:4 says, the apostles "were all filled with the Holy Spirit and began to speak with other tongues, as the Spirit gave them utterance."

Now after the theory of the Trinity had become widespread, some Christians read biblical passages like these thinking of the Holy Spirit as a person distinct from Yahweh. But it seems more reasonable to interpret those passages in the older way, as simply talking about God leading people, inspiring them, and sanctifying them. The Bible, to repeat, never describes the Holy Spirit as a person. When "the Holy Spirit" is mentioned, *God* is having an effect on someone. So why not just say that references to the Spirit of God and the Holy Spirit are references to God doing things in people's lives?

The phrase "the Holy Spirit" is different from the word "God," of course, but that doesn't mean they refer to different *persons*. The phrase "vice-president of the United States" and the phrase "president of the U.S. Senate" are different, too, but they both refer to one person, currently Joe Biden. The president of the U.S. Senate *is* the vice-president of the United States—when he is presiding over the Senate. Similarly, while "God" and "the Holy Spirit" are different words, they can both refer to the same being—Yahweh, the God of the Bible.

For further reading:

George S. Hendry. *The Holy Spirit in Christian Theology*. Rev. ed. Philadelphia: Westminster John Knox, 1965.

C. DOES THE BIBLE SAY THAT GOD IS THREE PERSONS IN ONE SUBSTANCE?

The Bible doesn't say that God is three persons in one substance for the simple reason that the writers of the Bible didn't have the concepts of *person* and *substance*. Those are from Greek, Roman, and later European cultures, not the Hebrew culture that produced the Bible. The biblical writers had the concept of a human being, of course, and the meaning of "person" is "individual human being," but no Christian thinks that God is three individual human beings. As we noted, to say that God is three persons, you have to use person in an extended sense, something like "a thing that thinks, desires, makes choices, communicates, and acts."

The English word person is derived from the Latin word *persona*, which means "a mask worn by an actor on stage." *Per* is Latin for "through" and *sonare* means "to make a sound." In ancient Rome, an actor's *persona* was the mask through which he spoke his lines. Since one individual might play several parts in a play by switching masks, *persona* came to mean a character played by an actor, a role. We still have that idea today when we speak of the *personae* (plural) in a play or novel. The idea of role-playing is extended a bit when we talk about someone putting on a certain persona to impress one group of people and a different persona to impress another group.

The Christian thinker who first spoke of the Father, the Son, and the Holy Spirit as "Trinity" was Tertullian (160–225). He also introduced a phrase that would be repeated by advocates of the Trinity theory: "*Una substantia, tres personae.*" That is sometimes sloppily translated as "One substance, three persons," but, as we've said, *personae* meant masks or roles, not persons. So, as Alister McGrath points out, "It is quite possible that Tertullian wanted his readers to understand the idea of 'one substance, three persons' to mean that the one God played three distinct yet related roles in the great drama of human redemption. Behind the plurality of roles lay a single actor."[8]

Today if we say, "God is three persons," we mean something quite different from what Tertullian may have meant. In modern English, masks and role-playing are not part of the meaning of "person"—that word simply means an individual human being. So if we say, "God is three persons," we do not mean that a single center of thought, desire, choice, communication, and action performs several roles. We mean instead that God is three centers of thought, desire, choice, communication, and action.

The writers of the Bible thought of God as similar to a human being, and therefore like what would later be called a "person." But they would not allow for thinking of God as similar to *three* human beings, because that is thinking of three things rather than one thing, and the writers of the Bible insisted on monotheism, the belief that God is one thing. They were familiar with people who believed in many gods—Baal, Asherah, Zeus, Hera, Jupiter, and so on. The common understanding of these gods was that they were, like human beings, centers of thought, desire, choice, communication, and action, only they were supernatural. Using the word "person" in the extended sense of "center of thought, desire, choice, communication, and action," the gods were thought of as supernatural persons rather than human persons. For the writers of the Bible, someone who believed in three supernatural centers of thought, desire, choice, communication, and action—three persons, in short—believed in three gods, and so was a pagan. Responding to that objection with something like "But the three persons are *one* God, not *three*" would not have persuaded the biblical writers. They understood a god to be a supernatural person. One supernatural person is one god, two supernatural persons are two gods, and three supernatural persons are three gods.

In trying to think about how the writers of the Bible might respond to the claim that God is three persons in one substance, we have gotten ahead of ourselves. As we said at the beginning, the biblical writers didn't have the concepts of *person* and *substance*. So we need to move forward in time, and from Hebrew culture to Greek culture, to look for other possible sources of the claim that God is three persons in one substance.

For further reading:

Luke Timothy Johnson. *The Creed: What Christians Believe and Why It Matters*. New York: Doubleday, 2005.

D. DO THE EARLY CREEDS SAY THAT GOD IS THREE PERSONS IN ONE SUBSTANCE?

Some of the creeds have neither the concept of substance nor the concept of person. The Apostles' Creed says simply:

> I believe in God, the Father almighty, creator of heaven and earth. I believe in Jesus Christ, his only Son, our Lord. He was conceived by the power of the Holy Spirit and born of the Virgin Mary. . . I believe in the Holy Spirit.

The Nicene Creed of 325 doesn't have the concept of person either, but does have the concept of substance. To the claim in the Apostles' Creed that Jesus Christ is the Son of God, it adds the claim that they are "of one substance":

> We believe in one God, the Father Almighty, Maker of all things visible and invisible; and in one Lord Jesus Christ, the Son of God, begotten from the Father, God from God, Light from Light, true God from true God; begotten, not made; being of one substance with the Father. . . . And in the Holy Spirit.

Notice that both the Apostles' Creed and the Nicene Creed simply mention the Holy Spirit as something Christians believe in, without saying what "the Holy Spirit" refers to. That is compatible with the Bible's understanding and the early church's understanding of the Holy Spirit as God in action.

The Council of Constantinople of 381 expands the simple reference to the Holy Spirit in the Nicene Creed this way:

> And in the Holy Spirit, the Lord and Giver of life, who proceeds from the Father, who with the Father and the Son together is worshiped and glorified, who spoke by the prophets.

That expanded creed then became the basic statement of Christian belief. Today it is often called the Nicene Creed, though a more accurate title is the Nicene-Constantinopolitan Creed. While it says that Jesus Christ is "of one substance with the Father," it doesn't say that the Holy Spirit is of one substance with either the Father or the Son. And, like the earlier creeds, it doesn't use the word person at all.

The bishops who wrote the Chalcedonian Creed of 451 were preoccupied with the human and divine natures of Christ and were not concerned with the Trinity. So while they repeated the claim that Jesus Christ is "of the same substance with the Father," they didn't even mention the Holy Spirit. They said nothing about God being three persons in one substance.

If the claim that God is three persons in one substance isn't in the Bible or in the early creeds, where did it come from? The answer is that it is a mistranslation of a questionable theory developed by three bishops in Cappadocia, a region now in Turkey. They were the brothers Basil of Caesarea and Gregory of Nyssa and their friend Gregory of Nazianzus.

The word used by these men that has often been translated as "person" was the Greek *hypostasis*. The word often translated as "substance" was the Greek *ousia*. *Hypostasis* comes from two words meaning "that which stands under." The corresponding Latin word is *substantia*. *Hypostasis* did not mean person, but something like "individual being."

Before the Cappadocian theologians wrote about the Trinity, *hypostasis* and *ousia* had the same meaning: an individual thing, a substance—such as a tree or a horse. Those words are synonymous in the Nicene Creed and in some of the writings of Athanasius, the leader of the majority at Nicaea.[9] But the Cappadocians changed the meanings of *hypostasis* and *ousia* so that they could say that God is three *hypostaseis* (plural) in one *ousia*. That would not have made sense when the two words were interchangeable.

Basil of Caesarea distinguished between the two words this way: "The distinction between *ousia* and *hypostasis* is the same as that between the general and the particular."[10] So, for example, "human being" is a general term referring to many individuals, while "Peter Brown" is the name of one of those individuals. Applied to the Trinity, the Cappadocians said that God is three *hypostaseis* (plural)—three particular things—in one *ousia*—one general kind of thing. Eventually, the claim that God is "three *hypostaseis* in one *ousia*" got translated sloppily into Latin as "three *personae* in one *substantia*," and centuries later that was sloppily translated into English as "three persons in one substance."

There are many problems with both these translations, and so with the doctrine of the Trinity as we know it today. We'll consider six of these problems.

First, even if the Cappadocian theologians had said—in today's English—"God is three persons in one substance," other Christians need not agree with them. Those men didn't observe God's nature directly, and they didn't claim they were divinely inspired to write what they did. They weren't commissioned by a church council to write their theory of God's nature. They were simply trying to work out a coherent explanation of how God could be three in one. If what they came up with was clear, coherent, and credible, then it would be reasonable for Christians to believe it. But if it was not clear, coherent, or credible, nothing forced anybody to agree with them.

A second problem is that "three persons in one substance" is a mistranslation of what the Cappadocians wrote. In fact, they *did not* say, "God is three persons in one substance" or the Greek equivalent. For them, *hypostasis* did not mean "person." It meant an individual thing that has a nature or essence in common with other things. And *ousia*, in their special use of that term, meant the general kind of thing to which those individual things belonged. Three individual human beings, for example, are three *hypostaseis* within the *ousia* of humanity.

A third problem is that the Cappadocians' explanation of how God is three *hypostaseis* in one *ousia* implies that there are three gods. Gregory of Nyssa explains that in God three individuals share a common divinity in the same way as "Peter, James, and John are called three humans, even though they share a single common humanity."[11] The difficulty here is that Peter, James, and John share a single *humanity* by being three *human beings*. If the Father, the Son, and the Holy Spirit share a single *divinity* in the same way, they do it by being three *divine beings*, that is, by being three gods! Gregory saw the implication of polytheism in his theory, as did several critics, and so he wrote a defense, "On Not Three Gods." That's the work from which the statement above about Peter, James, and John is taken. Unfortunately, at least in the eyes of his critics, Gregory's defense only confirmed the implication of polytheism in his theory of the Trinity.

Centuries later, the Cappadocians' word *hypostasis* was mistranslated into *person*, via the Latin *persona*. That's a fourth problem with the theory of the Trinity. *Hypostasis* meant a particular thing that belongs to a general kind of thing. *Person* is a much more specific word than that. It means an individual human being—or, in an extended sense, a center of thought, desire, choice, communication, and action.

A fifth problem is that the new expression "God is three persons in one substance" implies polytheism, as the original Greek from which it was mistranslated had implied polytheism. A person, in our extended sense, is something that thinks, desires, makes choices, communicates, and acts. And a god is a supernatural person. Those who think of the Father, the Son, and the Holy Spirit as three persons think of them as three supernatural persons—distinct beings that think, desire, make choices, communicate, and act. If a god is a supernatural person, and the Trinity is *three* supernatural persons, then the Trinity is three gods. People who think of God the Father and his Son Jesus Christ as two persons sitting next to each other on a throne in heaven, for example, are thinking of two gods, just as Hindus who think of the god Shiva and his son Ganesha as two persons are thinking of two gods.

The formula that "God is three persons in one substance" is questionable in English for yet a sixth reason. As we use the words *person* and *substance*, a person is a perfect example of a substance. If I asked you to point to two substances, you couldn't do better than to point to me and yourself. One person is one substance, two persons are two substances, three persons are three substances. If you told me that you, I, and that woman standing over there are one substance, you would be speaking incoherently. Three persons, to repeat, are three substances: three persons cannot be one substance.

By now, you may feel like you're swimming in a whirlpool of confusing words, finding it hard to keep your head above water. If so, you're not alone. The doctrine of the Trinity was supposed to provide a clear explanation for a few passages in the Bible. But the dozens of explanations that were produced under the name "Trinity" provided more confusion than clarity. Since the late fourth century, Christians have been trying to make sense of what claims about the Trinity even mean. The most popular interpretation—"God is three persons in one substance"—has serious problems, as we've seen, both in how it was arrived at and in what it implies. Its big implication, polytheism, is as serious as a problem can be for Christianity, a religion that proclaims itself to be monotheistic. If the dominant interpretation of the doctrine of the Trinity has in fact turned millions of Christians into polytheists over the last sixteen centuries, it has obviously been deeply harmful. That's why groups like the Unitarians have explicitly rejected the doctrine of the Trinity.

For further reading:

Apostles' Creed.
Nicene Creed.
Nicene-Constantinopolitan Creed.
Chalcedonian Creed.
G. L Prestige. *God in Patristic Thought*. Eugene, OR: Wipf & Stock, 2008.

E. IS THE TRINITY A MYSTERY?

One clear-headed, knowledgeable contemporary theologian who tries hard to make sense of the Trinity is Alister McGrath. In *Christian Theology: An Introduction*, he writes, "The doctrine of the Trinity . . . is a remarkably difficult area of Christian theology." Then he describes "six approaches, classic and modern, to this doctrine," which he also calls "Six Models."[12] But these are not six ways to present one well-formed set of ideas. In the words they use and in the claims they make, they are six different theories about God, Jesus Christ, and the Holy Spirit.

McGrath's first model is that of the Cappadocians: God is three *hypostaseis* in one *ousia*. He translates *hypostaseis* as *persons*, which, as we've seen, is misleading. What the Cappadocians meant is that God is three individual things that belong to a general kind of thing. In either translation of *hypostaseis*, "persons" or "individual things," unfortunately, the explanation of the Cappadocians implies that there are three gods.

The second model discussed by McGrath is that of Augustine, who identifies "the Son" with wisdom and "the Spirit" with love. As McGrath explains it, "The Spirit appears as a sort of glue, binding Father and Son together, and binding both to believers."[13] Augustine rejects the Cappadocians' comparison of the three individuals in the Trinity to three men, because it implies polytheism. Augustine is also wary of the term "person," usually substituting for it "relation."[14] The three so-called persons in the Trinity, he says, are not different from one another: in relation to the divine substance, they are identical.[15] Augustine compares the Trinity to three operations of the human mind—memory, understanding, and will—which he calls "traces of the Trinity."[16] A natural way to understand this claim is that God is just one person, and the three are modes in which that one person acts. That, of course, yields a theory quite contrary to the standard theory of "three persons in one substance."

McGrath's third model is that of Karl Barth, whose says that the Father is God revealing himself to humans, the Son is the self-revelation of the Father, and the Holy Spirit is "the means by which Jesus is *recognized* as the self-revelation of God."[17]

In Karl Rahner's theory of the Trinity, McGrath's fourth model, "the entire work of salvation is the work of one divine person. Despite the complexity of the mystery of salvation, a single divine person can be discerned as its source, origin, and goal. Behind the diversity of the process of salvation there is to be discerned only one God."[18]

Robert Jensen's explanation of the Trinity, McGrath's fifth model, is that the five-word phrase "Father, Son, and Holy Spirit" is the proper name of God.[19] This claim seems dubious, since the Bible says that the proper name of God is "YHWH," often written "Yahweh." At most, "Father, Son, and Holy Spirit" seems to be what Jensen calls an "identifying description." We cannot get into linguistics here, but notice how different Jensen's explanation is from the other five.

McGrath's sixth model of the Trinity comes from John Macquarrie, who "appears to argue that the doctrine of the Trinity is to be viewed as the revelation of three modes of Being within God."[20] The Father is "primordial Being. . . . 'the ultimate act or energy of letting-be, the condition that there should be anything whatsoever.'" The Son is expressive being: "Primordial being needs to express itself in the world of beings, which it does by 'flowing out through expressive Being.'" The Holy Spirit is unitive Being in that it "is the function of the Spirit to maintain, strengthen and, where need be, restore the unity of Being with the beings."[21]

In describing the writings of these theologians, McGrath is treating them as six models of a single reality, the Trinity, and so he emphasizes what they have in common. Even so, it is very difficult to see them as explanations of the same thing. If you read the original writings of these theologians, that difficulty grows. They have the idea that God is one, and the idea that God is three, and they try in very different ways to make those ideas fit together. Their ideas of what is "three" about God are diverse—modes of being, relations, operations, and so on—and none of them say that God is "three persons" in the familiar sense in which 99 percent of Christians today say that God is "three persons." If the Cappadocians' explanation had been successful, after all, we would have had a clear doctrine of the Trinity sixteen hundred years ago, and there would have been no need for the hundreds of later attempts.

A common way of responding to all the confusion generated by the diverse explanations of the Trinity is to say, "The Trinity is a mystery." This approach assumes that "the Trinity" refers to a real phenomenon and the problem is that we don't understand the phenomenon well. An early practitioner of this "mystery" approach was Gregory of Nazianzus. When asked how the Father begat the Son, he replied that his questioners don't even know how they were begotten by their own fathers, so who are they to ask how God was begotten?

> The begetting of God must be honored by silence. It is a great thing for you to learn that he was begotten. But the manner of his generation we will not admit that even angels can conceive, much less you. Shall I tell you how it was? It was in a manner known to the Father who begat, and to the Son who was begotten. Any more than this is hidden by a cloud, and escapes your dim sight. [22]

This isn't an explanation of what "Trinity" is supposed to mean, but a condescending evasion of that question. The claim that the nonphysical God literally begot anyone is incoherent on the face of it, because God does not reproduce sexually. So anyone who is puzzled by the phrase "God the Father begot God the Son" is utterly rational to ask how this could be. Gregory saying that those ask don't even know how they were begotten, and that they are lucky to even have heard that God the Son was begotten by God the Father, is not an answer to the question. It's simply an attempt to silence the questioners.

As Gregory shows, appeals to mystery can be genuine or bogus. Some things are genuinely deep and hard to ponder, like the nature of time and what happens when we dream. With them we may want to talk of "mystery." But with "the Trinity," the difficulty comes less from God and more from people's fuzzy thinking. The problem arose because some theologians in the fourth and fifth centuries constructed some poorly thought-out theories that were then mistranslated several times, until the result was our incoherent English phrase "God is three persons in one substance."

It's good to remember that "Trinity" is not the name of a revealed truth. The word is not found in the Bible or even in an early creed. It's just a word used by people trying to explain some passages from the Bible. Explanations are only as reliable as the reasoning of the people who construct them. The theory of the Trinity is not well constructed. Its sloppiness is evident, for example, in the way it treats the threefold metaphor "The Father begot the Son" as if it were a literal statement. It also distinguishes between the way the Son is "begotten" by the Father and the way the Holy Spirit "proceeds" from the Father, but gives no clue as to what that difference might be.

If a group of words lacks a clear, coherent meaning, the problem lies with the people saying those words and not with their confused listeners. Recalling the example from chapter 1, suppose that my wife told me, "It's noon on the sun," and I responded, "How can that be, since noon is when the sun is overhead, and the sun can't be over *itself*?" It would be bogus of her to reply, "Our tiny human minds cannot grasp the mystery of Solar Noon." If there were any mystery here, it would be that she expected me to accept what she said as a real statement.

The same goes for appeals to "the mystery of the Trinity." Thousands of Christians over the centuries have put words together in dozens of confusing, often incoherent ways to explain how God is somehow three. Many of their formulas implied polytheism. The problem lies not with those who ask them to make sense; it lies with them for not thinking and talking clearly.

For further reading:

Alister E. McGrath. *Christian Theology: An Introduction*. 3rd ed. Oxford: Blackwell, 2001, 319–44.
John Morreall. "Can Theological Language Have Hidden Meaning?" *Religious Studies* 19 (1983): 43–56.

6

THE FALL

While "the Trinity" is difficult to make into a clear idea, the fall is not. The idea is that God created the first human beings in a paradise where they would live forever, but they ruined everything by disobeying God. He punished them by expelling them from paradise, making their lives difficult and painful, and declaring that they must eventually die. Their human nature, which had shone with intelligence, natural goodness, and self-control, was now corrupted. No longer brilliant, with a natural tendency to love God and do good, they were now intellectually and morally flawed bumblers who did not see good clearly or will it natural- ly. Adam and Eve had fallen from an unending life in a perfect world to a few decades of toil and suffering followed by death.

As the parents of the human race, moreover, Adam and Eve had ruined things for all their descendants, since their corrupted human nature, and the guilt and punishment for their original sin, were passed down from generation to generation, making each new human being just as fallen as they were. Just by being born, all humans were now sinful and guilty, and so when they died, they could not live with God in heaven. That would require that they be forgiven by God for Adam's original sin. Fortunately, that forgiveness was eventually secured for the human race by Jesus Christ when he died on the cross.

Familiar as these ideas are to Western Christians, they were not taught by Jesus. He is called Savior in the Gospels, but not for saving people from the guilt of original sin. The New Testament writer usually cited to back up teachings about original sin is Paul, who in his letter to the Romans wrote these lines:

> Therefore, just as sin came into the world through one man, and death came through sin, and so death spread to all because all have sinned—sin was indeed in the world before the law, but sin is not reckoned where there is no law. Yet death exercised dominion from Adam to Moses, even over those whose sins were not like the transgression of Adam, who is a type of the one who was to come (5:12–14).

> Therefore just as one man's trespass led to condemnation for all, so one man's act of righteousness leads to justification and life for all. For just as by the one man's disobedience the many were made sinners, so by the one man's obedience the many will be made righteous (5:18–19).

In the first passage, "The one who was to come" is Jesus Christ, who, Paul says in the second passage, secured "justification and life for all" by his "act of righteousness" and "obedience." Paul sees Jesus Christ as the second Adam who corrects the mistake of the first Adam by obeying rather than disobeying God. In his First Letter to the Corinthians, Paul connects that idea to Jesus' resurrection, which makes possible the resurrection of everyone else: "But in fact Christ has been raised from the dead, the first fruits of those who have died. For since death came through a human being, the resurrection of the dead has also come through a human being; for as all died in Adam, so all will be made alive in Christ" (15:20–22).

While these three statements of Paul's contain some ideas found later in the doctrine of original sin, they do not say that everyone inherits Adam's guilt. Nor did the first theologian who used the term "original sin," Tertullian, think that human beings inherit that guilt. The church fathers of the Eastern Orthodox tradition, too, such as Gregory of Nyssa, Gregory of Nazianzus, and John Chrysostom, did not teach that Adam's descendants inherit his guilt. They, in fact, said that babies are born free of sin.[1] John Chrysostom rejected the whole idea of one person being guilty for what someone else did: "For unless a man becomes a sinner on his own responsibility, he will not be found to deserve punishment. . . . That one man should be punished on another's account seems to most people unreasonable."[2]

The first theologian to develop the idea that the human race inherited Adam's guilt was Augustine in the late 300s. His idea of original sin, in turn, was the foundation for Anselm's atonement theory around 1100, and then Martin Luther's and John Calvin's atonement theories in the 1500s. It was to atone for original sin, they said, that Jesus Christ became a man and died on the cross. Of all the ideas in Christian theology, then, Augustine's teachings about original sin are among the most influential.

According to Augustine, before the fall, Adam was a perfect creature having the "highest excellence of wisdom" with "no imperfection whatever."[3] That perfection was what made his choice to disobey God such a serious sin. Augustine also says that all human beings *are* Adam, so his sin is their sin too.[4] "In the misdirected choice of that one man all sinned in him, since all were that one man, from whom on that account they all severally derive original sin."[5]

The claim that all human beings are guilty of Adam's sin because they *are* Adam is puzzling to most people. So is the idea that all human beings *sinned in* Adam. What could either of these claims mean?

In identifying the human race with Adam, Augustine quoted Paul's Letter to the Romans 5:12: "Just as sin came into the world through one man, and death came through sin, and so death spread to all because all have sinned." The idea Augustine got here was that Adam was the "father" of the human race, and so all his descendants were "in the loins" of Adam—that is, in his testicles.[6] Since all human beings came ultimately from Adam's loins, we were all in him. When he sinned, therefore, we all sinned "in him." Thus, babies are born guilty of Adam's sin.

Augustine's doctrine of original sin influenced virtually every Western theologian after him. In the atonement theories of Anselm, Luther, and Calvin, it is original sin that required the death of Jesus Christ to "pay the debt" owed for that sin. In Luther and Calvin, the human race fell so far when Adam sinned that we are all born as depraved slaves of sin, without free will, unable to do anything good on our own, and deserving of eternal punishment in hell.

While these ideas about original sin have been important in the history of Christian thought, many liberal Protestant and Roman Catholic thinkers have rejected some or all of them, and so have Eastern Orthodox theologians. To see why, we can explore five questions.

A. DID THE HUMAN RACE START OUT PERFECT?

Before Charles Darwin proposed his theory of evolution, if you asked most Christians how the human race got started, they would talk about Adam and Eve as described in the Book of Genesis. Even a century and a half after Darwin, millions of Christians still insist that Genesis is literally true. In many polls taken in the United States, over half of respondents say that God created human beings directly, as it says in Genesis, rather than through an evolutionary process.

The idea that the human race started out perfect but then declined is found not just in the Bible but in many ancient cultures. Often the ideal early time is called the golden age. If we want to use golden age stories to contrast the way humans actually are with the way they could be or should be, that can be illuminating. But if we read them literally, as historical accounts of actual events, we face big problems. One is that the very language of Genesis suggests that the story of the fall is an allegory, a parable, or some other nonliteral use of language. As we saw in chapter 3, section E, as early as the third century, Christian thinkers like Origen pointed out that the Hebrew word "Adam" means "man," suggesting that the story is about the human race, not about an individual person. Consider, too, the description of the forbidden "tree" in Genesis.

> The Lord God took the man and put him in the garden of Eden to till it and keep it. And the Lord God commanded the man, "You may freely eat of every tree of the garden, but of the tree of the knowledge of good and evil, you shall not eat, for in the day that you eat of it, you shall die" (Genesis 2:15–17).

Those who want to read this story as literal history need to explain what Adam could have thought when God talked about "the tree of the knowledge of good and evil." Let's suppose that Adam knew which trees were the *apple* trees and which were the *walnut* trees. "The tree of the knowledge of good and evil" obviously doesn't name another kind of tree alongside those trees. They bear apples and walnuts. What would be dropped by the tree of the knowledge of good and evil? If we were in an orchard and I told you, "Don't eat from the apple tree," you'd know which tree to avoid. But if I said, "Don't eat of the tree of the knowledge of good and evil," you would wonder what I was talking about.

Saying that God told Adam not to eat from the tree of the knowledge of good and evil seems to be not a literal statement but a poetic way of saying that God told people not to do something that would give them direct experience of evil. It seems to be part of an allegory, not a historical report.

The rest of the story of how Adam came to disobey God is also easy to understand as allegory but hard to understand as history. If Genesis is literally true, then the human race started from scratch—as one adult male and no females or children. Then God made an adult female out of one of the man's ribs. The woman got into a conversation with a snake and believed what the snake told her. In fact, both she and the man took the snake's word for it that the creator of the universe, who had put them in this perfect world, was lying to them about the danger of eating of the tree of the knowledge of good and evil! And these people who trusted the talking snake, Augustine tells us, were much smarter than we are—with the "highest excellence of wisdom" and "no imperfection whatever."[7] As literal history, this story seems unbelievable, in the literal sense of that word.

Another problem with treating Genesis as literal history is that it contradicts the scientific evidence we have about the origins of human beings, from biology, archaeology, and anthropology. Thousands of scientists have spent millions of hours doing research around the globe on how humans got started and how they developed and migrated. None of it suggests that the human race began as one adult male in a perfect world; all of it suggests that early human beings evolved from lower primates. And instead of being *more* intelligent, self-controlled, and moral than we are now, the evidence suggests that early humans were far *less* of all of these. Modern genetics shows that the genes of current humans are 98 percent identical to the genes of chimpanzees, and that our lineage split off from chimpanzees six to seven million years ago. Some three million years ago, australopithecines walked upright but weighed only about fifty pounds and had brains one-quarter the size of ours. From them evolved *Homo habilis*, who used tools, and then *Homo erectus*, who used fire. Finally came *Homo sapiens*, our species. To say that humans did not evolve, but popped into existence with Adam, we would have to give some explanation of the hundreds of skulls, skeletons, and tools that these creatures left behind.

Today many Christian churches accept the findings from biology and archaeology that support the theory of evolution. The largest is the Roman Catholic Church. The Book of Genesis, they say, is true but not in the way a history or science book is true. Different churches have different teachings, but they tend to be variations on this basic account: What Genesis tells us is that God created the universe, loves his creatures, and expects them to live according to his plan. He has a special relationship with human beings, whom he gave freedom, including the freedom to either return the love he shows them or not. Unfortunately, they often turn away from him.

Some Christian thinkers say that to this basic story we need to add that the first humans disobeyed God, and their sin damaged human nature, so that every human being since then has inherited a corrupted nature and the guilt of that first sin. We'll discuss these ideas in the next question.

For further reading:

Jean Delumeau. *History of Paradise: The Garden of Eden in Myth and Tradition*. Champaign, IL: University of Illinois Press, 2000.
Walter R. Mattfeld. *The Garden of Eden Myth*. Raleigh, NC: Lulu, 2010.

B. ARE BABIES BORN DEPRAVED AND DESERVING OF HELL?

According to the traditional doctrine of original sin, each newborn baby inherits a corrupt human nature along with Adam's guilt for disobeying God. Since Augustine, the Catholic Church (but not the Orthodox churches) has taught that all human beings inherit the sin of Adam along with his fallen nature, but that they retain a basic goodness and free will. Luther and Calvin, however, taught that human nature was so totally corrupted by Adam's sin that we are utterly unable to will any good action or refrain from sinning. Luther said that because we inherit original sin, in us "there is nothing left that can turn toward the good, but only toward evil."[8] Calvin taught that the human will "cannot aspire after anything that is good."[9] These ideas were incorporated into the Westminster Confession of Faith, a creed for the Reformed tradition. Because of original sin, it says, we are "wholly defiled in all the faculties and parts of soul and body," and "we are utterly indisposed, disabled, and made opposite to all good, and wholly inclined to all evil."[10]

People sometimes appear to be performing good actions, Luther and Calvin admitted, but those are not really their actions—rather, God is acting in them. According to the Westminster Confession, "Their ability to do good works is not at all of themselves, but wholly from the Spirit of Christ."[11] By ourselves, we only sin. Each person is vile, deserving no praise or reward but only, as the Westminster Confession says, "the wrath of God."[12]

These teachings of Luther and Calvin are called the doctrine of total depravity. Each baby deserves damnation from the first moment of its existence. In Calvin's words,

> We derive an innate depravity from our very birth . . . Every descendant . . . from the impure source is born infected with the contagion of sin: and even before we behold the light of life, we are in the sight of God defiled and polluted. . . . From a putrefied root . . . have sprung putrid branches . . . there was in Adam such a spring of corruption, that it transfused from parents to children in a perpetual stream.[13]

I don't know how many babies Calvin ever held in his arms, but his judgment that they are all putrid, defiled, polluted, and infected with the contagion of sin does not seem based on direct observation. Nor does it reflect Jesus' attitude toward little children. As we saw in chapter 1, he welcomed them and said, "It is to such as these that the kingdom of God belongs" (Mark 10:14). Babies occasionally stink, it's true, but a change of diapers is usually enough to fix that. The idea that they are guilty of the sin of their most distant ancestor, committed thousands of years before they were born, seems hard to make sense of, much less to justify. Jesus certainly never taught that.

Augustine, Luther, and Calvin tried to explain original sin by appealing to Paul's Letter to the Romans 5:12–14 and 18–19. But, as we've seen, Paul does not say that all human beings inherit Adam's guilt, or that we all *are* Adam, or *are in* Adam. Those nonbiblical ideas are Augustine's, and they are neither clear nor credible.

Let's assume for the sake of argument that there was a first man called Adam, from whom we are all descended. Each baby, then, comes from a sperm which came from a man who himself came from a sperm, which came from a man who himself came from a sperm—and so on, back to the sperm in Adam. We might even say that each baby born today was *potentially* in Adam. But the baby was not *actually* in Adam, as a person guiding Adam's actions, because the baby did not even exist when Adam was alive.

To see what's questionable in Augustine's claim that each baby inherits Adam's guilt, consider the thousands of people alive today who are descended from Vlad the Impaler, the fifteenth-century ruler of the House of Drăculeşti, from whom Bram Stoker got the name for his novel *Dracula*. As his name suggests, Vlad the Impaler became famous for his excessive cruelty to his enemies. He killed tens of thousands of people, torturing many of them beforehand. Vlad's children had children who had children who had children, all the way down through the centuries to the people who call Vlad the Impaler their ancestor today. Would anyone punish any of these people for the crimes of Vlad the Impaler, by putting them in prison or executing them, because they came ultimately from Vlad's sperm?

One early critic of the idea of inherited guilt, Bishop Julian of Eclanum, wrote this to Augustine:

> "Tiny babies," you say, "are not weighed down by their own sin, but they are burdened with the sin of another." Tell me then, tell me, who is this person who inflicts punishment on innocent creatures? . . . You answer God. God, you say. . . . You have come so far from religious feeling, from civilized thinking, so far, indeed, from mere common sense, in that you think that the Lord God is capable of committing a crime against justice such as is hardly conceivable among barbarians. [14]

If it would be irrational and unjust to punish the descendants of a wrongdoer, then, it would be irrational and unjust for God to punish the descendants of Adam just for being his descendants. The doctrine that babies are born depraved and deserving of hell rests only on Augustine's questionable ideas that babies *are* Adam and *sinned in* him. Since those claims are not clear and credible, neither is the doctrine.

While the issues we've been discussing may seem pretty dry and academic, they have real-life implications. In the terrorist bombing of the Oklahoma City Federal Building in 1995, for example, seventeen infants and toddlers in the day-care center on the second floor were killed. At a service held for their parents, Reverend Billy Graham assured them of God's love for their little ones. "Someday there will be a glorious reunion with those who have died and gone to heaven before us, and that includes all those innocent children that are lost. They're not lost from God because any child that young is automatically in heaven and in God's arms."

R. C. Sproul Jr., a well-known Presbyterian theologian and radio show host, was so upset by what Graham had said that he wrote an article in the Christian magazine *World* accusing Graham of preaching a new gospel, "justification by youth alone." All babies are born guilty of original sin, Sproul insisted, and the only way to be saved from that sin is to profess faith in Jesus Christ. Since infants and toddlers aren't capable of professing faith in Christ, they aren't capable of being saved at their young age. In Sproul's words,

> Though Scripture is clear that in sin we are conceived, though it affirms that outside of faith in Christ alone there is no salvation, we comfort ourselves in the face of grim images of the dead children carried from the rubble with the biblically unwarranted assurance that if one only dies young enough, one will be saved. [15]

According to this Calvinist understanding of original sin, anyone who dies before they are old enough to make a faith commitment to Jesus Christ—age six or seven, most churches say—is damned forever to hell. Here I think Rev. Sproul needs to reread the Gospels, especially the story of how Jesus welcomed the little children, saying "Let the little children come to me, and do not stop them; for it is to such as these that the kingdom of heaven belongs" (Matthew 19:14).

For further reading:

Alan Jacobs. *Original Sin: A Cultural History*. New York: HarperCollins, 2009.

C. IS DEATH A PENALTY FOR SIN?

One of the most famous lines in the King James Bible is in Paul's letter to the Romans 6:23: "The wages of sin is death." ("Wages" was a singular noun when this Bible was written.) In the Genesis story, God warned Adam not to eat of the tree of the knowledge of good and evil because if he did, he would die. Those who read this as an historical account conclude that since Adam's disobedience caused him to die, if Adam had not eaten of that tree, he would not have died. Fundamentalists often quote Paul's letter to the Romans 5:12–14, above, to reinforce that idea. God's intention, they say, was that there would be no death.

All of this was made church doctrine by the Council of Carthage in 417: "If anyone says that Adam, the first man, was created mortal, so that, whether he sinned or not, he would have died from natural causes, and not as the wages of sin, let him be anathema [cursed by church authority]."[16]

The idea that death began only after Adam sinned, however, is implausible for a number of reasons. First, if Adam lived in a world where nothing died, how would he even understand God's warning that he would "die" if he ate of a certain tree (Genesis 2:17)? What could "die" mean to someone living in a world where nothing had ever died?

Another reason it's hard to accept the claim that death began after Adam's sin is that we know from biology that death has always been a natural feature of life on this planet. All bacteria, microbes, and plant and animal cells age and eventually either divide or die. So do entire plants and animals. The claim that death was introduced with the sin of Adam implies that nothing died before Adam sinned. But all animals have always lived by killing and eating other animals and plants. How, then, did animals nourish themselves before Adam sinned? What could they eat, if not plants and animals? The fossil record shows that millions of years before any human beings existed, dinosaurs were eating other dinosaurs, obviously killing them in the process. But those who insist that death is a penalty for sin have to say that no animal died before Adam sinned.

There is another biological fact that shows the implausibility of things living forever before Adam's sin. It is that the death of some plants and animals makes room for others. If there were no death, then as plants and animals reproduced, the earth would soon be overrun with them. In a world of immortal plants and animals that reproduce, it would soon be hard to even move. Consider just one of the nine million animal species on earth, the housefly. Entomologists calculate that with the short time it takes these flies to mature, and the great number of eggs they lay, one pair that began mating in April would produce 191,010,000,000,000,000,000 flies by the end of August—if all of them survived. That's enough flies to cover the earth forty-seven feet deep— in just four months! The mind boggles in trying to calculate a world in which flies lived not for four months but forever! To that, add immortal mosquitoes, immortal rats, and nine million more immortal species. A world with reproduction but no death is simply a biological impossibility.

Here a defender of the claim that death is a penalty for sin might respond that what Genesis is talking about is not death *in general*, but only *human* death. God designed plants and animals to be mortal, so they died before Adam sinned, this defense would say, but he designed human beings so that they would naturally live forever. It was human immortality that changed when Adam disobeyed God.

This scenario would explain how Adam could understand what the word die means—he would have seen animals die. And it would eliminate the problem of the earth being buried in immortal flies. But is it at all plausible?

One problem with this scenario is that while we talk about human beings as distinct from animals, they are in fact a kind of animal. Aristotle and Thomas Aquinas called us "rational animals." Like other animals, we are composed of cells, and every known kind of cell, as we said, ages and eventually divides or dies. Human genes are 98 percent identical to those of chimpanzees, which is why we can catch diseases from them and they from us. Organs such as hearts and livers have also been transplanted from chimps to humans. Given our overwhelming similarity, it's hard to picture the original Garden of Eden as a place where chimps die but humans live forever.

Another problem with the idea that God designed humans to live forever is that we grow and age, and with age come the slowing and eventually the breakdown of bodily processes. Death is the natural conclusion of that breakdown. A newborn baby weighs a few pounds and its organs are undeveloped. Over the next few years, it grows and develops into a child, then an adolescent, then a young adult, then a middle-aged adult, then an old adult. This process of aging involves significant changes in body structure and functioning, so that at age forty, we can't do some of the things we could do at twenty, and at eighty some people can't do much of anything. Assuming that humans would grow and age in the hypothetical Eden, how could they avoid these natural eventualities? Would they grow from babies to children to adolescents to young adults, and then remain young adults forever? It's hard to see how that could be if they had human bodies with human cells and organs.

The claim that death is a penalty for sin, then, seems to be like other ideas people have gotten when they read Genesis as a history book—a misinterpretation.

For further reading:

Rudolf Bultmann. "The New Testament and Mythology." In *The New Testament and Mythology and other Basic Writings*, ed. Schubert M. Ogden. Minneapolis, MN: Augsburg Fortress, 1984.

D. CAN WE DO GOOD ACTIONS BY OURSELVES?

In this chapter so far, we have been discussing beliefs shared by many Protestants and Catholics. But in our last two questions, we'll focus on two beliefs of Protestant thinkers like Luther and Calvin that are not shared by Catholic theologians. Luther and Calvin taught that humans inherit from Adam a completely corrupt human nature. This is called the doctrine of total depravity, and it implies two things. First, humans cannot do anything good by themselves. And second, humans no longer have the free will that Adam had. We'll look at the first of these in this question and the second in the next question.

Starting with Augustine, theologians who have taught the doctrine of original sin have emphasized the evil tendencies of human beings. Calvin, for example, puts this question to readers of his *Institutes of the Christian Religion*:

> Can you exempt yourself from the number of those whose feet are swift to shed blood; whose hands are foul with rapine and murder, whose throats are like open sepulchers; whose tongues are deceitful; whose lips are venomous; whose actions are useless, unjust, rotten, deadly; whose soul is without God; whose inward parts are full of

wickedness; whose eyes are on the watch for deception; whose minds are prepared for insult; whose every part, in short, is framed for endless deeds of wickedness?[17]

Calvin, and before him Luther, was so taken with the ability of humans to sin that he seems unable to recognize any human ability to do good. Here both follow Augustine, who said that humans can do good only when God's grace is operating within them. By themselves, they can only do evil.

A lot of Augustine's thinking here was in opposition to Pelagius, a British theologian who had a more optimistic view of human nature. People, Pelagius said, are basically good and can choose to do good actions as well as bad. It is because they have free will that they are responsible for their actions. Pelagius rejected the idea that babies are born with guilt from Adam's sin. Augustine condemned Pelagius as a heretic, insisting that we inherit original sin and, in our fallen state, naturally sin.

Luther and Calvin then put these ideas at the center of Protestant theology. Luther said the sin of Adam destroyed the ability of humans to initiate good actions; by ourselves, we are controlled by Satan and do only evil.

> If we believe that original sin has so ruined us that even in those who are led by the Spirit it causes a great deal of trouble by struggling against the good, it is clear that in a man devoid of the Spirit there is nothing left that can turn toward the good, but only toward evil.[18]

Calvin saw human beings as utterly depraved and disgusting in the sight of God. Commenting on Jesus' saying in John 15:5 that "Apart from me you can do nothing," Calvin argues, "He says not that we are too weak to suffice for ourselves; but, by reducing us to nothing, he excludes the idea of our possessing any, even the least ability. . . . Our Savior's words simply mean, that when separated from him, we are nothing but dry, useless wood, because, when so separated, we have no power to do good."[19]

Because Augustine, Luther, and Calvin saw human beings as incapable of doing anything good, they emphasized God's grace—God acting in us—and the redemptive work of Jesus Christ. Everything good, they said, comes from outside human nature, from God. If a human being appears to do something good, it is really God doing it, so God deserves all the praise. On this point Calvin cites Paul's Letter to the Philippians, in which

> he attributes the whole operation to God, "It is God who is at work in you, enabling you both to will and to work for his good pleasure" (Philippians 2:13). The first part of a good work is the will, the second is vigorous effort in the doing of it. God is the author of both. It is, therefore, robbery from God to arrogate anything to ourselves, either in the will or the act. [20]

Despite the centrality of the idea that humans can do nothing good by themselves in Protestant thought, the claim seems highly questionable. Jesus never said that human beings are incapable of good actions; indeed, he spent a lot of time encouraging people to do good actions. And while he does say in John 15:5, "Apart from me you can do nothing," that figure of speech does not mean that humans by themselves do only evil and not good. After all, if humans could "do nothing" by themselves, they could not even do evil.

What could it mean to say that all human beings, all the time, naturally do only evil when acting on their own, so that if anyone does anything good, the motivation must be coming from God? Most of the time when we call an action good, we are referring to how it shows concern for other people. That's why Jesus' central moral principle is "Love your neighbor." But such concern, especially toward our family and friends, seems natural to our species. Hundreds of scientific studies have shown that compassion, altruism, and a desire to contribute to the group are deep-seated in human nature and have been essential to our survival as a species.

If humans really were as antisocial as Calvin describes above—"swift to shed blood; whose hands are foul with rapine and murder"—our species would have died out long ago. We have survived and flourished because, though we are individually weak, especially in our early years, we cooperate and help one another. That is the essence of good actions.

A simple example of natural human goodness is parental love. When a baby cries at 3:00 a.m. and her mother or father gets up to care for her, the parent's motivation seems both natural and good. Who would say that only through an infusion of divine grace could parents do what they appear to be doing themselves? Babies are the most helpless creatures on the planet, and if parents lacked the natural desire to care for them, they would die within hours. Without this natural parental love, the human race could not have gotten started, much less flourished.

Jesus refers to this natural goodness of parents in his Sermon on the Mount, comparing it to the love of God:

> Is there anyone among you who, if your child asks for bread, will give a stone? Or if the child asks for a fish, will give a snake? If you then, who are evil, know how to give good gifts to your children, how much more will your Father in heaven give good things to those who ask him (Matthew 7:9–11).

When Jesus says, "even you then, who are evil," he means only that we are somewhat evil. His point is that while we do bad things, we also do good things, such as give good gifts to our children. And he is clearly attributing good actions to human beings themselves, not to God acting in us, because he is comparing the good actions of human beings to the much greater good actions of God. The idea that we cannot do good actions by ourselves would have struck Jesus as odd, and it clashes with his preaching about how our dominant motive should be love.

Contrary to what Calvin implies in the long quotation above, there is simply no such thing as a person with 100 percent evil inclinations. Even horrendously evil monsters like Adolf Hitler had *some* good motives. After Martin Bormann gave the Führer a German Shepherd dog in 1941, Hitler named her Blondi and took good care of her until the end of his life. When he moved into the bunker in 1945, he even allowed Blondi to sleep in his bedroom, something he didn't permit his mistress, Eva Braun. Were none of Hitler's acts of kindness toward Blondi good? And if any of them were good, did the motivation have to come from God rather than from Hitler's natural affection for the dog?

For further reading:

Michael Shermer. *The Science of Good and Evil: Why People Cheat, Gossip, Care, Share, and Follow the Golden Rule*. New York: Henry Holt, 2004.

E. DO WE HAVE FREE WILL?

Free will is a topic that has engaged theologians and philosophers for thousands of years, but we cannot go into all the issues it raises. We will concentrate on the big question that has concerned Christian thinkers: After Adam sinned, did human beings have free will? "Will" is tradition- ally thought of as the ability of a person to choose, especially to choose actions. That's why free will is also called free choice. If I find a Rolex watch on the sidewalk, there are at least three things I could do: leave it where it is, in case the owner comes back looking for it; put it in my pocket, saying, "Finders keepers"; or take it home and put an advertise- ment in the "lost and found" section of the newspaper. My decision to do the third thing, or the second, or the first, is said to be an act of will. I am choosing one among several possibilities. The "free" in "free will" is understood to be a lack of coercion or necessity in choosing; nothing outside of me is forcing me to choose one of these alternatives.

Part of choosing freely, then, is having at least two possibilities and not having to do what I in fact do. A standard exercise in hypnotism is to tell the hypnotized person that when she awakes, she will have an over- powering thirst and will immediately look for something to drink. When the person is brought out of the trance and asks for a glass of water, we would probably say that she didn't have free will, because something outside her—the hypnotist's suggestion—caused her to ask for the wa- ter. In the grip of that mental manipulation, she could not have done otherwise. For that reason, too, we would not blame the person for asking for the water, if there were something objectionable about doing that. It is fair to blame people for an action only if they could have avoided that action.

A related idea in ethics is that if a person has a moral responsibility to do something—tell the truth, say—he is able to do it. This is often expressed in the motto "Ought implies can." It would be irrational for someone to tell me I have a moral responsibility to compete in the next Olympics, for example, when I am too old to even be considered for the tryouts. Blaming me for not doing something I cannot do would make no sense.

With this basic understanding of free will and moral responsibility, let's turn to the big theological question: Do people after Adam's sin have free will? Catholic and Orthodox theologians generally answer yes;

Protestants following Luther and Calvin generally answer no. In theological discussions, by the way, free will is generally understood to involve choices of good and evil, choices that matter to a person's salvation, and not nonmoral choices such as what to eat for lunch or what color shoes to buy.

In the Gospels Jesus doesn't talk about "free will," but many of the things he says imply that people have control over their actions and are free to choose between alternatives. What God expects us to do, Jesus thinks we can do. Many of his parables, such as that of the prodigal son, are about people making choices and living with the consequences. In the Gospel of Luke, when the rich young ruler asks Jesus what he must do to inherit eternal life, Jesus tells him to keep the commandments. When the man says he has done that since his youth, Jesus says, "There is still one thing lacking. Sell all that you own and distribute the money to the poor, and . . . come, follow me" (Luke 18:18–25). The Gospel says that he did not choose to give away his fortune, but the point of Jesus' advice was to get him to make that choice. If Jesus thought that the selfish choice was the only choice the man could make, there would have been no point in encouraging him to make the opposite choice.

Following Jesus, most early Christian theologians thought of human beings as able to choose between alternatives and able to do good actions. Several also taught that if someone does something without freely choosing it, she is not blameworthy for it. As Clement of Alexandria said, "Actions which are not the result of free will are not imputed."[21] In the late 300s, however, Augustine came up with new ideas about moral responsibility in his teachings about original sin. Because of Adam's sin, he said, humans are born fallen and depraved, able to sin but unable to do good. Only when God is acting in us can good actions result, and then it is God who deserves the credit, not we.

Augustine realized that there was a problem in saying that we are naturally unable to do the good actions that God tells us we should do. Isn't it true that "Ought implies can"? His solution was to say that after the fall we still have free will, but in exercising that free will, we always sin. For Augustine's critics, that was not a clear explanation but a confused way of talking, because people don't have free will if they automatically sin and can't do otherwise.

When Luther and Calvin adopted Augustine's ideas about original sin in the 1500s, they spoke in less confusing ways by admitting that free will had no place in their theology. In *The Bondage of the Will*, which Luther considered his greatest work, he said that after the fall of Adam, the human will is "enslaved to sin" and so is not free. "When God is not present and at work in us, everything we do is evil."[22] Later in that book he wrote, "Original sin itself, therefore, leaves free choice with no capacity to do anything but sin and be damned."[23]

To this argument against free will, Luther added a quite different one—that free will is ruled out by God's foreknowledge of human actions:

> If we believe it to be true that God foreknows and predestines all things, that he can neither be mistaken in his foreknowledge nor hindered in his predestination, and that nothing takes place but as he wills it (as reason itself is forced to admit), then on the testimony of reason itself there cannot be any free choice in man or angel or any creature.[24]

Earlier in *The Bondage of the Will*, Luther wrote simply, "The proposition stands, and remains invincible, that all things happen by necessity."[25] While we humans may in our ignorance feel that we are free to choose between alternatives, in reality, all of our choices and actions have been predetermined by God from all eternity.

John Calvin agreed with Luther that there is no such thing as free will in human beings. In book 2 of his *Institutes of the Christian Religion*, chapter 5 is "The Arguments Usually Alleged in Support of Free Will Refuted." His and Luther's denial of free will is less confusing than Augustine keeping the words while denying the reality. But these leaders of Protestantism face the same question Augustine faces of how human beings can be blamed for choosing what it is utterly natural for them to choose. As we've said, it doesn't seem rational to blame someone for an action unless she could have done otherwise. "You ought to avoid evil" implies "You can avoid evil," but Luther and Calvin insist that choosing evil is as natural to human beings as eating and drinking.

In their responses to critics, Luther and Calvin tried to solve this problem, but in doing so they had to appeal to Augustine's idea that all human beings are guilty of Adam's sin. Calvin, arguing against those who say that if we do evil necessarily, we should not be blamed, writes,

> Adam voluntarily subjected himself to the tyranny of the devil . . .
> Hence the corruption by which we are held bound as with chains,
> originated in the first man's revolt from his Maker. If all men are
> justly held guilty of this revolt, let them not think themselves excused
> by a necessity in which they see the clearest cause of their condem-
> nation.[26]

Here Calvin says that we sin necessarily, but maintains that Adam
brought that necessity on himself by revolting against God, and all of
Adam's descendants are "justly held guilty of this revolt." For us to
complain about being blamed for what we do unavoidably, then, is like
heroin addicts complaining about being blamed for using the drug they
got themselves addicted to. You brought this necessity on yourself, Calvin would say. Replying to the criticism that "Exhortations are vain,
warnings superfluous, and rebukes absurd, if the sinner possesses not
the power to obey," Calvin borrows an argument from Augustine: "O
man! . . . it is your own fault you have not the power [to obey exhortations, warnings, and rebukes]."[27]

The trouble with Calvin's argument here is that he assumes "All men
are justly held guilty of this revolt" (Adam's disobeying God). He does
that by lumping together all human beings with the first human being
as if they were a single person. Only under that assumption can he say,
"O man! . . . it is your own fault." But, as we saw in question C, a
newborn baby is quite distinct from the first man who ever lived and
had nothing to do with his moral choices. Blaming a baby for Adam's sin
is like executing a descendant of Vlad the Impaler for the murders Vlad
committed. While the Hebrew word "Adam" means "man," it is neither
logical nor fair to hold the human race responsible for what Adam did.

Calvin's argument that it is just for God to punish human beings
even though they lack free will, then, is highly problematic. It is doubt-
ful that Jesus would agree.

For further reading:

Luther and Erasmus. *Free Will and Salvation.* Edited by E. Gordon Rupp and Philip S.
  Watson. Atlanta: Westminster John Knox, 1995.
John Calvin. *Bondage and Liberation of the Will.* Grand Rapids, MI: Baker, 2002.
R. C. Sproul. *Willing to Believe: The Controversy over Free Will.* Grand Rapids, MI: Baker,
  2002.

7

LIFE AFTER DEATH

In earlier chapters we saw how some Christian beliefs changed under the influence of Greek thinkers. Christians came to say things that would have puzzled Jesus, such as that God is three persons in one substance and Mary is the mother of God. In this chapter, we'll discuss another topic in which Greek-influenced Christians made big changes to the ideas of Jesus—life after death.

In the minds of first-century Jews like Jesus, the natural fate of human beings was to be destroyed by death. As God said to Adam in evicting him from paradise, "By the sweat of your face you shall eat bread until you return to the ground, for out of it you were taken; you are dust, and to dust you shall return" (Genesis 3:19). The idea that death destroys human beings was the standard belief of the people of Israel for a thousand years. As the speaker in Psalm 6:5 says to God, "In death there is no remembrance of you; in Sheol [the grave] who can give you praise?" The speaker in Ecclesiastes is even harsher:

> The fate of humans and the fate of animals is the same; as one dies, so dies the other. They all have the same breath, and humans have no advantage over the animals; for all is vanity. All go to one place; all are from the dust, and all turn to dust again. . . . the dead know nothing; they have no more reward, and even the memory of them is lost. Their love and their hate and their envy have already perished; never again will they have any share in all that happens under the sun (3:19–20; 9:4–6).

Jesus agreed with the idea that death destroys people, but he also held a new belief in life after death. In the second century BCE, some Jews had started talking about a resurrection in which God would bring Jews back to life, while leaving their enemies rotting in the dust. This idea was controversial—the Pharisees believed in it, while the Sadducees did not. Jesus made the resurrection central to his teaching and expanded the idea to include all human beings, not just Jews. At the end of the world, he said, God will bring all the dead back to life, judge them, and then reward or punish them. The resurrection will not be a natural event, but the miraculous intervention of God in history.

The Greek understanding of life after death was quite different. Greek thinkers, especially in the tradition following Plato (424–347 BCE), thought of living human beings as made up of two parts, one essential and one nonessential. That idea is called dualism, from *duo*, the Latin word for "two." The essential part of a human being is the soul, which is identified with the mind. It is nonphysical and naturally immortal—it will live forever. The nonessential part of a human being is the physical body. Greek dualists believed that while the body is destroyed at death, the human being survives death, because the essential part, the immortal soul, lives on. The human being had been a nonphysical soul living in a physical body, but after death is a soul living on its own.

As Greek philosophy influenced Christian thinkers more and more, their understanding of death gradually changed from Jesus' Jewish idea—that we will be destroyed by death but then resurrected at the end of the world—to a Greek understanding of life after death—that we will survive death because our immortal souls survive death. Without announcing the change, they switched from Jesus' idea that we will live *again*, to the Greek idea that we will live *forever*. And so today, Christians talk about people's immortal souls going to heaven when they die, and about missionaries saving people's immortal souls from hell, as if these were teachings of Jesus, not realizing that he had very different ideas about life after death. For us to understand the differences, it will help to ask some questions.

A. AM I A SOUL OR SPIRIT?

Death is puzzling for young children, especially the death of family members. It's common to explain it to them by saying that the person "went to heaven." When I was four, my grandmother died, and that's the explanation I got. So for years I thought heaven was two blocks away at Bauman's Funeral Home. If I had been more philosophical, I would have asked a follow-up question: "If Grandma is in heaven, what's in that big box?" There's a stock answer for that one, too—"What's in the casket is only Grandma's body. It's her soul that went to heaven." Had I been even more philosophical, I would then have asked, "What is a soul? And how can Grandma's soul be Grandma?"

Notice that if Grandma's soul went to heaven, and that counts as Grandma going to heaven, then Grandma's soul must count as Grandma. If something less than Grandma—say her heart—went to heaven, then it wouldn't be Grandma in heaven, only one of her organs. When we think of a dead person being in heaven, especially ourselves, we think of the whole person—what we are now—being in heaven. If someone could guarantee the endless preservation of just my heart after I die, I wouldn't be even slightly interested: what I'm looking for is the endless survival of me, the whole person I am now. If, then, when our souls go to heaven, that is us going to heaven, our souls must be us.

The evangelist Billy Graham is a good example of someone who thinks this way. When asked about death in an interview with *Newsweek* magazine, Graham answered, "I do not fear death. I may fear a little bit about the process, but not death itself, because I think the moment that my spirit leaves this body, I will be in the presence of the Lord."[1] Graham speaks of his "spirit" as many Christians speak of their "souls" here, and the same reasoning applies to Graham's "spirit" as to Grandma's "soul." Both are thought of as something nonphysical that is equivalent to the person. When Graham says that as soon as his spirit leaves his body, he will be in God's presence, he means that his spirit in heaven will be Billy Graham in heaven.

Christians today talk about "soul" and "spirit" in several ways, but in all of them the soul or spirit is supposed to be distinct from the body. Living as a soul or spirit after death is supposed to be living without the body that was cremated or that is rotting in the ground.

But how could Billy Graham, or anyone else, be the human being he is without his body? My soul or spirit doesn't have eyes, and seeing is a big part of my life. My soul or spirit doesn't have ears, a nose, a tongue, or fingers, and with them I experience the world and other people.

Not only do we experience with our bodies, but we act with them. It is with my fingers and arms that I prepare and eat meals, play the piano, shake people's hands, and do hundreds of other things. It is with my legs that I run, dance, and propel my bicycle. With my tongue I talk; with my face I smile, frown, laugh, and cry.

If I try to imagine myself without my head, torso, arms, and legs, I don't imagine anything like the person I am. It's hard to see how what is left would even be a human being, much less be me. Without a body, whatever is left would not be able to perceive or move. Even if it had some kind of awareness, it would not be the rich, sensory, interactive awareness I have of the world and other people. It would be more like the awareness of Helen Keller—the famous woman who was both blind and deaf—only after Ms. Keller had suffered another catastrophe in which she was completely paralyzed and lost her abilities to touch, smell, and taste, as well as her feelings of body orientation! Was that what Billy Graham was looking forward to when he talked about being a spirit after death?

People like Billy Graham who talk about going to heaven as spirits or souls, I suggest, have not thought carefully about what they are saying. They do not really imagine themselves as disembodied spirits or souls. Instead, they confusedly imagine themselves and others as still having bodies. That's how heaven is pictured in hundreds of paintings, movies, and hymns—as a physical place inhabited by physical people who can see, hear, touch, smell, and taste, as well as communicate and move around. In the familiar image of Saint Peter standing at the gates of heaven greeting people who have just died, for instance, Peter and the newly dead all have bodies. At many funerals, people say things like, "Bob sure loved to play golf—I'll bet he's practicing his putt right now, in heaven." The answer to our question "Am I a soul or spirit?", then, is no. And leading theologians like Thomas Aquinas agree. "It is clear that man is not a soul only," Thomas wrote, "but something composed of soul and body."[2]

None of our criticisms of the idea that a person is a soul or spirit apply to what Jesus taught about the resurrection, because he didn't say that human beings are souls or spirits, nor that in heaven we will be souls or spirits. In fact, Jesus appears to have had no conception of people without bodies—in heaven or anywhere else.

For further reading:

Thomas Aquinas. *Summa Theologiae*, question 75. In *The Basic Writings of Saint Thomas Aquinas*, ed. Anton C. Pegis. Indianapolis: Hackett, 1997, 682–94.

B. DID JESUS SAY THAT OUR SOULS GO TO HEAVEN OR HELL WHEN WE DIE?

The description of death as the person's soul going to heaven is so familiar to Christians that many think it's in the Bible, but it isn't. Neither Jesus nor any writer of the Bible says anything about the soul going anywhere when they describe death. Nor do they identify the soul with the mind, or with the whole human being, as Christians began doing in the fourth century. Jesus certainly taught that there will be life after death—the resurrection—but he didn't teach that there will be life right after death, which is what most Christians now believe.

In the last question we kept saying "soul or spirit" because Christians sometimes say "soul" and sometimes say "spirit" when they talk about what "goes to heaven." For simplicity and clarity, in this question, we will ask just about souls going to heaven. By "soul" we mean what most Christians mean by "soul" and by "spirit"—the nonphysical essential part of a human being that will exist in heaven or hell after death.

Jesus talked about souls, but he did not think of them in the way most Christians today do. Like other first-century Jews, he thought of a person's soul as what made him or her be alive. Common words for soul at the time were *nefesh* and *ruach* in Hebrew, and *spiré* and *pneuma* in Greek. Like the words for soul in most languages, these came from words for breath, wind, air that's moving. The reason words meaning air that's moving were used for what makes us alive is probably that people noticed that as long as we are alive, we breathe, but when we "breathe our last breath," we die. So they thought that our breath is what keeps us alive. Nothing was thought of as immortal here, as the soul is immortal in Greek dualism. The soul was understood to be mortal just like the rest of the person, and at death, both were destroyed.

Many Christians today think of soul or spirit as the opposite of matter, as something nonphysical. But the writers of the Bible didn't think this way. They thought of spirit as the finest, lightest kind of matter, like what we now call vapor or gas.

If Jesus thought of the soul as what makes a person alive, and not as the person's nonphysical, immortal mind, where did the now popular idea that the soul is the nonphysical, immortal mind come from? That idea came not from the Bible but from Greek philosophy, especially from Plato. While the first Christians were Jews who thought of each human being as one thing, Greek-influenced Christians tended to be dualists, thinking of each person as two things: a mortal body being controlled by an immortal soul. The most influential of those dualists was Augustine, who defined a human being as "a rational soul using a mortal and earthly body."[3] As we said in chapter 1, that definition would have puzzled Jesus, because he thought of a human being as one thing—a living body, not as two things—a soul, plus a body that it "uses."

In switching to Platonic ideas about death liberating the immortal soul, Christian thinkers quietly put aside Jesus' idea, which he shared with the writers of the Bible, that death destroys us. The polite way of saying that in the Bible is that the dead are "asleep in the dust." Psalm 13:3 asks God to "Give light to my eyes, or I will sleep the sleep of death, and my enemy will say, 'I have prevailed.'" In First Corinthians 15:6, Paul says of the five hundred people who saw Jesus after his resurrection, that most "are still living, though some have fallen asleep." What Jesus added was that the destruction of death is not permanent because at the end of the world God will intervene in the natural order of things and resurrect everyone, judge them, and reward or punish them.

In Jesus' day, this idea of the resurrection was less than two centuries old and was not accepted by all Jews. The Sadducees rejected it because it was not well grounded in the Scriptures. If you read through the whole Old Testament—over one thousand pages—God says nothing at all about anyone living after they die. And just before he drives Adam and Eve out of the garden, he scolds Adam, saying, "You are dust, and to dust you shall return."

There are just two sketchy prophetic passages in the Old Testament that suggest a future resurrection, and it is not a resurrection of the human race. These passages were written at a time when Jews were being persecuted, and in both of them only Jews—maybe only some Jews—will be resurrected. The first is Isaiah 26:14–15. Here the first lines seem to refer to the people who have oppressed the Israelites:

The dead do not live; shades do not rise—
Because you have punished and destroyed them, and wiped out all memory of them.

But then, a few lines down, Isaiah prophesies a resurrection for the people of Israel:

> Your dead shall live, their corpses shall rise.
> O dwellers in the dust, awake and sing for joy!
> For your dew is a radiant dew,
> and the earth will give birth to those long dead (26:19).

The other prophesy in the Old Testament of a resurrection is an apocalyptic vision at the beginning of chapter 12 of the Book of Daniel:

> At that time Michael, the great prince, the protector of your people, shall arise. There shall be a time of anguish, such as has never occurred since nations first came into existence. But at that time your people shall be delivered, everyone who is found written in the book. Many of those who sleep in the dust of the earth shall awake, some to everlasting life, and some to shame and everlasting contempt.

Any Jew who believed in the resurrection of the dead at the time of Jesus, then, had very little to base it on. Jesus is vague about what it will involve, except to suggest that everyone, not just some Jews, will be resurrected, and there will be a judgment after the resurrection, followed by happiness for the good people and suffering for the bad. But whatever he said about the resurrection of the dead, it is clear that he did not say that people's souls go to heaven or hell when they die.

For further reading:

Oscar Cullman. *Immortality of the Soul or Resurrection of the Dead? The Witness of the New Testament.* Eugene, OR: Wipf & Stock, 2000.

John Morreall. "Perfect Happiness and the Resurrection of the Body." *Religious Studies* 16, no. 1 (1980): 29–35.

C. ARE THERE PEOPLE IN HEAVEN AND HELL RIGHT NOW?

Jesus preached that the resurrection would occur at the end of the world, which he and many others believed would be within a few decades. In three of the Gospels, as we saw in chapter 2, he says it will be within the lifetime of some people listening to him: "For the Son of Man is to come with his angels in the glory of his Father, and then he will repay everyone for what has been done. Truly, I tell you, there are some standing here who will not taste death before they see the Son of Man coming in his kingdom" (Matthew 16:27–28; see Luke 9:26–27 and Mark 9:1).

Suppose you lived around the year 30 and heard Jesus say these words, and you were only twenty years old. You might well expect to be alive at the end of the world when Jesus returns, so that you would be judged and go to the next life without dying. When Jesus Christ "come[s] to judge the living and the dead," as the Apostles' Creed says, you might expect to be among the living. And if you died before the end of the world, you would be "asleep in the dust" for only a few years before being resurrected. Either way, you would hope to be in heaven within, say, seventy years.

If you were dead for seventy years before the resurrection, that was not a problem, either, because during that time you would be out of existence, so you wouldn't notice the passage of time—or anything else. As Ecclesiastes says, "The dead know nothing" (9:5). When you died, you would lose consciousness, and the next thing you knew—literally— you would be at the Last Judgment. It would be like going to sleep, having no dreams, and then waking up. The best-known Christian who thought of the period between death and resurrection as like sleep is Martin Luther. He wrote,

> As soon as your eyes have closed, you shall be woken; a thousand years shall be as if you had slept but a little half-hour. Just as at night we hear the clock strike and know not how long we have slept, so too, and how much more, are in death a thousand years soon past. Before a man should turn round, he is already a fair angel. [4]

With that understanding of death, it's not surprising that early Christians thought of death as "rest." We still talk that way, as in the expression "May she rest in peace." As Christianity spread into cultures influenced by Greek dualism, however, the idea of the immortal soul, and the identification of the soul with the mind, gradually replaced Jesus' ideas about death and resurrection. Ultimately, death was no longer thought of as going unconscious, to be "asleep in the dust." Instead, it was thought of as the immortal soul/mind being freed from the body to join God in heaven. In this new way of thinking, the dead are not unconscious but fully conscious. Indeed, those who are saved are perfectly happy.

In the last question, we said that it seems impossible to imagine a human being without a body. But even if we could imagine such a thing, that is not what Jesus taught about life after death. Nonetheless, Christians influenced by Greek dualism gradually came to think of their dead friends and relatives as living in heaven with God, rather than as "asleep in the dust" awaiting the resurrection.

This change in thinking got an extra push when Christians were persecuted by the Romans. When Christians in Rome saw friends and family members herded into the Coliseum and mauled to death by lions for the entertainment of the crowd, they naturally wanted to think that these martyrs would be rewarded for their faithfulness to Jesus Christ. And since it seems best if a reward comes soon after the meritorious action, it was natural for them to want their friends and family members to be rewarded right after they died, rather than at the end of the world. So, gradually, Christian martyrs were said to be in heaven immediately after death, rather than after the resurrection. Those who had been killed for their faith became "saints"—people living in heaven with God. Christians held annual celebrations of the dates of their deaths, calling those their *dies natalis*—their days of birth into heaven. Christians collected relics of the saints, such as their bones, and eventually named churches after them.

Later, prominent Christians who had not been martyred, such as bishops and theologians, were called saints, too. As praying to saints became popular, the church assigned them "feast days" on the calendar, usually the day they had died and "gone to heaven." Eventually, the church developed a system for officially declaring that a dead person is a saint in heaven. That process of canonization is currently being conducted for Mother Teresa of Calcutta, among others.

Not all Christians went along with the cult of saints. In the early 400s Vigilantius argued for the original Christian belief that when people die, they are "asleep" until the resurrection.[5] By that time, though, the veneration of saints had become too popular for most people to question.

A big part of the appeal of the idea of saints was that people on earth could pray to them, asking for favors. Then the saints would ask God to fulfill those requests. Saint Joseph, the foster father of Jesus, had been a carpenter, so it was assumed he would be especially willing to help carpenters. Saint Cecilia was martyred under Emperor Marcus Aurelius around 180. Before she died she sang to God, so she became a patron saint of musicians. Saint Christopher is the patron saint of travelers, and Catholics still pray to Saint Anthony to help them find lost possessions.

The most important saint of all was Mary. In the fifth century she was officially declared "the Mother of God," and since then many other claims have been made about her power. Dozens of Catholic churches are named "Mary, Queen of Heaven," and the Second Vatican Council declared Mary "Advocate, Auxiliatrix, Adjutrix and Mediatrix."

Once the belief was widespread that martyrs and other famous dead Christians were in heaven, people naturally wondered about the fate of everyone else who had died, such as their relatives and friends. Were they in heaven, too? Would it do any good to pray for them? Obviously, if they were in hell, there was no hope, but over the centuries many Christians came to believe in a third state after death for people who were not damned, but who had not been purified of the effects of all their sins, and so could not enter heaven immediately. That state was called "purgatory," because in that state they were "purged" of the effects of their sins. Many descriptions spoke of flames like those in hell, with the big difference being that the suffering in purgatory was for a limited time, after which the person would enter heaven. Origen, for instance, wrote about a "fire" that burns away sins.[6] By the sixth century, Pope Gregory the Great would say that belief in purgatory is "established" and "to be believed." In the Middle Ages theologians discussed many details about purgatory, and it was made doctrine at the First and Second Councils of Lyon (1245 and 1274), the Council of Florence (1438–1445), and the Council of Trent (1545–63).

One of the teachings of the medieval church was that people could pray for those in purgatory in order to shorten their periods of suffering. People tended to be most concerned about their family and friends, but prayers could also be offered for all "the Poor Souls in Purgatory." November 2 was made a special day to pray for them—All Souls' Day. To provide a concrete way to help those in purgatory, the medieval church created "indulgences," something that would greatly trouble Martin Luther and help spur the Protestant Reformation. Coming from a Latin word meaning the canceling of a debt, an indulgence was granted by the pope or a bishop. It cancelled some or all of the time a person would have to spend in purgatory to atone for his sins. This system is still in place in the Roman Catholic Church. Saying the short prayer "My Jesus, Mercy," for example, carries an indulgence of one hundred days; saying "Jesus, meek and humble of Heart, make my heart like unto Thine" carries an indulgence of three hundred days. A plenary indulgence cancelled all the time a person would have to spend in purgatory, allowing her to enter heaven immediately when she died. The first plenary indulgences came from Pope Urban II in 1095 to all who would join his First Crusade to liberate the Holy Land from the Muslims.

One of the things that bothered Luther about the granting of indulgences in the early 1500s was that the church was selling them to finance the rebuilding of Saint Peter's Basilica in Rome. John Tetzel, a Dominican managing indulgence sales, composed and sent to parish priests sermons they could us to persuade people to buy indulgences. Here is part of one of those sermons:

> Do you not hear the voice of your parents and other deceased loved ones crying loudly and saying, "Have mercy, have mercy on me, especially you my friends, because the hand of the Lord has touched me! We are in strong punishment and torment, from which you are able to rescue us with only a little money, but yet you do not want to!" Open your ears, as the father says to his son and the mother says to her daughter, "Why do you punish me, and are not satisfied with my flesh?" It is as if they were saying, "We gave you birth, we fed you, we raised you, we left you our earthly goods, and yet you are cruel and hard to us. You are able to free us easily, but you let us lie in flames, and you delay the glory promised to us."[7]

Besides the crassness of the sale of indulgences, Luther and other reformers pointed out that the whole idea of purgatory was not in the

Bible. As Huldrych Zwingli wrote in his Ten Berne Theses, "There is nothing in Scripture about a purgatory after this life. Consequently, all services for the dead, such as vigils, requiems . . . are vain."[8] The teaching of Jesus, as we have said, is that the next life does not begin until the resurrection at the end of the world.

Some Christian theologians realized that their picture of the dead as already living in heaven, hell, and purgatory conflicted with Jesus' teaching about the resurrection and Last Judgment occurring at the end of the world. So they came up with the idea of an earlier judgment called the Particular Judgment, which happens right after the individual dies. After that private, individual judgment, they said, the person immediately goes to heaven or hell or purgatory.

There are at least three problems with this idea of a Particular Judgment for each person right after death. First, it is not what Jesus taught. He taught only the Last Judgment for everyone, at the end of time, as in Matthew 25:31–46.

Secondly, according to the idea of the Particular Judgment immediately after death, people will exist in heaven and hell *without bodies* before the resurrection. But Jesus had no conception of a person without a body, especially in the state of happiness he promised heaven would be. When Jesus talks about hell, too, his images are of fire and physical pain: "They will throw them into the furnace of fire, where there will be weeping and gnashing of teeth" (Matthew 13:42). How could something without a body be thrown into a furnace, be hurt by flames, weep, or gnash its teeth?

Thirdly, the idea that people are judged individually right after death makes the resurrection and the Last Judgment pointless. If, at the end of the world, there are people already in heaven, perfectly happy as disembodied souls, there would be no point to "giving" them bodies again. God couldn't make them any happier than perfectly happy, so there would be no point to resurrecting them. Jesus taught that there will be a resurrection at the end of the world, and he certainly did not think it would be pointless.[9]

If we go back to the Gospels, then, we see that centuries of church teaching about immortal souls going to heaven, hell, or purgatory conflict with what Jesus taught. And even those Christians today who speak of death as the soul going to heaven show by their actions that their deeper intuition is closer to the biblical belief that dying is perishing. If we really believed that a terminal cancer patient, for instance, was going to be instantly transported at death from agonizing pain to heavenly bliss, why would we go to so much trouble to delay the bliss and prolong the pain through surgery and other treatments that extend the person's life a few weeks or months? Is it so we can spend more time with the person? Or is it because we don't think of death as instant transport to bliss?

For further reading:

N. T. Wright. *Surprised by Hope: Rethinking Heaven, the Resurrection, and the Mission of the Church*. New York: HarperOne, 2008.

D. COULD I BE RESURRECTED AS JESUS WAS?

Ever since Paul began preaching, the resurrection of Jesus has been a model for the resurrection of the human race. The idea is that Jesus rose from the dead, so we can too.

> Now if Christ is proclaimed as raised from the dead, how can some of you say there is no resurrection of the dead? If there is no resurrection of the dead, then Christ has not been raised; and if Christ has not been raised, then our proclamation has been in vain and your faith has been in vain. We are even found to be misrepresenting God, because we testified of God that he raised Christ—whom he did not raise if it is true that the dead are not raised. For if the dead are not raised, then Christ has not been raised. If Christ has not been raised, your faith is futile and you are still in your sins. Then those also who have died in Christ have perished. If for this life only we have hoped in Christ, we are of all people most to be pitied. But in fact Christ has been raised from the dead, the first fruits of those who have died (1 Corinthians 15:12–20).

In Paul's metaphor of resurrection as harvest, Jesus is the "first fruits of those who have died" at the beginning of the harvest, and the rest of the human race will be harvested after him.

When Paul was writing this in the middle of the first century, the idea of resurrection was only two centuries old and was accepted by only some Jews. Having grown up as a Pharisee, Paul believed in it, but other Jews, such as the Sadducees, denied the resurrection because they found no convincing evidence for it in the Scriptures. Jews who believed in a resurrection usually linked it to the justice of God, especially to his rewarding and punishing people fairly. In the Old Testament, God blesses the people of Israel when they follow his will and punishes them when they don't. When they lose battles, for instance, they often attribute those losses to disobeying God. While the historically early books of the Bible generally see reward and punishment as applying to the people of Israel as a group, later books also consider individual persons. The Book of Job is the most famous. When we look at individual lives, it seems that while some good people may be rewarded before they die, many are not. Similarly, while some evil people may get what they deserve before death, many live comfortably all the way to the end, dying painlessly in their sleep. How can we explain these facts if God is just? For God to reward and punish people fairly, it seems there must be some time *after death* for reward and punishment.

This issue became acute in the second century BCE, when the people of Israel were part of the empire created by Alexander the Great. Under King Antiochus, Jews were being martyred for being faithful to their God and practicing their religion. Some people probably reasoned that if God lets his followers be tortured to death for being faithful to him, and there is nothing after death, then those martyrs are not rewarded for their faithfulness. On the other hand, people who renounce their religion to escape persecution may live out their days in comfort and prosperity, without being punished. In either case—unrewarded virtue or unpunished vice—God would not be just if death is the permanent end of human experience. So there must be something after death—a time when the good are rewarded and the evil punished.

That time for God to reward and punish would be provided by a resurrection of the dead. The Hebrew Bible merely hints at such a time, and only in the two places we mentioned in question B—Isaiah 26:14–15, 19 and Daniel 12:1–2. By the time of Jesus, many Jews had come to believe in a resurrection followed by judgment and then reward and punishment. Jesus, as we've seen, made these beliefs central to his preaching and added that everyone would be brought back to life. Jesus also taught another idea popular in the first century—that the world was going to end soon. So after he was gone, his followers expected him to return within decades, at which time everyone would be resurrected, judged, and rewarded or punished. Though that didn't happen, belief in his return and in a general resurrection like his own have remained part of Christianity.

Few Christians, however, have thought about the differences between the way Jesus came back to life and the possible ways the rest of us could come back to life. According to the Gospels, Jesus was dead for less than forty hours, from late Friday afternoon to early Sunday morning, at the latest. People have fallen into icy lakes and gone into a state of suspended animation for longer than that. During the time Jesus was dead, his organs, most importantly his brain, remained intact. For the billions of other people who have died, however, resurrection would not be so simple. Many of them have had their corpses completely destroyed by fire, for example. Cremation is the traditional way of disposing of the dead in many cultures and is now common among Christians. Billions of other corpses have completely decomposed in the soil, with their molecules becoming part of the soil, microbes, mold, fungi, plants, or animals.

Assume for the sake of argument that after I die, my body is completely destroyed, say by cremation. For me to look forward to being resurrected, I have to imagine God somehow bringing me back to life, making me—the person I am today—exist again. What could that process be like?

In thinking about a future world of resurrected people, some Christians have asked how old people will be. Someone who dies at age 105 would probably prefer to be resurrected at a younger age; a child who dies at age 8 might want to be older. Several medieval theologians said that in the next life everyone will be around 33. We might also imagine other improvements. If we had a large mole on our nose, we might like to have it gone. If we had a fair complexion, we might like to have bronze-colored or brown skin. But whatever changes I might imagine for myself in the next life, there is one thing I would not want to change—my consciousness. I want the person in heaven to think with the very same consciousness I have right now. It would not be enough for there to be a future person whose thoughts are merely similar to mine. It wouldn't do me any good even to have a future person who has my name and lots of memories and personality traits similar to mine. I wouldn't be happy even with a perfect copy of myself—a replica—that looked and acted and spoke just as I do, and remembered, liked, and hated all the things I remember, like, and hate. What I want in heaven is not some future person that is *just like me*. I want it to *be me*, with the very same consciousness that is thinking these thoughts right now.

If at death I am destroyed, and in the future God makes a replica of me, that replica is not me living again, but only a copy of me living its brand-new life. If that were to happen, I wouldn't even know that it happened, because I wouldn't exist.

To understand what's unsatisfactory about being replaced by a replica, let's do a little thought experiment. Imagine an amazing new machine that makes perfect copies of human beings. The device is eight feet tall and has two compartments, one on the left called the scanner and one on the right called the fabricator. You walk into the left compartment and stand there motionless as electronic sensors scan every one of your ninety trillion cells, including the eighty-five billion neurons in your brain. All that information is fed into a computer, which then sends signals to the fabricator. Using reserves of molecules as raw materials, the fabricator then makes a perfect copy of you, molecule for molecule. When the copying is complete, you walk out of the left door, and the replica walks out of the right door.

If you were copied by this machine and everything went smoothly, you would undoubtedly be amazed when you first met your double. And the replica, being exactly like you, would be equally surprised. But suppose that the process did not go smoothly, and in the scanning operation, you were exposed to a mega-dose of harmful radiation, so that by the time the copying process was finished, your corpse was slumped on the floor in the scanner. The fabricator did its work flawlessly, however, so the replica emerged from the machine in perfect condition.

Would it be any comfort to you that although you had been killed by the radiation, there was a replica of you that could now take over your job and your personal relationships? If you hadn't told anyone that you were going to be replicated, and the operators of the machine kept your death a secret, perhaps no one would ever know the difference. So if this happened, would it be all right with you?

Of course it wouldn't, because the existence of a *replica* of you after you have died isn't anything like the continued existence of *you*. And this lesson applies directly to the idea that you will be resurrected at the end of the world after every part of you has been destroyed. Once you have been destroyed, it seems that all that could be made—even by the all-powerful God—is a replica of you.

As I try to imagine a world like heaven in which I exist again—not a replica of me, but the very same person I am now—there is one huge problem: the destruction of my brain. From everything known about the brain and the mind, consciousness is dependent on a functioning brain. And *my* consciousness is dependent on *my* brain—the brain that's in my head right now—functioning. If there is another brain somewhere right now thinking about the same things I'm thinking about, that is not *my* consciousness because it is not a function of *my* brain. And the same holds for another brain created in the future to replicate my brain.

So the big question is: Once my brain is destroyed, could anything after that be my consciousness? If not, then it seems that I cannot exist again; the best God could do is make a replica of me.

Anyone who wants to follow Jesus' teachings about life after death, then, should study his ideas about the resurrection. In doing that, we need to realize that the resurrection of most people could not be as simple as Jesus' "waking up" on Easter morning.

For further reading:

Peter van Inwagen. "The Possibility of Resurrection." *International Journal for Philosophy of Religion* 9 (1978): 114–21.

E. COULD GOD PUNISH PEOPLE FOREVER?

As in most contemporary discussions of life after death, we've focused on heaven and have said little about hell. The number of books and sermons on hell has declined greatly from past centuries. But through most of Christian history, doctrines about hell were central to many churches, and hell is still part of the teaching of many churches. So it's worth considering the idea of hell, especially the claim that it is punishment that goes on forever.

Jesus never talked about "hell"—that's a northern European word taken from Hel, the fierce Norse goddess ruling the underworld. When Jesus preached about punishment after death, he talked about "Gehenna," which was not a word used literally, but a figure of speech. At the time Gehenna was a valley just south of Jerusalem used for burning trash where, it was said, children had been burned as sacrifices in earlier times. Like much of what Jesus says in the Gospels, his talk about being "thrown into Gehenna" is not a doctrine being announced, but preaching based on a metaphor. That's important to keep in mind as we interpret what he says about Gehenna, where "the worm never dies and the fire is never quenched" (Mark 9:48). For centuries some Christians have read the second part of that phrase literally and concluded that hell is punishment that lasts forever. But the same people never read the first part literally and conclude that there will be a worm in hell that lives forever. Being thrown into Gehenna is a metaphor and, as we've seen in earlier chapters, we have to be careful about drawing literal conclusions from metaphors. Just as "the worm never dies" is a figure of speech, "the fire is never quenched" may be one, too.

There are ten places in the Gospels where Jesus talks about Gehenna, but only two of them give any indication that "Gehenna" might go on forever, and those are reports of a single sermon by Jesus. The first is Matthew 18:8–9:

> If your hand or your foot causes you to stumble, cut it off and throw it away; it is better for you to enter life maimed or lame than to have two hands or two feet and to be thrown into the eternal fire. And if your eye causes you to stumble, tear it out and throw it away; it is better for you to enter life with one eye than to have two eyes and to be thrown into the hell [Gehenna] of fire.

Here Jesus is using a figure of speech common in sermons—hyperbole, exaggeration. Christians do not read this literally as commanding them to chop off their hands and feet. The vast majority of them have done something wrong involving one or both hands, and they have walked to at least one place where they did something wrong. So if Jesus meant these words literally, most of the world's two billion Christians should have stumps at the ends of their arms and legs. Similarly, the vast majority of Christians have done something wrong which they could not have done without their eyes. But they don't tear out their eyeballs and throw them away. The fact that they haven't torn out their eyes and chopped off their hands and feet shows their ability to recognize hyperbole in sermons.

The other passage from which Christians have gotten the idea that hell lasts forever is Mark 9:43–50. It says what Matthew 18:8 says about chopping off hands and feet and tearing out eyeballs, but it adds some words at the end:

> It is better for you to enter the kingdom of God with one eye than to have two eyes and to be thrown into hell, where the worm never dies, and the fire is never quenched. For everyone will be salted with fire. Salt is good; but if salt has lost its saltiness, how can you season it? Have salt in yourselves, and be at peace with one another.

Bible scholars tell us that the writers of the Gospels got their material from several sources, among them collections of sayings attributed to Jesus. What the last three sentences above show, I think, is that the person who wrote them was carelessly running together several unrelated sayings attributed to Jesus that had the word "salt" in them. If in preaching Jesus, or anyone else, actually said, "For everyone will be salted with fire. Salt is good; but if salt has lost its saltiness, how can you season it? Have salt in yourselves, and be at peace with one another," people would probably scratch their heads and walk away. The incoherence of this section of Mark should alert us to be careful in drawing conclusions from it, such as that hell lasts forever.

If being thrown into Gehenna is a metaphor for being punished after death, then what about "the worm never dies, and the fire is never quenched"? Those words are not new with Jesus, but are taken from the Book of Isaiah (66:21–24), where God says that he will make "the new heavens and the new earth," and "all flesh shall come to worship before me." The disgusting corpses of his enemies, God continues, will lie rotting and burning: "And they shall go out and look at the dead bodies of the people who have rebelled against me; for their worm shall not die, their fire shall not be quenched, and they shall be an abhorrence to all flesh." As a masterful preacher, Jesus used these words from the prophet Isaiah to strengthen his message that sin will lead to punishment in the next life. The idea of worms consuming the corpses as they smolder in flames was in turn strengthened by saying that the worms won't die and the fire won't go out. But in both Isaiah and Jesus' preaching, all of this is rhetorical language used to impress on the audience the importance of doing God's will. It is not a literal prediction that either the corpses of God's enemies, or the living bodies of people in hell, will be infested by immortal worms and burn forever.

Until around 1800, almost all churches taught that hell is a place of unending punishment, but since then many have either abandoned belief in hell, or kept the idea of hell but said that the punishment will eventually end, and all people will be reconciled with God. That second idea is a form of universalism—the belief that all will ultimately be saved. One of the earliest universalists was Pantaenus, the first head of the school for catechumens in Alexandria, around 190. Two centuries later, Gregory of Nyssa predicted in his *Sermo Catecheticus Magnus* (*Large Catechetical Sermon*), "the annihilation of evil, the restitution of all things, and the final restoration of evil men and evil spirits to the blessedness of union with God, so that he may be 'all in all,' embracing all things endowed with sense and reason." Universalism was not popular in the Middle Ages or during the Protestant Reformation, but it started to grow in the mid-1600s. In the 1700s the Universalist Church in America was founded.

Another theory about what happens to evil people at death is called *annihilationism* or *conditionalism*. Taking lines from the Bible such as Jesus' warning to "fear him who can destroy both soul and body in hell" (Matthew 10:28), and Paul's Second Letter to the Thessalonians (1:9), in which he says that those persecuting Christians "will suffer the punishment of eternal destruction," annihilationists say that life after death is not for everyone, but is conditional. Those who have been accepted by God will go to heaven, but those rejected by God will be annihilated. That idea is easy to reconcile with the idea that death destroys human beings. All God would have to do is resurrect the people destined for heaven, but not resurrect the others.

One of the reasons some Christians have adopted these beliefs contrary to the traditional belief in an unending hell is that it seems to make no sense to punish anyone *forever*. Over the course of history, different cultures have understood punishment as serving different functions. There have been four main ones. The oldest is retribution, "paying back" the offending person for the harm they have done. The biblical verse about "an eye for an eye, a tooth for a tooth" (Exodus 21:24; Leviticus 24:20) captures this idea.

The second function of punishment is deterrence. The idea here is that people who are considering doing something wrong will think twice when they consider the punishment that may follow. Someone planning a murder, for example, will decide against it when he considers that it may put him in prison for the rest of his life, or even get him executed.

The third function of punishment is reformation, rehabilitation. This idea is that the wrongdoer can be changed into a better person, the kind who is not likely to repeat the offense. Notice that in modern times the word "prison" has been largely replaced by "reformatory" and "correctional institution."

The fourth function of punishment is also discussed a lot today: restraint. Here the idea is not that imprisonment will make the offender a better person. But while behind bars, at least he won't be out on the street committing more crimes.

If we examine the idea of hell as unending punishment, it doesn't seem to fulfill any of these four functions of punishment. First, consider retribution. A basic feature of "paying someone back" is that "the punishment fits the crime," that is, the suffering inflicted on the wrongdoer is proportional to the wrong committed. But unending punishment is infinite, and so it seems to be too much—infinitely too much—for any offense. Even if the worst human being—Hitler, say—deserves to suffer horribly for a very, very, very long time, he would seem to reach a point—say, after a trillion years—when his debt has been paid. But if hell goes on forever, then after a trillion years, Hitler would still have an infinite length of time left to suffer.

The second function of punishment is deterrence, scaring potential wrongdoers into not going through with their evil plans. While the fear of hell may have deterred many people from evil actions, after the Last Judgment there would be no possibility of deterrence. Neither those in heaven nor those in hell would be deterred from doing evil by the thought of unending punishment. So making hell last forever doesn't seem to fit this function of punishment.

The third function of punishment—reformation, rehabilitation— also doesn't seem compatible with *unending* punishment. Reforming someone's behavior by punishing her assumes that the punishment will end and she will again live a normal life in which she can be good. But if hell lasts forever, no one gets out to live a reformed life.

Lastly, punishment as restraint wouldn't explain eternal punishment. It's not as though the people in heaven need to be protected from evildoers in a gated community. Certainly an omnipotent God has other means than unending torture to keep bad people away from good. As we said above, God could judge some people as hopelessly evil and simply annihilate them. Just letting them stay dead, which is what Isaiah 66:21–24 predicts, would accomplish that.

Many Christians who raise objections like these to the traditional idea that hell is eternal punishment are guided by a simple insight: if billions of people suffer in hell, totally separated from God, infinitely into the future, that frustrates God's purpose in creating them, and frustrates it forever. God created every person to be happy in a relationship with him. Who would say that God's purpose is going to be permanently frustrated?

For further reading:

William Crockett, ed. *Four Views of Hell*. Grand Rapids, MI: Zondervan, 1992.
Richard Swinburne. "A Theodicy of Heaven and Hell." In *The Existence and Nature of God*, ed. Alfred Freddoso. South Bend, IN: University of Notre Dame Press, 1983.

8

ANGELS AND DEMONS

In the last few decades there has been a lot of popular interest in angels and demons. The title of this chapter comes from a Dan Brown novel that was made into a movie. Films and TV shows about angels abound in the United States, and demons have been a hot subject in movies since *Rosemary's Baby*, a novel inspired by the founding of the Church of Satan in 1966. Traditional Christian theology has a lot to say about angels and demons, too. The medieval theologian Thomas Aquinas acquired the title Angelic Doctor for his extensive writings about them. Billy Graham, the most popular preacher in history, published *Angels: God's Secret Agents* in 1994, and Satan is a popular topic for sermons among evangelical Christians.

According to standard theological descriptions, angels and demons are personal beings—they are rational and intelligent creatures who make moral choices and act. In those ways, they are like human beings. But unlike us, angels are nonphysical and so not male or female. They are also naturally immortal—they don't die. One way to think about angels, Aquinas suggests, is as minds that are not in bodies: "Not all intellects, then, are joined with bodies; there are some that exist separately, and these we call angels."[1]

The Bible says nothing about when God created angels, but most theologians think it was before he created the universe. Some books of the Bible speak of thousands of them. The Book of Revelation (5:11) puts the number in the millions. Jesus says in Matthew 26:53 that if he asked his Father, "he will at once send me more than twelve legions of angels." There were about five thousand soldiers in a legion at the time, so that's sixty thousand angels. Curiously, though, in the various Christian Bibles only four angels have names—Michael, Gabriel, Raphael, and Satan. The first three of these names include "el," which is Hebrew for "God." "Micha-el" means "Who is like God?" "Gabri-el" means "strong man of God." And "Raphael" means "God heals." In the Roman Catholic, Orthodox, Anglican, and Lutheran churches, those angels are counted as saints.

Medieval theologians wrote about hierarchies of angels. Aquinas counted nine orders in three groups. From highest to lowest, they are seraphim, cherubim, and thrones; dominions, virtues, and powers; and principalities, archangels, and angels (regular). Michael, Gabriel, and Raphael are all archangels, the second-lowest order.

Several Hebrew words are translated into English as "demons" or "devils," and Christians interpret many names and phrases in the Bible as referring to Satan, the chief demon: Beelzebub, Lucifer, Belial, the Enemy, the Evil One, and the "serpent" in Genesis. The standard way of understanding demons is that they were created by God as angels, but then under the leadership of Satan they rebelled against God. The writers of the New Testament seem to assume that this turning against God was irreversible, so that Satan and his followers could not be redeemed as the human race was redeemed by Jesus Christ.

Our word *angel* comes from the Latin *angelus*, which is from the Greek *aggelos*, itself a translation of the Hebrew *mal'ach*, meaning messenger. In the Bible, angels bring messages to people from God and serve people in other ways, as by protecting them. That's where the idea came from that God assigns a guardian angel to watch over each human being. Charles Wesley, cofounder of Methodism, captured that idea in a song:

> Angels, where ere we go,
> Attend our steps what'er betide.
> With watchful care their charge attend,
> And evil turn aside.

Angels have been venerated since early Christianity. In Syria the sign "Χ Μ Γ" was frequently put on tombs, doorframes, and rings. Those are the first letters of the Greek words for "Christ, Michael, Gabriel." Some early Christians apparently went too far in their veneration of angels. In his letter to the Colossians (2:18), Paul warns, "Let no one who delights in humility and the worship of angels cheat you out of the prize."

A. DO ANGELS HAVE WINGS AND DEMONS HAVE HORNS?

Since the fourth century, Christians have represented angels in art and literature as looking like human beings with wings growing out of their backs. Since the twelfth century, Christian art and literature have represented demons as having the overall body shape of humans, but with grotesque body parts such as horns, pointed tails, and goat-like legs. However common these pictures and descriptions have become, though, they cannot accurately portray angels and demons for the simple reason that angels and demons are not physical beings. They are pure spirits without bodies and so are invisible. If something is *invisible*, then any *visual* description of it cannot be literally true. Pictures or words about wings, horns, tails, or other physical features cannot represent what angels actually are, any more than pictures or words about a bearded man sitting on a throne can represent what God actually is. Just as the nonphysical God can't have a beard, nonphysical angels can't have wings and nonphysical demons can't have horns, tails, goat legs, and so on. At most, such representations could be metaphorical interpretations of what someone had experienced. As the *New Catholic Encyclopedia* article "Angels" points out, "These descriptions of angel appearances to men are anthropomorphic accounts of supernatural experiences, and as a result, it is impossible to determine their material objectivity in detail."[2]

Anthropomorphism is describing something that is not a human being as if it were a human being. Anthropomorphic descriptions of angels are found throughout the Bible. The writers of the Bible had no concept of what would later be called the "purely spiritual," and so they described even God as having a face and hands, walking, sitting on a throne, and so on. Joshua 10:11 even says that to help the Israelites defeat the Amorites, "The Lord threw down huge stones from heaven on them."

Several Bible stories go beyond anthropomorphism to present angels and men as interchangeable. Here is how the book of Genesis describes

God's revelation to Abraham that his elderly wife Sarah would bear a son:

> The Lord appeared to Abraham by the oaks of Mamre, as he sat at
> the entrance of his tent in the heat of the day. He looked up and saw
> three men standing near him. . . . They said to him, "Where is your
> wife Sarah?" And he said, "There, in the tent." Then one said, "I will
> surely return to you in due season, and your wife Sarah shall have a
> son." . . . Sarah laughed to herself, saying, "After I have grown old,
> and my husband is old, shall I have pleasure?" The Lord said to
> Abraham, "Why did Sarah laugh, and say, "Shall I indeed bear a
> child, now that I am old?" Is anything too wonderful for the Lord? At
> the set time I will return to you in due season, and Sarah shall have a
> son." . . . Then the men set out from there, and they looked toward
> Sodom. . . . The two angels came to Sodom in the evening
> (18:1–19:1).

In this story, the messengers are sometimes called "men" and other
times called "angels." That naturally leads readers to think of angels as
physical beings. The confusion continues as the story goes on. When
the angels met Lot in Sodom, he brought them to his home for dinner.
Then, as they were about to go to bed, "the men of the city . . . surrounded the house; and they called to Lot, "Where are the men who
came to you tonight? Bring them out to us, so that we may know [have
sex with] them" (19:4–5). Lot begged the crowd not to rape his guests,
and even offered his two virgin daughters as a substitute, but the crowd
refused. Then "the men" inside Lot's house pulled him inside and mi-
raculously struck the would-be rapists blind. The next morning "the
angels" urged Lot to get his family out of Sodom because God was
going to destroy the city.

Adding to the men/angels confusion here is the way the men/angels
are presented as interchangeable with God himself. The first two verses
say that *"The Lord* appeared to Abraham . . . He [Abraham] looked up
and saw *three men.*" One of *the men* said, "I will surely return to you in
due season, and your wife Sarah shall have a son." Then, after Sarah
laughed in disbelief, *the Lord* asked Abraham why Sarah doubted the
news that she would have a baby. "Is anything too wonderful for the
Lord? At the set time I will return to you, in due season, and Sarah shall
have a son." I have added all the italics here, to show the confusing

interchangeability of men, angels, and the Lord. As *The New Oxford Annotated Bible* points out, "The relation of the three visitors to the Lord or Yahweh is difficult. All three angels may represent the Lord."[3]

The New Testament, too, has passages that encourage us to think of angels and men as interchangeable. The four Gospels say that when Mary Magdalene and the other women went to the tomb of Jesus on Easter morning, they were told that he had been raised. In Mark 16:5, that message is spoken by "a young man, dressed in a white robe." Matthew 28:2–3 says that the women saw "an angel of the Lord . . . whose appearance was like lightning, and his clothing white as snow." In Luke 24:4, the message comes from "two men in dazzling clothes," and in John 20:12, from "two angels in white." If we try to read these as literal descriptions of an actual event, the obvious questions are: Was there one figure or two? Was it/were they a man/men or an angel/angels?

Rather than reading the Gospel passages as contrary descriptions of what one man, two men, one angel, and two angels did, it seems better to treat them as four literary ways of conveying a single message. That message is that God revealed to the women that Jesus had been raised from the dead. We can attribute the variations between the four stories to literary choices made by the four storytellers.

The problem of anthropomorphism in the Bible's portrayal of angels all but disappears when we turn to consider demons in the Bible. While the appearances of angels in the Bible are often indistinguishable from the appearances of men, demons are never described as looking like men. In fact, they aren't described as looking like anything at all. The three Gospel accounts of Satan tempting Jesus in the desert (Matthew 4:1–11; Mark 1:12–13; and Luke 4:1–13), for example, attribute no visual features to Satan. Similarly, the stories of Jesus expelling unclean spirits from possessed people give no visual description of those spirits. So the Bible's descriptions of demons turn out to be more "spiritual" and less misleading than its anthropomorphic descriptions of angels.

It was only in the twelfth century that Christians began representing Satan and his fellow demons in the now familiar form of grotesque monsters with horns, bat wings, pointed tails, cloven hooves, and so on. Many of these colorful images were borrowed from European and Middle Eastern mythologies, and others came from people's imaginations. The horns and goat legs are probably derived from the Greek god Pan.

But, as with the wings of angels, none of these features of demons comes from the Bible.

The answer to our question "Do angels have wings and demons have horns?" then is no. Not only *don't* they have physical features, but they *can't* have physical features, because they are nonphysical beings.

But what about the *appearances* of angels, as when Mary and Joseph were told by angels that Mary would have a baby? The simple answer is that these are *appearances*, not perceptions of actual physical bodies. Matthew 1:20 says of Joseph that "An angel of the Lord appeared to him in a dream." That was a dream image, not a solid body being seen by Joseph. Luke 1:26–38 says that the angel Gabriel "came to" Mary, but it gives no visual description of the angel or the encounter. Although medieval artists painted Gabriel as a young man with wings, all that Luke tells us is what the angel *said*. So Mary's whole experience could have been of a voice. And even if she experienced a visual appearance of a young man, there was not a real young man standing in front of her, because angels are not physical beings. An angel could *appear as* something physical—a young man, a fierce warrior, even an animal— but that doesn't mean that the angel *is* a young man, fierce warrior, or animal. Exodus 3:2 describes a vision Moses had on Mount Horeb: "There an angel of the Lord appeared to him in a flame of fire out of a bush." In verse 4, "God called to him out of the bush, 'Moses, Moses!'" But while the angel and God *appeared as* a burning bush, of course neither *was* a burning bush. As the *New Catholic Encyclopedia* says, an appearance like that is not of God or an angel "in his true form, but in a special form suited to the apparition."[4]

For further reading:

Gustave Davidson. *A Dictionary of Angels, Including the Fallen Angels*. New York: Free Press, 1967.
James D. Collins. *The Thomistic Philosophy of Angels*. Washington, DC: Catholic University of America Press, 1947.

B. DO ANGELS LIVE IN HEAVEN AND DEMONS LIVE IN HELL?

Our anthropomorphic thinking about angels, demons, and God includes thinking of them as living in particular places, as human beings do. Just as we have homes, angels and God are thought to have their home in heaven and Satan and other demons to have their home in hell. In the Bible, and in popular imagination until recent centuries, heaven is a place above us in the sky, and hell is a place under the earth. Isaiah 63:15 asks God to "look down from heaven and see, from your holy and glorious habitation." A standard picture of heaven is a city with God as its king sitting on a throne and being served by angels as his courtiers. Psalm 103:19–21 says, "The Lord has established his throne in the heavens, and his kingdom rules over all. Bless the Lord, O you his angels, you mighty ones who do his bidding, obedient to his spoken word. Bless the Lord, all his hosts, his ministers that do his will."

While in this picture heaven is where God and angels live, they sometimes visit the earth. In Genesis 3:8, God comes down to check on Adam and Eve: "They heard the sound of the Lord God walking in the garden at the time of the evening breeze." When God leaves Adam, and later when he leaves Abraham, he "goes up" to heaven, the Greek verb *anabaino* being the same word as for going upstairs in a house. In the Book of Job 1:7, when Satan (an angel serving God) reports to heaven and God asks, "Where have you come from?" Satan answers, "From going to and fro on the earth, and from walking up and down on it."

However natural it is to associate persons with homes, however, this anthropomorphism doesn't work with nonphysical persons like angels and God. Only what is physical is located in a place. Being in a place is taking up a certain amount of space and having boundaries. Right now, for instance, the desk I'm working on is sixty inches long and thirty inches wide, and it is located four inches from the north wall of my house and three feet from the east wall of my house. None of this location and measurement is possible with nonphysical things like angels and God. They do not have edges, take up a certain amount of space, or have boundaries. Not being physical, they are not located anywhere. In the Bible, heaven is described as a physical place in the sky, above the clouds. Since angels and God are not located anywhere, they cannot be located in the sky above the clouds. They cannot be located in heaven.[5]

To be located in a place is to be limited by that place. The belief that God is not limited by a place began early with Justin Martyr, who wrote in the mid-second century, "God is uncontained either in one place or in the whole universe, since he existed before the universe came into being."[6] A bit later, Theophilus of Antioch said that "It belongs to God, the highest and almighty and the truly God, . . . not to be contained in space."[7] Clement of Alexandria, early in the third century, said simply that God is "beyond place."[8] While angels are not unlimited in the absolute way God is unlimited, they are not contained in space. And so they, like God, cannot live in a place, such as heaven.

The same point applies to the idea that demons live in hell. Like good angels, bad angels are nonphysical beings. Since only physical beings are located anywhere, demons are not located anywhere. Hell is a place, so they are not located in hell.

There are at least two more reasons to question the traditional idea that demons live in hell. First, just as heaven was traditionally located above the earth, hell was located below the earth. But now we know from geological exploration that there is no such place as hell under the earth.

The second problem is that over the centuries, Satan and his demons have been thought to already live in hell, but the Bible says that they will be cast into hell at the end of the world (Revelation 20:10). As with the claim that dead humans are already in hell, or heaven, some Christians have jumped the gun in thinking that demons are there now.

Further confusing things, many Christians have pictured Satan and his demons as the managers and staff of hell, torturing the damned. Artists like Hieronymus Bosch are famous for painting demons in hell taking sadistic glee in their work. That idea is pure imagination. It's not biblical, and it's contrary to Jesus' idea that Satan and his demons will be punished in hell. If they were to enjoy poking people with hot irons and the like, then for them hell would be fun rather than punishment. Further, if the demons were carrying out the operations in hell, they would be working for God. But Christian teaching is that Satan rejected God permanently, so there is no reason that he would serve God in this way.

For further reading:

Mortimer Adler. *The Angels and Us*. New York: Macmillan, 1982.

C. IS THERE A GUARDIAN ANGEL FOR EACH PERSON?

> Angel of God, my guardian dear
> to whom God's love commits me here.
> Ever this day be at my side
> to light, to guard, to rule and guide. Amen.

This lovely prayer, which many people learned as children, expresses the widespread belief that God has assigned an angel to protect and guide each of us. The idea of angels helping people was common in the ancient world. In Persia, Zoroastrianism taught about Arda Fravaš—holy guardian angels who guide people through their lives. Later, some Muslims came to believe that each person has two guardian angels, one on each side. In the Hebrew Bible, angels carry out God's wishes, including helping people. In Genesis 28–29, for example, angels deliver Lot from danger. The New Testament also has angels assisting people. In Matthew 4:11, after Jesus resists the temptations by Satan, "The devil left him, and suddenly angels came and waited on him." On the night before he died, Jesus prayed to God to "'remove this cup from me; yet, not my will but yours be done.' Then an angel from heaven appeared to him and gave him strength" (Luke 22:41–43). Acts 12:6–11 tells of how an angel liberated Peter from prison.

To the biblical idea that God sends angels to help people, early Christians added the idea that *each person* has been assigned an angel *for his whole life.* That's what is usually meant by guardian angels. In a fifth-century mosaic in the Basilica of Saint Mary Major in Rome, two guardian angels protect the child Jesus. Angels as personal guardians are not mentioned in the Bible, but many people infer their existence from Jesus' warning in Matthew 18:10: "Take care that you do not despise one of these little ones; for I tell you, in heaven their angels continually see the face of my father in heaven." In his *Commentary on Matthew,* Saint Jerome in the fourth century wrote, "The dignity of a soul is so great, that each has a guardian angel from its birth."

In the Middle Ages Christians venerated and prayed to guardian angels just as they prayed to patron saints. A major advocate of that practice was Bernard of Clairvaux, the founding abbot of Clairvaux Abbey in France. Thomas Aquinas offered a rationale for believing in guardian angels in his *Summa Theologiae* (part 1, question 113, articles 2–5). Of the nine ranks or "orders" of angels, he said, only the lowest serves as guardian angels. John Duns Scotus, another medieval theologian, disagreed, arguing that any rank of angel could accept such an assignment.

Belief in guardian angels has continued to our own day, especially in the Catholic Church, which celebrates the Feast of the Guardian Angels on October 2. The Catechism of the Catholic Church (336) says, "From infancy to death human life is surrounded by their watchful care and intercession. Beside each believer stands an angel as protector and shepherd leading him to life." In his 1997 *Regina Caeli* (Queen of Heaven) address, Pope John Paul II referred to guardian angels twice, ending his talk this way: "Let us invoke the Queen of angels and saints, that she may grant us, supported by our guardian angels, to be authentic witnesses to the Lord's paschal mystery."

Starting with medieval morality plays, Christian writers sometimes pitted personal angels against personal demons. In Christopher Marlowe's *The Tragical History of Doctor Faustus*, written around 1592, Faustus gets conflicting advice from a "good angel" and a "bad angel." In modern pop culture, that motif shows up in cartoons, where, for instance, Donald Duck has a tiny demonic duck on his left shoulder and a tiny angelic duck on his right.

While belief in a divinely appointed personal protector and guide is comforting, it raises at least six questions. The first is that if it's true, why didn't God reveal this important fact in the Bible? Living with a powerful spirit protecting and guiding you at all times is very different from living without such help. Why would God leave such a crucial feature of human life to be inferred from a single unclear passage in the New Testament? Why aren't guardian angels described in the stories of the creation of humans in Genesis? For the same reason, why haven't Christian churches made guardian angels a central part of religious education? Why hasn't the Roman Catholic Church made guardian angels a matter of dogma? Why, too, does that church reject "all names of angels except Michael, Gabriel and Raphael," none of whom is a guardian angel?[9]

A second group of questions has to do with the number of guardian angels. It is standard Christian teaching that God created angels before he created the earth and human beings. Unlike us, they do not reproduce and they live forever, so the number of angels would remain constant. But the number of human beings isn't constant. According to

Genesis, the human race started with Adam. Then there was Eve, Cain and Abel, and so on, until today, when there are over seven billion of us. Even if we say that Genesis isn't literally true and humans evolved from lower primates, the earliest human groups numbered at most only in the hundreds. If God made one guardian angel for each human being, then at the creation of the angels, he made at least seven billion guardian angels. Were the vast majority of those billions not assigned to anyone for tens of thousands of years, until the human birthrate started to accelerate a few centuries ago? And if God did create one angel for each person who would ever be born, are there still billions of unassigned angels waiting for new humans to be born?

We can ask another question about how guardian angels are assigned: What happens to them when the people they are protecting die? Are they reassigned to babies being born? Can they retire?

The fourth question is that if all human beings have these powerful helpers protecting them 24/7, how is it that people are harmed all the time? According to the United Nations, thirty-five thousand children starve to death each day. What are their guardian angels doing as they go through their death throes? Is it beyond those angels' power to get food for the children? A human babysitter who let a child starve to death would be prosecuted, and guardian angels are supposed to be babysitters extraordinaire.

A fifth question is related to the fourth. If each of us has this ultimate best friend who cares about us at least as much as our families and friends do, why does almost no one get any communication from them? What, for instance, is the name of your guardian angel? How has your angel helped you recently? A few Christian mystics have talked about their guardian angels, but mystics are famous for having visions that are not accurate representations of reality. Saint Gemma Galgani, a Roman Catholic mystic, said that her guardian angel sometimes stopped her from speaking up at the wrong moment.[10] Maria Valtorta wrote *The Book of Azariah* based on things she said her guardian angel dictated to her. But such mystics are extremely rare, even in Christian countries. In China, India, and Africa, before the arrival of missionaries, none of the indigenous people had even considered that they might have guardian angels. How could that be, if every person has such a wonderful friend? How can billions of people be guided by beings they don't know about?

The last question is that if guardian angels protect and guide human beings full-time, how can they at the same time be fully aware of God? Anyone who has babysat a frisky two-year-old knows that they require full attention. And what about evil adults? What would it be like to be the guardian angel of Adolf Hitler, Joseph Stalin, or Pol Pot? How could such angels be perfectly happy with God, as angels are supposed to be, if they were trying their best to keep their charges out of trouble?

None of these questions makes a knock-down argument, but together they should make us pause before accepting the simple traditional picture of guardian angels.

For further reading:

Mitch Finley. *Everybody Has a Guardian Angel . . . And other Lasting Lessons I Learned in Catholic Schools*. New York: Crossroad, 1993.

D. IS SATAN AN ANGEL WHO LED A REBELLION AGAINST GOD?

The story that demons were created as good angels but then turned against God is at least two thousand years old. But the events in the story are supposed to have taken place before the creation of the world, so no human could have witnessed it. And there is no physical evidence or historical record we can check to see if it really happened. If we are to believe this story, then, it seems we must trace it to divine revelation—in the Bible. The Old Testament and New Testament, however, say nothing about the creation of angels or demons, and nothing about how demons came to be evil. More problematic is the fact that the standard picture of Satan as the archenemy of God is nowhere in the Old Testament, where Satan is mentioned only a few times. The only Old Testament book that provides any details about Satan is Job. Here is how he is described in that book:

> One day the heavenly beings [Hebrew: sons of God] came to present themselves before the Lord, and Satan also came among them. The Lord said to Satan, "Where have you come from?" Satan answered the Lord, "From going to and fro on the earth, and from walking up and down in it." The Lord said to Satan, "Have you considered my servant Job? There is no one like him on the earth, a blameless and

upright man who fears God and turns away from evil." Then Satan answered the Lord, "Does Job fear God for nothing? Have you not put a fence around him and his house and all that he has, on every side? You have blessed the work of his hands, and his possessions have increased in the land. But stretch out your hand now, and touch all that he has, and he will curse you to your face" (1:6–11).

Here Satan is not God's enemy but a "son of God," that is, an angel who serves God. The word *satan* in Hebrew means "accuser," and Satan's service to God appears to be investigating people and reporting what he finds. That's what he was doing "going to and fro on the earth." Since the Book of Job is part of the Bible, it is authoritative. So its description of Satan as serving God at the time when Job lived is true. But Job lived long after the creation of the earth. Satan's turning against God, however, was supposed to have taken place before the earth was created, and to be irreversible. So how could Satan have turned against God before the creation of the earth if he is a servant of God long after the creation, during Job's lifetime?

If all the Bible's references to Satan were in the Old Testament, then there would be no biblical foundation for the idea of Satan's rebellion, or for the idea that Satan is the enemy of God and of the human race. But the New Testament has several references to Satan and demons in which they are portrayed as hostile to God and to people. The Second Letter of Peter 2:4 has a warning against being seduced by false teachers, who, it says, will be punished just as the fallen angels were punished, as sinners at the time of Noah were punished, and as Sodom and Gomorrah were punished: "For if God did not spare the angels when they sinned, but cast them into hell[11] and committed them to chains (or pits) of deepest darkness to be kept until the judgment." The Letter of Jude (6–7) has a similar warning:

And the angels who did not keep their own position, but left their proper dwelling, he has kept in eternal chains in deepest darkness for the judgment of the great day. Likewise, Sodom and Gomorrah and the surrounding cities, which, in the same manner as they, indulged in sexual immorality and pursued unnatural lust, serve as an example by undergoing a punishment of eternal fire.

The writers of these warnings assume that their readers are familiar with the story of how some angels sinned, just as they assume familiarity with the stories of the great flood and God's destruction of Sodom and Gomorrah. So the story of the fall of the angels must have been widely known in the first century CE. Jesus implies that he knows the story when he predicts how at the Last Judgment the Son of Man is going to condemn evil people: "Then he will say to those on his left, "Depart from me, you who are cursed, into the eternal fire prepared for the devil and his angels" (Matthew 25:41).

If the story of the fall of the angels was popular when the New Testament was written, but is not found in the Old Testament, where did it come from? Scholars tell us that it came from the Book of Enoch, which was written between 300 BCE and the end of the first century BCE. When the New Testament was written, the Book of Enoch was considered to be scripture, like Genesis, Exodus, Psalms, and so on. The letter of Jude (14–15) quotes from it. Many early church fathers, including Clement of Alexandria, Irenaeus, and Tertullian, considered it scripture, too. Remember that the canon—the official list of books that compose the Bible—was not decided upon until the late fourth century. By that time, most Christian leaders had rejected the Book of Enoch as scripture, and so today it is found in no Christian Bible except that of the Ethiopian Orthodox Church. Many things in the Book of Enoch, however, had already influenced Christian thinkers, including the writers of the books that did become the New Testament. Calling the Messiah the Son of Man, for example, and saying that the Son of Man will conduct the Last Judgment, as Jesus does in the Gospels, are found in the Book of Enoch.

More important for our discussion here are the passages in the Book of Enoch that trace the evil on earth to two hundred angels who mated with women on earth to produce a race of evil giants. That was how the writers of the Book of Enoch interpreted the story of the Nephilim in Genesis 6, which we quoted in chapter 4, section D.

Though such stories in the Book of Enoch are now rejected by Christians as folklore, they helped to shape the Christian tendency to link sexuality, sin, and demons. Consider the warning above in Jude 7 about how both the bad angels and the people of Sodom and Gomorrah "indulged in sexual immorality and pursued unnatural lust."

In the early Christian centuries, a document called the *Clementine Homilies* extended the Book of Enoch's explanation of the two hundred lustful angels mating with women to produce evil giants. Those giants, the *Clementine Homilies* said, were drowned in the great flood, but their souls lived on—to become the pagan gods!

Later, in the Middle Ages, many theologians wrote about incubi and succubi, lustful demons who were said to climb into bed with men and women to seduce them as they slept. Incubi were male demons who climbed on top of women, and succubi were female demons who crawled under men. As the *New Catholic Encyclopedia* article "Demon (Theology of)" says, "the impact of the apocryphal book of Enoch on early Christian demonology cannot be overestimated." [12]

For further reading:

New Catholic Encyclopedia. S.v. "Demon (In the Bible)," and "Demon (Theology of)." New
    York: McGraw-Hill, 1967, 4:752–56.

E. DO DEMONS POSSESS PEOPLE?

Many cultures in the ancient world believed that a spirit can take control of a human being. In ancient Greece a standard explanation for how poets write and musicians compose was that spirits called Muses breathe the words and tunes into them. *Spiré* is Greek for breath; to be *in-spired* was to have a Muse breathe into you. Our word *music* comes from the Greek *mousiké*, which meant all the human activities governed by the Muses.

When the writers of the Bible thought of spirits taking control of people, it was almost never this benign. In the Bible, the spirits who take control of people are not Muses but demons, and what they cause is not poetry or music, but something bad like blindness, seizures, unstoppable cursing, or antisocial behavior. If we take the Bible to be divinely revealed, and we read its passages about these spirits literally, as we would read a medical textbook, then it seems we have to say that demons do possess people, or at least they did two thousand years ago. But if we consider the primitive level of people's understanding of biology and psychology in the first century, and how the writers of the

Bible often use metaphor, allegory, and other figures of speech, we can interpret the stories of demonic possession in other ways.

The maladies mentioned in the Gospels are still with us—blindness, the inability to speak, epileptic seizures, and so on—but the Gospel writers attribute those maladies to demons far more often than we do. When was the last time a doctor diagnosed blindness or epilepsy as caused by demons? It is conceivable that first-century Palestine was infested with far more demons than bother us today. But isn't it more likely that people back then were more ready to explain problems by appealing to demons than we are? After all, what *other* explanations were available to them? They knew nothing about microbes, the endocrine system, the nervous system, or the brain. When someone whose eyes appeared normal could not see, how could that be explained? Blindness is a kind of evil, as are epilepsy and other disabilities. Where does evil come from? One source is demons. So what is causing this person's disability? It could be demons. And when someone was cured of a malady, wasn't it reasonable to say that the demons had left him or her? Without our modern medical and psychological explanations, was there a better hypothesis than demons?

A natural way for persons to understand events has always been to think of them as the actions of persons. That's part of our natural anthropomorphism. Even today we talk of Mother Nature and Mother Earth, and we give hurricanes personal names like Katrina and Andrew. With all our sophisticated medical science, we still think of diseases as enemies we are fighting. A popular advertising campaign for cancer clinics features pictures of recovering patients holding signs like "Bob 1, Cancer 0" and "Nice try, Cancer." When people in the first century attributed maladies to demons, they were thinking in a similarly anthropomorphic way.

Consider three typical stories of Jesus healing people, from the Gospel of Matthew:

> Matthew 9:32–33: A man who was demon-possessed and could not talk was brought to Jesus. And when the demon was driven out, the man who had been mute spoke.
> Matthew 12:22: Then a demon-possessed man who was blind and mute was brought to Jesus, and he healed him, so that the mute man spoke and saw.

Matthew 17:14–18: When they came to the crowd, a man ap-
proached Jesus and knelt before him. "Lord, have mercy on my
son," he said. "He has seizures and is suffering greatly. He often
falls into the fire or into the water. I brought him to your disciples, but they could not heal him." "O unbelieving and perverse
generation," Jesus replied, "how long shall I stay with you? How
long shall I put up with you? Bring the boy here to me." Jesus
rebuked the demon, and it came out of the boy, and he was
healed from that moment.

In these stories, a person had a malady. The writers of the first two
tell us what the problems were and that the people were "demon-
possessed." In the third case, the writer says what the problem was but
says nothing about demons or possession. Then in the first case the
writer says, "The demon was driven out." In the second case, the writer
says simply, "He healed him," without saying that a demon was expelled. And in the third case, where no demon had been mentioned, it
says, "Jesus rebuked the demon, and it came out of the boy, and he was
healed from that moment." Only in the first case does the writer *both*
attribute the malady to a demon *and* say that the demon was "driven
out."

What all three cases have in common, though, is that Jesus showed
compassion for suffering people and healed them. That seems to be
what the writer of Matthew is conveying to the reader, regardless of the
details.

Notice that in all three stories the demons are not persons with
names who first communicate with human beings and then possess
them. The demons aren't even observed; they are just assumed to be
causing the trouble. They are what explains the malady, and their being
"driven out" is what explains the recovery.

What do these assumed entities add to the stories of how Jesus
healed people? If the point of these stories is to show Jesus' compassion
and power, is possession by demons necessary to do that? Would anything of the lesson of Jesus' compassion and power be lost in Matthew
12:22, for instance, if the author had written: "Then a man who was
blind and mute was brought to Jesus, and he healed him, so that the
mute man spoke and saw"?

There is no denying that the author of Matthew and other Gospel
writers believed in demonic possession. In ancient Palestine almost

everybody did. But that belief does not seem essential to the lessons of the Gospels. There are many beliefs expressed by writers of the Bible that we today reject as scientifically inaccurate. But since they do not compromise the lessons of the books in which they are found, we don't fault them. The first chapter of Genesis (6–8) says that God made a sky-dome ("firmament" in the King James translation), with some water flowing above the dome and some flowing under it. There is no sky-dome in modern meteorology and astronomy, but that doesn't compromise the lesson in Genesis that God created the universe. Genesis 1:19 says that the sun was created on the fourth day, which is puzzling, since we reckon days by sunrises and sunsets. But again, that doesn't weaken the message of Genesis, and so no one complains. Just as we need not believe in a sky-dome, or believe in days before there was a sun, to accept Genesis as scripture, I do not think we need to believe in demonic possession to accept the Gospels.

I chose the three stories of demonic possession above because they are easy to tell without reference to demons. But it seems harder to dispense with the demons in other such stories, especially the one about the Gadarene swine. Here is Matthew's version (9:28–32):

> When he reached the other side [of the lake], in the country of the Gadarenes, he was met by two men who came out of the tombs; they were possessed by devils, and so violent that no one dared pass that way. "You son of God," they shouted, "what do you want with us? Have you come here to torment us before our time?" In the distance a large herd of pigs was feeding; and the devils begged him: "If you drive us out, send us into that herd of pigs." "Begone!" he said. Then they came out and went into the pigs; the whole herd rushed over the edge into the lake, and perished in the water.

In this story, the demons seem essential. They speak to Jesus, they ask him for a favor, and they are not just expelled from the two men but are "sent" into the pigs. In Mark's and Luke's versions of this story, Jesus asks their name and the response is "Legion." But these very details about the demons lead to troubling questions. One is about nonphysical beings being located and changing their location. As we saw in question B above, only physical things are located. So what does it mean to say that the devils were *in* the two men and that Jesus *sent* the devils into the pigs?

You might wonder, too, what possible advantage there could be for the demons to be "sent into" a herd of pigs that were about to drown? What would a demon do "inside" a pig, even if that idea made sense? Also, the doomed herd was large—Mark's Gospel (5:13) says about two thousand. Was there one devil possessing each pig? That would mean that a total of two thousand devils had possessed the two men. How would a thousand devils control one man? Would they vote on what awful prank to do next? Or can one devil possess several pigs or people at the same time?

If we try to read this story literally, moral questions also come up. Why would Jesus agree to the devils' request to send them into the pigs if he knew that would cause the pigs' death by drowning? Presumably, this story is told to show Jesus' compassion, so what about compassion for the drowning pigs? And compassion for the swineherds who lost two thousand animals and so their livelihood?

A larger moral question is why God would ever allow demons to take control of any human being, thereby eliminating that person's free will. Such a condition would be far worse than slavery, because the possessed person would not even be in control of his own body. He would be like a puppet controlled by the demons. In Luke's version of the story (8:26–33), it was one man possessed by devils instead of two, and "for a long time he had neither worn clothes nor lived in a house, but stayed among the tombs." Imagine what such a life would be like. People in the area were understandably frightened by him, so "for safety's sake, they would secure him with chains and fetters; but each time he broke loose, and with the devil in charge made off to solitary places." If demonic possession was not merely a colorful way of describing what we now call mental illness, but was literally the cause of this man's miserable state, then for years demons took control of his body away from him, so that "his actions" were not his. Would an all-good God let some of his creatures—devils—do that to other creatures—humans?

While we can read the story of the Gadarene swine, then, as a literal description of an event in Jesus' ministry, that reading conflicts not only with what we have learned about biology and psychology over the last two thousand years, but with what we believe about the goodness of Jesus and the goodness of God. It seems more reasonable to read the story as a scientifically uninformed interpretation of an event in Jesus' life that showed his remarkable compassion for suffering people and his miraculous power to heal them.

For further reading:

William M. Alexander. *Demonic Possession in the New Testament: Its Historical, Medical, and Theological Aspects*. Eugene, OR: Wipf & Stock, 2001.

9

THE GOOD LIFE

In many of our discussions so far, we've focused on questions that grew out of Greek metaphysics—the branch of philosophy concerned with what things exist and what their natures are. Whether Jesus is *homoousios* with God is a metaphysical question, for example, and so is whether human beings are souls living in bodies. While such questions were of great importance to many Greek-speaking Christians in the Eastern Empire, however, they were far less important to Latin-speaking Christians in the Western Empire. As mentioned in chapter 1, at the First Ecumenical Council in 325, which produced the Nicene Creed, only six of the three hundred bishops were from the West; and at the Second Ecumenical Council in 381, none of the bishops were from the West. Jesus was not a Latin-speaking Western Christian, of course, but he, too, showed no interest in metaphysical issues. What concerned him, and what he preached, was not metaphysics but morality—what it is to live a good life. His overarching theme was the Kingdom of God—people living the way God wants them to live. In chapter 1 we presented his Ten Tenets; in these last two chapters, we will go into more detail about the way of life he preached.

A. IS BEING GOOD OBEYING A SET OF COMMANDS?

If you ask many Christians what living a good life is, they will start talking about the Ten Commandments. The idea that being good is obeying commands, and being bad is disobeying commands, is found not just in religion but in children's moral training. When most of us were three or four, we were praised as "good" when we obeyed our parents and were criticized as "bad" when we disobeyed them. "Do what you're told" was the foundation of right and wrong.

In the ancient Near East, where the Bible was written, too, powerful rulers like the pharaohs of Egypt and the emperors of Rome demanded obedience from their people, much as some fathers demand obedience from their children. We call this kind of ruler a patriarch—from the Greek *pater*, father, and *archon*, ruler. Just as for a young child, being good is doing what Father says, many ancient peoples understood being good as doing what the ruler said. To add to the force of their commands, many of these patriarchs claimed to be divine.

The people of Israel thought of their god Yahweh as the greatest ruler of all—a supreme lawgiver and judge who rewards obedience and punishes disobedience. Christians often refer to the "Ten Commandments" given by God in the Old Testament, but the Bible has hundreds more. Orthodox Jews count 613. As the website Judaism 101 says, "According to Jewish tradition, God gave the Jewish people 613 *mitzvot* (commandments). All 613 of those *mitzvot* are equally sacred, equally binding, and equally the word of God."[1] Here are thirteen of the 613:

> Circumcise all males on the eighth day after their birth (Genesis 17:10).
> A rapist must marry his victim if she is unwed (Deuteronomy 22:29).
> Do not eat blood (Leviticus 3:17).
> Do not cook meat and milk together (Exodus 34:26).
> Do not wear a garment woven of wool and linen (Deuteronomy 22:11).
> Release all loans in the seventh year (Deuteronomy 15:2).
> Do not stand idly by if someone's life is in danger (Leviticus 19:16).
> Break the neck of a calf by the river valley following an unsolved murder (Deuteronomy 21:4).
> Do not insult or harm anyone with words (Leviticus 25:17).
> Pay wages on the day they were earned (Deuteronomy 24:15).
> Respect your father or mother (Exodus 20:13).
> Destroy the seven Canaanite nations (Deuteronomy 20:17).
> Wipe out the descendants of Amalek (Deuteronomy 25:19).

One of these laws—"Respect your father or mother"—is familiar to Christians from the Ten Commandments. Others seem like reasonable moral guidelines, such as "Do not stand idly by if someone's life is in danger." But others seem unreasonable, especially "A rapist must marry his victim if she is unwed." Still others don't seem like moral guidelines at all, such as "Do not cook meat and milk together" and "Do not wear a garment woven of wool and linen." The command to "Break the neck of a calf by the river valley following an unsolved murder" just seems bizarre to most Christians.

The hundreds of commandments in the Old Testament govern not only what we call morality—such as respecting one's parents and not stealing—but also purity, such as not mixing meat and milk and not wearing garments made of mixed fibers. There are also commandments about performing rituals correctly. The Old Testament itself does not distinguish morality from purity and from ritual correctness, but simply commands certain actions and forbids other actions.

If we went through the entire list of God's 613 commandments in the Bible, we would find that Christians do not consider themselves bound by the vast majority of them. Instead, they follow only a few, and what those have in common is that they are related to loving God and loving other people. In that way, most Christians are like Jesus.

As a Jew, Jesus grew up with hundreds of commandments, but as an adult, he overlooked most of them, especially the ones about purity and about not working on the Sabbath. As mentioned in chapter 1, one Sabbath day when he and his followers were walking through a grain field, some of them were hungry and picked grain to eat. When some Pharisees asked why they were violating the law about not working on the Sabbath, Jesus told them, "The Sabbath was made for humankind, and not humankind for the Sabbath." As an illustration, he talked about how, when King David and his friends were hungry, they went into the house of God and ate the bread that was intended only for the priests (Mark 2:23–27). To reinforce Jesus' principle, the writer of Mark's Gospel follows that with a story about Jesus in the synagogue on the Sabbath curing a man with a withered hand. The Pharisees were so incensed by this "working on the Sabbath" that they started plotting "how they might destroy him" (Mark 3:1–6).

Jesus was also criticized for ignoring purity rules about eating. The Pharisees followed not just the Bible's laws about "clean" and "unclean" foods, but also their own rules about hand washing before meals. Jesus and his friends largely ignored these rules (Matthew 15:2; Mark 7:2, 5; Luke 11:38). His explanation was:

> Do you not see that whatever goes into the mouth enters the stomach, and goes out into the sewer? But what comes out of the mouth proceeds from the heart, and this is what defiles. For out of the heart come evil intentions, murder, adultery, fornication, theft, false witness, slander. These are what defile a person, but to eat with unwashed hands does not defile (Matthew 15:17–20).

Jesus' list of evil actions here reveals his understanding of what makes immoral actions wrong: they harm people. Unlike purity rules and rules about not working on the Sabbath, commandments against murder, fornication, adultery, stealing, bearing false witness, and slander forbid people to harm others.

Although Jesus was familiar with dozens—perhaps hundreds—of commandments from the Hebrew Scriptures, he did not consider most of them binding. Those he did follow were the ones that served the two "greatest" commandments: "You shall love the Lord your God with all your heart, and with all your soul, and with all your mind" and "You shall love your neighbor as yourself." "On these two commandments," he says, "hang all the law and the prophets" (Matthew 27:37–39).

As mentioned in chapter 1, Jesus was opposed to legalism—venerating laws for their own sake. For him what made a law valuable was that it helped people live lives based on love. Even if a law was beneficial in one time or place, it might not be beneficial in another time or place. The commandment "Pay wages on the day they were earned," for instance, was good for workers in the ancient Near East, many of whom were paid in food that they needed for their evening meal. But if all employers today tried to follow that commandment, it would create accounting nightmares. So we ignore it.

One of the Ten Commandments—the second—is ignored by all Christians today because it wouldn't benefit anyone and would make our lives much less interesting. "You shall not make for yourself an image in the form of anything in heaven above or on the earth beneath or in the waters below" (Exodus 20:4, New International Version). In ancient Israel, that was a useful rule because it kept people from carving statues to use as idols and thus reduced the worship of pagan gods.

But today, when idol worship is no longer a problem, most Christians violate the second commandment dozens of times a day by making or looking at drawings, photographs, videos, movies, paintings, sculptures, and other images. We are not bound even by all of the Ten Commandments, then, much less by all of the 613.

Even the other nine of the Ten Commandments we do not follow unconditionally. In most situations, it's wrong to lie, for example, but when telling the truth would harm someone and not help anyone, we often say what we know is false. Suppose that a friend of yours has gotten a new haircut to cheer herself up after a period of mourning, and she asks if you like it. You wouldn't be much of a friend if you said, "No, it makes you look fatter than your old haircut did." The right thing to do here is to say something nice, even though you don't believe it.

The hundreds of commandments given by God, then, are not moral absolutes to be followed rigidly without considering whether they will benefit or harm anyone. Hundreds of the 613 commandments are not about morality, but about purity or ritual correctness. And even the Ten Commandments don't hold for all times, places, and situations. We have to think, as Jesus did, about whether applying a particular commandment at a particular time will foster the two kinds of love he made central to living a good life: love of God and love of other people. When telling the truth or obeying another commandment serves love, then it's the right thing to do. When obeying a commandment—say "A rapist must marry his victim if she is unwed"—would not serve love, then it's not the right thing to do.

Morality, to conclude, is not a simple matter of obeying God's commands. Those commands do not by themselves make actions right or wrong. What makes actions right or wrong is whether they serve the love of God and the love of other people.

For further reading:

Mary Douglas. *Purity and Danger: An Analysis of the Concepts of Pollution and Taboo.* London: Routledge, 1984.
Joseph Fletcher. *Situation Ethics: The New Morality.* Philadelphia: Westminster, 1966.

B. WOULD JESUS OPPOSE GAY MARRIAGE?

Once we understand Jesus' preaching about love as the basis of morality, we can consider moral questions that are not mentioned in the Gospels, such as homosexuality. Jesus says nothing about gay people in the Gospels, and many scholars say that the concept of a homosexual person did not yet exist when the Bible was written. For the ancients there were homosexual *actions*, they say, but not homosexual *persons*.

Since Jesus did not condemn homosexuality, Christians opposed to it often turn from the Gospels to other parts of the Bible. One problem here is that there are many rules about sexual morality in the Bible that we reject today and that Jesus may well have rejected. Several biblical verses talk of women as the sexual property of men, for instance, as with King Solomon's three hundred concubines (sex slaves) and even his seven hundred wives (1 Kings 11:3). Obviously, polygamy is acceptable in the Bible. There are also verses condemning mixed marriages (Ezra 9:1–4), sex during menstruation (Leviticus 18:19), and nudity in the home (Genesis 9:21–25).

In the Old Testament, a few verses refer to homosexual acts, but none to homosexual persons. The one cited most often is Leviticus 18:22: "You shall not lie with a male as with a woman. It is an abomination." Leviticus has dozens of similar laws, however, that Christians do not consider binding. In chapter 11, it declares dozens of animals to be unclean, "an abomination." Among the forbidden birds are the eagle, osprey, kite, raven, ostrich, nighthawk, seagull, little owl, great owl, desert owl, stork, heron, hoopoe, and bat (11:13–19). The only land animals that are not unclean are those which have a split hoof and chew the cud. Further, Leviticus says, "Whatever in the water does not have fins or scales—that shall be an abomination to you" (11:12). These laws are repeated in Deuteronomy, chapter 14, which uses the same word *tow'ebah* for the "abomination" of eating shellfish as for the "abomination" of men having sex (the Bible says nothing about lesbian relationships). So eating shrimp is an abomination, just as men's having sex with each other is an abomination. The obvious question for Christians is: If we don't agree with the first judgment, why should we agree with the second?

One prominent opponent of homosexuality who bases her position on the Bible is Dr. Laura Schlessinger, the popular American radio show host and author of thirteen books, including *The Ten Command-ments: The Significance of God's Laws in Everyday Life* (New York: HarperCollins, 1998). Her position is that gay people are "biological errors" who should undergo therapy to change into heterosexuals. On her radio show and on her website www.drlaura.com, she said,

> I'm sorry—hear it one more time, perfectly clearly: If you're gay or a lesbian, it's a biological error that inhibits you from relating normally to the opposite sex. The fact that you are intelligent, creative and valuable is all true. The error is in your inability to relate sexually intimately, in a loving way to a member of the opposite sex—it is a biological error (December 8, 1998).

For her public statements on homosexuality, Dr. Laura was given an award by National Religious Broadcasters in February 2000. In June 2000, the delegates to the Southern Baptist Convention overwhelming-ly adopted a motion commending her staunch opposition to the homo-sexual lifestyle.[2]

A letter to Dr. Laura opposing her position on homosexuality was signed by a hundred clergy and dozens of medical, child-welfare, and civil rights organizations. It included these lines:

> The anti-gay beliefs you espouse on a regular basis—that homosexu-ality is "deviant" and that gays can and should be cured—are entirely outside the mainstream of scientific thought. . . . Your claim that homosexuality is a tragic pathology and that gays and lesbians can and should be "cured" by "reparative therapy" is not only inaccurate but also promotes the idea that there is something wrong with being gay.[3]

As more people spoke out against her, Dr. Laura released a statement on March 10, 2000, in which she said that she never intended to "hurt anyone or contribute in any way to an atmosphere of hate or intoler-ance . . . Regrettably, some of the words I've used have hurt some people, and I am sorry for that. Words that I have used in a clinical context have been perceived as judgment."[4] After more criticism, she published a full-page statement in *Variety* on October 11, 2000, in which she said that "in talking about gays and lesbians some of my words were poorly chosen" and that she was sorry that anyone was hurt by what she said. What she did not say, then or later, however, is that she had changed her mind about homosexual acts being wrong because they are forbidden by the Book of Leviticus. On this issue, Kent Ashcroft composed an ingenious "Letter to Dr. Laura" that was widely circulated on the Internet, especially in response to opponents of gay marriage:

Dear Dr. Laura,

Thank you for doing so much to educate people regarding God's Law. I have learned a great deal from your show, and I try to share that knowledge with as many people as I can. When someone tries to defend the homosexual lifestyle, for example, I simply remind him that Leviticus 18:22 clearly states it to be an abomination. End of debate. I do need some advice from you, however, regarding some of the specific laws and how to best follow them.

a) When I burn a bull on the altar as a sacrifice, I know it creates a pleasing odor for the Lord (Lev. 1:9). The problem is my neighbors. They claim the odor is not pleasing to them. Should I smite them?

b) I would like to sell my daughter into slavery, as sanctioned in Exodus 21:7. In this day and age, what do you think would be a fair price for her?

c) I know that I am allowed no contact with a woman while she is in her period of menstrual uncleanliness (Lev. 15:19–24). The problem is, how do I tell? I have tried asking, but most women take offense.

d) Lev. 25:44 states that I may indeed possess slaves, both male and female, provided they are purchased from neighboring nations. A friend of mine claims that this applies to Mexicans, but not Canadians. Can you clarify? Why can't I own Canadians?

e) I have a neighbor who insists on working on the Sabbath. Exodus 35:2 clearly states he should be put to death. Am I morally obligated to kill him myself?

f) A friend of mine feels that even though eating shellfish is an abomination (Leviticus 11:10), it is a lesser abomination than homosexuality. I don't agree. Can you settle this? . . . I know you have studied these things extensively, so I am confident you can help.

Thank you again for reminding us that God's word is eternal and unchanging.

Your devoted disciple and adoring fan.[5]

The use of the Bible to condemn gay marriage as a union between "biological errors" is revealing, because for centuries the Bible was used in similar ways to outlaw interracial marriage in the United States. In 1664 Maryland made miscegenation—mixing of the races—illegal, and by 1750 all the southern colonies, along with Pennsylvania and Massachusetts, had such laws. Virginia's declared that "All marriages between a white person and a colored person shall be absolutely void without any decree of divorce or other legal process."[6] After the Civil War, the Georgia Supreme Court ruled that:

> Moral or social equality between the different races . . . does not in fact exist, and never can. The God of nature made it otherwise, and no human law can produce it, and no human tribunal can enforce it. There are gradations and classes throughout the universe. From the tallest archangel in Heaven, down to the meanest reptile on earth, moral and social inequalities exist, and must continue to exist through all eternity.[7]

In 1959, a judge trying an interracial married couple in Virginia ruled that:

> Almighty God created the races white, black, yellow, malay and red, and he placed them on separate continents. And but for the interference with his arrangement there would be no cause for such marriages. The fact that he separated the races shows that he did not intend for the races to mix.[8]

If some of the laws of the Old Testament seem outmoded, what about the parts of the New Testament other than the Gospels? Here there are just a few verses referring to homosexuality. Often cited is Paul's First Letter to the Corinthians 6:9: "Fornicators, idolaters, adulterers, male prostitutes, sodomites, thieves, the greedy, drunkards, revilers, robbers—none of these will inherit the kingdom of God." The trouble with appealing to Paul on moral questions is that he never even met Jesus, and he made moral judgments that are now rejected by all Christian churches and that Jesus may well have rejected. In chapter 1 we mentioned two of them. One was that slavery is a legitimate social institution: "Slaves, obey your earthly masters with fear and trembling, in singleness of heart, as you obey Christ" (Ephesians 6:5). Another was that all political leaders have been appointed by God: "Let every soul be subject to the governing authorities. For there is no authority except from God, and the authorities that exist are appointed by God. Therefore whoever resists the authority resists the ordinance of God" (Romans 13:1–2). If Paul is right about slavery, then, for example, people in India who protest the chaining of child weavers to their looms as slaves are wrong. If Paul is right about political authority, then no one should ever complain about any dictator, not even monsters like Adolf Hitler and Pol Pot, since God appoints all "governing authorities." If Paul is wrong about slavery and political authority, maybe he is wrong about homosexuality, too.

On the moral issue of homosexual acts, we must also remember that Paul's comments on "male prostitutes" and "sodomites" were made in the first century in the Roman Empire. The most common homosexual act then was pederasty—an older male penetrating a boy or adolescent. Paul's word for "sodomites" refers to the active role of the older men; his word for "male prostitutes" refers to the passive role of younger males. So what Paul may have been objecting to here is the unequal, manipulative relationship, the use of one person by another. Neither Paul nor any other writer of the Bible says anything about a same-sex couple in a mutual, committed relationship of love, such as what is now called gay marriage.

In the centuries since the Bible was written, we have learned a lot about homosexuality. In cultures around the world, about 5 to 10 percent of people are homosexual, and other animal species have homosexuals too. Another finding is that homosexuality is a psychological and physical condition that is determined from a young age—in the womb, according to many experts. If that's true, then what kind of all-good God would create hundreds of millions of people with desires for loving relationships with members of their own sex, but order those people to never act on those desires?

That question brings us back to Jesus. Though he never said anything about gays and lesbians, he was very clear about how we should treat people—with loving concern for their well-being. People's well-being includes having enough to eat and having a roof over their heads, but it also includes having people to love. And not just people to care about, but people to share their lives with intimately, as married couples do. About 90 percent of us desire that relationship with someone of the opposite sex, and 10 percent of us desire it with someone of our own sex. These desires seem as God-given as any other. If Jesus accepted all people who showed goodwill—rich and poor, Jews and Samaritans, even Romans and tax collectors, on what possible ground would he have rejected gays and lesbians?

The attitude of some contemporary Christians toward gays and lesbians seems especially un-Christlike. At antigay rallies, they often carry signs and wear T-shirts saying "God hates fags" and "You're going to hell." Right now on YouTube, a video has gone viral of a Baptist preacher in North Carolina calling from the pulpit for gays and lesbians to be put in concentration camps until they "die out." Wherever these people get their hatred, it's not from Jesus.

For further reading:

James B. Nelson. "Sources for Body Theology: Homosexuality as a Test Case." In *Body Theology*. Louisville, KY: Westminster John Knox, 1992, 55–74.
Robin Scroggs. *The New Testament and Homosexuality*. Minneapolis: Fortress, 1984.

C. WOULD JESUS FAVOR CAPITAL PUNISHMENT?

Although Christians who cite Leviticus 20:13 to condemn gay sex seldom mention it, that verse prescribes a punishment for gay sex: death. "If a man lies with a male as with a woman, both of them have committed an abomination; they shall be put to death." Verses before and after that stipulate the death penalty for other sexual offenses, too: adultery, bestiality (the animal must also die), and a man having sex with his father's wife, his daughter-in-law, or his mother-in-law. Though stoning is the usual method, the punishment for that last offense is being "burned to death"—for the man, his wife, and her mother (20:14).

Leviticus and other Old Testament books also prescribe execution for many religious offenses, such as blasphemy (Leviticus 10:16); worshiping a god other than Yahweh (Exodus 22:20; Leviticus 20:1–5; Numbers 25:1–9; Deuteronomy 17:2–7); false prophesy (Deuteronomy 13:1–10; 18:20–22); being a medium, witch, or wizard (Leviticus 20:27); and not keeping the Sabbath (Exodus 31:14; 35:2; Numbers 15:32–36).

Most Christians know that "Honor your father and your mother" is one of the Ten Commandments; fewer know that the penalty for cursing or striking one's parents, or just being "a stubborn and rebellious son who will not obey his father and mother," is being stoned to death

(Exodus 21:15, 17; Deuteronomy 21:18–21). The Old Testament also prescribes capital punishment for murder (Genesis 9:6; Exodus 21:12–14; Leviticus 24:17) and for kidnapping (Exodus 21:16; Deuteronomy 24:7). If an ox has gored people but the owner has not restrained it after that "and it kills a man or a woman, the ox shall be stoned, and its owner also shall be put to death" (Exodus 21:29). If an engaged woman who is a virgin is raped within a town, "you shall bring both of them to the gate of that town and stone them to death, the young woman because she did not cry for help in the town and the man because he violated his neighbor's wife" (Deuteronomy 22:23–24).

If the Bible's statements about executing people consisted of only verses like these, then capital punishment would seem not just acceptable, but required. In the New Testament, however, Jesus has a completely different attitude not just toward killing people, but even toward judging and punishing them. Two stories from the Gospels show his attitude toward wrongdoers. One is about the woman caught in adultery in John 8:3–11. The scribes and Pharisees brought her to Jesus and said, "In the law Moses commanded us to stone such women. Now what do you say?" If Jesus accepted the Mosaic law, he would have agreed that she should be killed. But instead he got the crowd to disperse, saying, "Let anyone among you who is without sin be the first to throw a stone at her." When just she and he were left, Jesus "said to her, 'Woman, where are they? Has no one condemned you?' She said, 'No one, sir.' And Jesus said, 'Neither do I condemn you. Go your way, and from now on, do not sin again.'"

Another wrongdoer in the Gospels is the convicted thief crucified next to Jesus (Luke 23:42–43). He admitted his guilt, but asked Jesus to "remember me when you come into your kingdom." If Jesus favored capital punishment, he might have scorned this criminal and told him he was only getting what he deserved. But instead Jesus "replied, 'Truly I tell you, today you will be with me in Paradise.'" That is something Jesus promised no one else, not even his mother!

If we consider Jesus' Love Ethic from chapter 1, we can see how different his attitude toward the adulteress and the thief was from other people's attitudes—at that time and also today. Most people's motive for killing wrongdoers has always been retaliation—"paying them back" for the harm they have done. That's obvious when the television news shows family members of a murder victim attending the murderer's execution. They often say that they "feel good he got what he de-served"—which was to be killed as he had killed. This ancient motive was incorporated into the Code of Hammurabi in Babylon around 1780 BCE, and then into the Hebrew Scriptures. The principle in Leviticus 24:20 is often called the law of talion: "The injury inflicted is the injury to be suffered." Exodus 21:22–25 says, "You shall give life for life, eye for eye, tooth for tooth, hand for hand, foot for foot, burn for burn, wound for wound, stripe for stripe." The law of talion was also found in early Roman law.

Throughout history, the pleasure of seeing criminals suffer the harm they have inflicted was often accompanied by simple sadism. Though governments often said that they made stonings, burnings, decapita-tions, and hangings public in order to deter others from committing the same crimes, many who attended public executions were there to be entertained. A recent story in the *New York Times* titled "Iran Resorts to Hangings in Public to Cut Crime" records this revealing moment:

> From behind a makeshift barrier of scaffolding, the crowd jostled for position. "Let's move to the other side," one spectator whispered to his wife, pointing to the spot where Iranian state television cameras had been set up. "I think we will have a better view from there."[9]

However good vengeance may feel, such pleasure is utterly incompat-ible with what Jesus preached. Most obviously, it violates five of the Ten Tenets presented in chapter 1:

> 1. Love Ethic. Love God and Love All People.
> 2. God's Children. All Human Beings Are Brothers and Sisters, with God as Their Father.
> 8. Divine Judgment. God Alone Is Judge.
> 9. Forgiveness. Be Ready to Forgive Anyone for Anything.
> 10. Pacifism. "Do Not Resist an Evildoer" (Matthew 5:39).

Jesus condemned the law of talion and so the biblical rationale for capital punishment:

> You have heard that it was said, "An eye for an eye and a tooth for a tooth." But I say to you, Do not resist an evildoer. But if anyone strikes you on the right cheek, turn the other also; and if anyone wants to sue you and take your coat, give your cloak as well; and if

anyone forces you to go one mile, go also the second mile (Matthew 5:38–41).

In place of retaliation, Jesus preached forgiveness: "Be merciful, just as your Father is merciful. Do not judge, and you will not be judged; do not condemn, and you will not be condemned. Forgive, and you will be forgiven" (Luke 6:36–37).

With his disciples and the people he met, Jesus instructed, guided, admonished, and cajoled, but he did not punish. And in his instructions for spreading his message after he was gone, Jesus did not say his followers should punish anyone. Instead he said to be merciful, to not judge or condemn, and to forgive. Other parts of the New Testament repeat Jesus' preaching. In Paul's Letter to the Romans 12:17–21, he writes, "Do not repay anyone evil for evil, but take thought for what is noble in the sight of all." In his First Letter to the Thessalonians 5:14–15, he says, "And we urge you, beloved, to admonish the idlers, encourage the fainthearted, help the weak, be patient with all of them. See that none of you repays evil for evil, but always seek to do good to one another and to all." Similarly, the First Letter of Peter 3:8–9 says, "Finally, all of you, have unity of spirit, sympathy, love for one another, a tender heart, and a humble mind. Do not repay evil for evil or abuse for abuse; but, on the contrary, repay with a blessing."

In the ancient world, where the law of talion dominated, turning the other cheek and repaying abuse with a blessing seemed bizarre to most people. But the first three centuries of Christians largely followed Jesus' principles of pacifism and forgiveness. In the fourth century, however, as the Roman emperors made Christianity the state religion, bishops began to approve of punishments like those in Roman law. As we saw in chapter 1, just five years after Christianity became the religion of the empire, Bishop Priscillian and six of his followers were beheaded for heresy. In the Middle Ages, Christian governments not only executed people, but hired skilled torturers to maximize the degree and time of suffering. Some methods, such as burning at the stake, they inherited from the Romans. On the breaking wheel, people's limbs were systematically broken. In quartering, their arms and legs were tied to four horses, which then moved away in four directions. In pressing, the person was slowly crushed to death as rocks or other heavy objects were slowly loaded on top of them; this method was still in use by the Puritans at the Salem witch trials of 1692–1693. Impalement was piercing the body with a long spear or pole, sometimes entering the rectum or vagina and exiting the mouth. Other methods perfected in Christian Europe were hanging, boiling, and decapitation by axe or sword. All of these show an utter rejection of the Love Ethic of Jesus. Were it not for the fact that he had been nailed to a cross, they might well have used that method, too.

Today, of course, most Christians who advocate capital punishment deny any desire for retaliation. Those who know modern theories of punishment often insist that punishment has three other functions besides retaliation—deterrence, reformation, and restraint. We considered those briefly in our discussion of hell in chapter 7, section E. Of the three, reformation could not apply to capital punishment, since killing people leaves them no time to reform. So we can consider deterrence and restraint as possible functions of capital punishment.

While it seems logical that attaching a penalty of death to a crime would deter people from committing it, research over decades has not borne out that intuition. As Judge Richard Nygaard says,

> Statistics uniformly show that the condemned on death row did not consider the possibility that they might die for their crimes. There may be others, of course, who thought of the consequences and did not kill. This possibility has been little researched, and as yet we simply do not know much about this aspect of deterrence. The incomplete data, however, indicate that of those disposed to kill, none seemed to fear the consequences. [10]

That leaves restraint as our last possible function for capital punishment. The idea of restraining criminals so that they could not repeat their crimes was first applied to imprisonment. Behind bars, they would be unable to hurt people outside the prison. Killing criminals, of course, also prevents them from repeating their crimes—and from doing anything else, forever. But execution is an extreme way to restrain people, one that makes their reform impossible. Opponents of capital punishment say that imprisonment is preferable, since it leaves open the possibility of the criminal's rehabilitation. And even life imprisonment, they point out, is cheaper than execution. As Nygaard says, "All current statistics indicate that it is . . . more expensive to execute a person than it is to imprison for life." [11]

Of the standard justifications of capital punishment, then, the only two plausible ones are retaliation and restraint. The first, as we showed, was rejected by Jesus, Paul, and the author of the First Letter of Peter. The second is unconvincing, since killing people is an extreme way to restrain them, and imprisonment is a cheaper alternative that leaves open the possibility of their rehabilitation.

For further reading:

Richard L. Nygaard. "'Vengeance is Mine' Says the Lord." *America*, October 8, 1994, 6–8.
Ernest Van den Haag. *Punishing Criminals: Concerning a Very Old and Painful Question.* Lanham, MD: University Press of America, 1991.
Howard Zehr. *Changing Lenses: A New Focus for Crime and Justice.* Harrisonburg, VA: Herald Press, 1990.

D. WOULD JESUS JOIN THE U.S. MARINES?

After what we've said about pacifism and forgiveness in Jesus' Love Ethic, the answer to this question might seem obvious. And it would have been obvious for the first three centuries of Christians, who rejected violence, did not fight back, and did not allow soldiers to join their communities. Their condemnation of the military was captured in the book *De corona militis* (*Concerning the Military Crown*) by Tertullian (c. 160–c. 220), the theologian often called the Father of Latin Christianity:

> Is it right to make an occupation of the sword, when the Lord proclaims that he who uses the sword shall perish by the sword? Shall the son of peace take part in the battle when it does not become him even to sue at law? Shall he apply the chain, and the prison, and the torture, and punishment, when he is not even the avenger of his own wrongs? . . . Putting all my strength to the main question, I banish us from military life.[12]

If later generations of Christians had continued to be forgiving pacifists, as a few small Christian groups were, there wouldn't even be such military forces as the U.S. Marines to ask the question about. But once Christianity became the state religion of the Roman Empire, most church leaders turned away from Jesus' Love Ethic to accept warfare as a good way to solve problems. The most influential was Augustine, with his just war theory around 400. Reversing four centuries of Christian pacifism, Augustine used that theory to justify attacking the Donatists, a Christian group he judged to be heretics. That just war theory, with modifications by Thomas Aquinas and others, has been used ever since by religious and governmental authorities wanting to attack someone. In the Middle Ages, bishops and popes commanded armies, most famously in the Crusades (1095–1291), which are estimated to have taken two hundred thousand lives in the name of Jesus Christ. Pope Urban II started recruiting troops for the First Crusade with an impassioned speech at the Council of Clermont:

> On this account I, or rather the Lord, beseech you as Christ's heralds to publish this everywhere and to persuade all people of whatever rank, foot-soldiers and knights, poor and rich, to carry aid promptly to those Christians [in the East] and to destroy that vile race [Muslims] from the lands of our friends. I say this to those who are present; it is also meant for those who are absent. Moreover, Christ commands it. All who die on the way, whether by land or by sea, or in battle against the pagans, shall have immediate remission of sins. I grant them this through the power of God with which I am invested. O what a disgrace if such a despised and base race, which worships demons, should conquer a people which has the faith of omnipotent God and is made glorious with the name of Christ!

Notice the pope's claim that it is Jesus Christ beseeching them to destroy the Muslims in Palestine and his granting of a plenary indulgence to those who become crusaders. That's the cancellation of all the debt incurred by their sins, so that they would enter heaven the instant they died on the battlefield, or died on their way there. In the Fourth Crusade (1202–1204), Christians from Western Europe attacked fellow Christians in Constantinople, the center of Eastern Christianity. They sacked the city and surrounding areas and established a new "Latin Empire" there.

When Protestants broke away from the Roman Catholic Church in the 1500s, and then split off from each other, there was still more violence in the name of Jesus Christ. A standard estimate of the number killed during the "Age of Religious Wars," 1560–1715, is one hundred thousand. In the last three centuries, millions more Christians have been killed by fellow Christians in various wars, most notably, World Wars I and II.

As with capital punishment, Jesus' attitude toward such killing is a radical break from the religious tradition he grew up in. The Hebrew Scriptures are full of violence and warfare, much of it coming from Yahweh himself. Over two hundred times Yahweh is called Lord of Hosts—"hosts" meaning "armies." As a military commander, he plans dozens of battles and campaigns. In the Second Book of Chronicles, Yahweh leads one Hebrew group against another Hebrew group—the army of Judah against the army of Israel! "The Israelites fled before Judah, and God gave them unto their hands. Abijah and his army defeated them with great slaughter; five hundred thousand picked men of Israel fell slain" (13:15–17). In the next chapter of Second Chronicles, Yahweh leads an attack against a million Ethiopians. "So the Lord defeated the Ethiopians . . . and the Ethiopians fell until no one remained alive" (14:9–13). That's a million and a half people killed in just two battles.

Not only is Yahweh violent, but by modern moral standards, his violence is indiscriminate. If some members of a group incur his wrath, he often punishes the whole group and their descendants. In the first commandment, he says, "for I the Lord your God am a jealous God, punishing children for the iniquity of parents, to the third and fourth generation of those who reject me" (Exodus 20:5).

Yahweh's punishing groups for the actions of individuals starts early in the Bible. When Adam sins, Yahweh punishes him plus all his descendants—the whole human race! A few chapters later, in Genesis 6, he gets so angry with humans that he decides to kill them all, along with all animals, in a great flood. "I will blot out from the earth the human beings I have created—people together with animals and creeping things and birds of the air, for I am sorry that I have made them" (6:7).

In the Book of Exodus, the Hebrews are led by Moses to escape slavery in Egypt. To motivate the pharaoh to let them go, Yahweh kills the firstborn of every Egyptian family, including the children of slaves and even young livestock (11:5). Being "passed over" in that mass slaughter is what Jews celebrate at Passover. Once out of Egypt, the Hebrews head toward Canaan, the land Yahweh had promised to give them. Moses describes their destination as "a land with fine, large cities that you did not build, houses filled with all sorts of goods that you did not fill, hewn cisterns that you did not hew, vineyards and olive groves that you did not plant" (Deuteronomy 6:10–11). Before they enter the promised land, Yahweh instructs Moses: "Speak to the Israelites, and say to them: When you cross over the Jordan into the land of Canaan, you shall drive out all the inhabitants of the land from before you . . . You shall take possession of the land and settle in it, for I have given you the land to possess" (Numbers 33:50–53). Deuteronomy 7:1–2 is similar, with Moses saying, "When the Lord your God brings you into the land that you are about to enter and occupy, and he clears away many nations before you . . . and when the Lord your God gives them over to you and you defeat them, then you must utterly destroy them. Make no covenant with them and show them no mercy." Deuteronomy 20:16–17 adds that "you must not let anything that breathes remain alive. You shall annihilate them."

Once in Canaan, the Israelites get further orders from Yahweh for wiping out city after city. The first is Jericho, one of the oldest cities in the world, where they slaughter "all in the city, both young and old, oxen, sheep, and donkeys" (Joshua 6:21). Next is Ai, where "the total of those who fell that day, both men and women, was twelve thousand— all the people of Ai" (Joshua 8:25).

Until they are conquered by invading empires several centuries later, the Bible says, the people of Israel continue to fight wars, and they gauge their approval in Yahweh's eyes by how successful they are in conquering their neighbors. Once they are themselves conquered to become colonies, they long to overthrow their masters and become an independent nation again. That is what the Messiah was predicted to lead them in doing. In the second century BCE, a Jewish revolt led by the Maccabees brought them a brief period of independence, and at the time of Jesus, a group called the Zealots fought skirmishes with Roman soldiers.

From their earliest days to the time of Jesus, then, the people of Israel embraced militarism—the belief that war is a good way to solve problems. So when Jesus rejected violence, he was opposing over a thousand years of religious ideology. Today, the vast majority of Christians, especially in the United States, ignore Jesus' pacifism. They see no incompatibility between their religion and their support for and fighting in war. Indeed, many talk about their militarism as if it were a Christian virtue. Patriotic assemblies often begin and end with prayers.

In the parking lot, bumpers with "GOD BLESS AMERICA" stickers are likely to also have stickers saying "SUPPORT OUR TROOPS." Thousands of Christian clergy are officers in the U.S. Armed Forces serving as chaplains, and they pray with the troops for God to help them defeat their enemies.

For decades, preachers on television have praised the U.S. military and have prayed for "our men and women in uniform." The United States not only spends more on the military than the next ten countries combined—over a million dollars a minute 24/7—but is by far the largest exporter of arms to other countries, fueling wars around the world.

What would Jesus say about Christian leaders blessing all this militarism? It seems obvious that he would condemn it. His Love Ethic was to show concern for everyone, to not resist the evildoer, to forgive, and to love one's enemies. Jesus would be especially disgusted, I think, by the celebration of killing so common in American Christian militarism. Again, a good place to find this ideology is on bumper stickers. Here are ten that are popular on U.S. Marine Corps bases, published on www.leatherneck.com, a website designed for Marines that has five hundred thousand visitors each month. [13]

U.S. Marines—Travel Agents To Allah

Marines—Providing Enemies of America an Opportunity to Die For Their Country Since 1775

The Marine Corps . . . When it Absolutely, Positively Has to Be Destroyed Overnight

God Bless Our Troops, Especially Our Snipers

A Dead Enemy Is a Peaceful Enemy—Blessed Be the Peacemakers

Life, Liberty and the Pursuit of Anyone Who Threatens It

Marine Sniper—You Can Run, But You'll Just Die Tired!

Water-boarding Is Out, So Kill Them All!

Naval Corollary: Dead Men Don't Testify

When In Doubt, Empty the Magazine

Four decades ago, when the United States carried on a disastrous war in Southeast Asia, a T-shirt popular among supporters of the war had the words "Kill 'em all. Let God sort 'em out!" This is like what a commander of Pope Innocent III's crusade against the Cathars said in 1209 when one of his officers asked how to distinguish Cathars from Catholics—"Kill them all. God will know his own." Have Christians learned anything since the Crusades? Have they learned anything since the Vietnam War?

For further reading:

Joshua, ch. 1–11.

John Driver. *How Christians Made Peace with War: Early Christian Understandings of War.* Harrisonburg, VA: Herald Press, 1988.

Mark J. Allman. *Who Would Jesus Kill? War, Peace, and the Christian Tradition.* Winona, MN: Anselm Academic, 2008.

A. James Reimer. *Christians and War: A Brief History of the Church's Teachings and Practices.* Minneapolis: Augsburg Fortress, 2010.

E. WOULD JESUS SHOP 'TIL HE DROPPED?

In case you're unfamiliar with the slogan "Shop 'til you drop," it's from Bloomingdale's department store in New York City. They use it on catalogs and advertising materials, and they have teamed up with the Waldorf-Astoria Hotel to sell the Bloomingdale's Shop 'til You Drop Package:

> The Waldorf-Astoria Hotel is offering shopaholics a reason to rejoice in one of the world's most coveted shopping destinations! Located just a few blocks from the array of top designers and fashion retailers lining Fifth Avenue as well as one of the city's most iconic department stores, the Bloomingdale's Shop 'Til You Drop Package offers guest VIP treatment with special offers and discounts from Bloomingdale's (located just a few blocks from the hotel on 59th Street and Lexington Avenue).

From 1991 to 2006, *Shop 'til You Drop* was also a television game show. It opened with this voiceover:

> How would you like to win the shopping trip of a lifetime to a fabulous city like Rome, Paris, New York, London, or Hong Kong? Well, that's what our contestants will be playing for today on the wildest shopping game ever, Shop 'Til You Drop!

In a chapter about moral issues, it's obvious that gay marriage, capital punishment, and war are appropriate issues. But shopping? Is that a moral issue?

While many Christians give it little thought, the way we make money and spend it has a lot to do with whether we are living the way Jesus preached. Accumulating money and possessions can seriously interfere with loving God and loving other people. The way of life called consumerism can even become a religion. That's why Jesus warned, "It is easier for a camel to pass through the eye of a needle than for someone who is rich to enter the kingdom of God" (Matthew 19:24). When a rich young ruler asked Jesus what he should do in order to have eternal life. Jesus told him to keep the commandments.

> The young man said to him, "I have kept all these; what do I still lack?" Jesus said to him, "If you wish to be perfect, go, sell your possessions, and give the money to the poor, and you will have treasure in heaven; then come, follow me." When the young man heard this word, he went away grieving, for he had many possessions (Matthew 19:16–22).

Even when he was preaching to peasants who had few possessions, Jesus told them, "Do not worry, saying, 'What will we eat?' or 'What will we drink?' or 'What will we wear?' . . . But strive first for the kingdom of God and his righteousness, and all these things will be given to you as well" (Matthew 6:31–33). If Jesus' followers are not supposed to worry even about where their next meal is coming from, how could they be "shopaholics" who pay 359 dollars for the Bloomingdale's Shop 'Til You Drop Package to "rejoice in one of the world's most coveted shopping destinations"?

> Where your treasure is, there your heart will be also. . . . No one can serve two masters: for a slave will either hate the one, and love the other; or be devoted to the one and despise the other. You cannot serve God and wealth (Matthew 6:21, 24).

Jesus' preaching about the danger of money and possessions was in line with a long line of Hebrew Scriptures. Ecclesiastes warns that "The lover of money will not be satisfied with money; nor the lover of wealth, with gain. This also is vanity. When goods increase, those who eat them increase; and what gain has their owner but to see them with his eyes?" (5:10–20). Proverbs says, "When you sit down to eat with a ruler, observe carefully what is before you, and put a knife to your throat if you have a big appetite. Do not desire the ruler's delicacies, for they are deceptive food. Do not wear yourself out to get rich: be wise enough to desist" (23:1–4).

In the New Testament, the Letter of James has a similar warning: "Your riches have rotted, and your clothes are moth-eaten. Your gold and silver have rusted, and their rust shall be evidence against you, and it will eat your flesh like fire" (5:2–3).

While the allure of possessions has always been a problem for Christians, our contemporary consumerism seems especially dangerous because it is so pervasive and unexamined by Christians. In the Middle Ages, perhaps a few dozen people in a city lived in luxury. Today in the same city, tens of thousands live with far more comforts and conveniences than medieval lords and ladies had. And while the wealthy in earlier times tended to hold onto their possessions for decades or for life, today all of us are constantly bombarded by messages telling us to replace our current possessions with new, more stylish and up-to-date things. In North America each day, there are twelve billion display ads, three million radio commercials, and two hundred thousand TV commercials.[14] Since World War II, a dominant marketing strategy has been "planned obsolescence." Sometimes products are designed to wear out quickly; more often, successive waves of newer models are designed to make items that are not worn out "out of date." This season your jeans have to look new and be skintight; next season you have to replace them with loose jeans that have preworn holes in them—or whatever else the manufacturers have told you is the latest style.

In spite of the embrace of consumerism by most Christians, it conflicts with Jesus' Love Ethic—both the love of God and the love of other people. For almost two millennia, an important way Christians showed love for God was by devoting Sunday to worship and rest from work and commerce. That's how they followed the commandment "Remember the Sabbath day, and keep it holy" (Exodus 20:8). But in the 1970s, as the United States was building thousands of shopping malls, large retail chains decided to open on Sundays to increase sales. A few churches challenged them and told their congregations to boycott Sunday sales. But most churches did nothing, and so millions of Christian sales clerks, managers, stock personnel, and truck drivers began working on Sundays, with millions more Christians as their customers. Within a decade, a significant percentage of American Christians were spending hours on Sunday shopping. Last Sunday morning, as I read through our local newspaper, the *Daily Press* of Newport News, Virginia, I made a pile of the advertising sections, most of which announced sales starting Sunday. There were thirty-two sections, with a total of 460 pages of advertising. That's far more pages than the rest of that newspaper, which itself had dozens of ads mixed in with the news and features. On Sunday afternoon, in this area and in the rest of America, tens of millions of Christians were at the shopping malls—as workers and shoppers—apparently oblivious to the commandment to keep holy the Sabbath day.

If the love of God is not fostered by consumerism, neither is love of neighbor. Jesus' Love Ethic is altruistic; the concern is for other people. But advertising and marketing encourage each consumer to think of herself or himself as the center of the universe. When ads mention people beyond me and my immediate family, it is usually in an invidious way. New, expensive, and stylish products are presented as appealing because my family will have them but my neighbors won't. The 2013 Neiman Marcus Christmas Book, for example, starts off with a woman lying in the grass in a magenta dress that costs $1,995, followed by a couple embracing—Her Jacket $2,495, His Jacket $3,295. On the next page is a woman holding a handbag for $7,200 with a charm for $700. Five pages later are two clutch purses that measure 3½ by 6½ by 2½ inches: the white rayon one with synthetic pearls is $4,030; the black one in python skin with synthetic pearls is $2,945. The next page shows a gold bracelet for $19,500. In the Fantasy Gifts section of the catalog, there is a "Wild Child" motorcycle built by "Indian Larry" for $750,000, and a trip to a DeBeers diamond mine in South Africa, where you'll receive a twenty-carat rough-cut diamond, for $850,000. As the tongue-in-cheek bumper sticker says, "The one who dies with the most toys wins."

Our consumer economy is based not only on luxury items, but also on things bought by middle-income and lower-income people. Here advertisers foster selfishness, too, by encouraging us not to share things. If groups of neighbors pooled their money to buy a single lawn mower, and took turns using it, sales of lawn mowers would plummet. If, as in the 1950s, there was just one television set and one car for each family, then electronics companies and automobile companies would be far less profitable. And so today millions of American homes have a television set in each bedroom, a car for each driver, and even his-and-hers sinks in each bathroom.

In the New Testament, all this emphasis on the individual and convenience is implicitly rejected and sharing is encouraged. As mentioned in chapter 1, the Acts of the Apostles says that early Christians practiced a radical kind of socialism. That passage deserves repeating:

> Now the whole group of those who believed were of one heart and soul, and no one claimed private ownership of any possessions, but everything they owned was held in common. . . . There was not a needy person among them, for as many as owned lands or houses sold them and brought the proceeds of what was sold. They laid it at the apostles' feet, and it was distributed to each as any had need (4:32–35).

To emphasize the importance of communal sharing, Acts 5:1–11 continues with a description of what happened to a married couple who sold a piece of property but secretly held back part of the money as they gave the proceeds to the apostles. When their deceit was discovered by Peter, first the man, and then the woman "fell down at his feet and died."

Christians who question consumerism seldom go so far as to advocate common ownership of all property, but they do make it clear that our current economic system is incompatible with the way of life Jesus preached. If over this century churches continue to ignore those criticisms and go along with the growth of consumerism, by the twenty-second century Jesus' warning that "You cannot serve God and mammon" may well be merely a quaint anachronism.

For further reading:

Act of the Apostles 2:44–45.
Acts of the Apostles 4:32–5:11.
Jay McDaniel. "Christianity and the Pursuit of Wealth." *Anglican Theological Review* 69, no. 4 (1987): 349–61.
Bethany Moreton. *To Serve God and Wal-Mart: The Making of Christian Free Enterprise.* Cambridge, MA: Harvard University Press, 2009.
Robert C. Roberts. "Just a Little Bit More: Greed and the Malling of Our Souls." *Christianity Today*, April 8, 1996.
John Morreall. "Serving God and Mammon? Consumerism and Religion in America." *Delta Epsilon Sigma Journal* 49 (2004): 100–12.
Jay McDaniel. *Living from the Center: Spirituality in an Age of Consumerism.* St. Louis, MO: Chalice Press, 2000.
James Twitchell. *Lead Us into Temptation: The Triumph of American Materialism.* New York: Columbia University Press, 1999.

10

CHURCHES

In a book about Christianity, it might seem odd to wait until the last chapter to discuss churches. Aren't churches what Christianity is all about? In the Bible, the word that gets translated as church is *ekklesia*, but that's misleading. The first meaning of *church* in most dictionaries is something like "a building used for public Christian worship." *Church* occurs over a hundred times in English Bibles, but it is used to translate *ekklesia*, which never refers to a building, but always to a group of people. Only in later centuries did the idea of a group of people get linked to the idea of the building where they worshipped, as they were both called "church."

Church is also a poor translation of *ekklesia* because *ekklesia* means "the people who have been called out," that is, the assembly or congregation. *Church* isn't derived from that word but instead from the Greek *kuriakon*, which means "of the Lord," as in "the day of the Lord." It was in the fourth century, when Emperor Constantine began constructing basilicas for Christian worship, that the word *kuriakon* was applied to them. Those buildings were "of the Lord," because they belonged to him. *Kuriakon* later came into German as *Kirche*, into Old English as *circe*, and into Middle English as *chirche*.

When Martin Luther translated the New Testament into German in 1521–1522, he didn't translate *ekklesia* as *Kirche*, the German word for church. Instead, he used the German *Gemeinde*, which means community. Similarly, when William Tyndale translated the New Testament into English in 1536, he translated *ekklesia* as *congregation*.

However important the words for church became in later centuries, Jesus didn't use *kuriakon* at all, and he used *ekklesia*, or its Aramaic equivalent, only in two verses in Matthew's Gospel. The first is Matthew 16:18: "You are Peter, and on this rock I will build my church." The other is Matthew 18:17, where Jesus is talking about how to handle offensive behavior within the community: "If your brother sins against you, go and point out the fault when the two of you are alone" (18:15). If he doesn't listen to you, Jesus continues, then "take one or two others along with you" (18:16). And if he "refuses to listen to them, tell it to the church; and if the offender refuses to listen even to the church, let such a one be to you as a Gentile and a tax collector" (18:17).

A. DID JESUS OR HIS FOLLOWERS GO TO CHURCH?

When most of us think of a church, we think of a building. Christians "go to church" on Sundays, for example. Jesus could not "go to church" because there were no such buildings in the first century. When he said, "You are Peter, and upon this rock I will build my church," he didn't mean a building, but a community. The first Christians didn't *go to* church—they *were* a church.

The only religious buildings Jesus spent time in were Jewish—the temple in Jerusalem and synagogues. Not only did Jesus not have a word for a church building—because there weren't any—but he never used the word "Christian," because it didn't exist until after he was gone. Jesus was born a Jew and remained a Jew his whole life. His family and his apostles were all Jews. His goal, he said, was "not to abolish but to fulfill" the law and the prophets—that is, the Jewish tradition in which he grew up (Matthew 5:17). The idea of the Messiah, as we saw in chapter 4, section A, was of a Jewish king descended from David. And when Jesus was executed by the Romans, the mocking inscription they put on his cross was "King of the Jews."

After Jesus was gone, his apostles, all Jews, continued to worship in the temple as he had (Acts 2:46; 3:1–3). They weren't a new religion, but a new Jewish sect. The Acts of the Apostles says that Paul, Peter, and John preached in the temple, addressing people as "Men of Israel." Other Jewish sects at the time were the Pharisees, Sadducees, Essenes, and Zealots. As a Jewish community, Jesus' followers agreed with each of these groups about some things but not others, just as those groups agreed and disagreed with each other. The followers of Jesus agreed with the Pharisees that there would be a resurrection of the dead, for example, and disagreed about the need to follow all of the Mosaic laws. As pacifists, Jesus' followers disagreed with the Zealots, a Jewish group who fought to overthrow the Roman government in Palestine. The most obvious difference between followers of Jesus and other Jews was their belief that Jesus is the Messiah—the long-awaited savior of the Jews. The other leading Jewish sects thought that the Messiah had not yet come.

Even when Jesus' followers began to be called "Christians," they were still Jews, not a new religion. In the New Testament, the word "Christian" appears just three times. "It was in Antioch [Syria] that the disciples were first called 'Christians,'" Acts 11:26 says. In Acts 26:28–31, the Jewish king Agrippa asks Paul, "Are you so quickly persuading me to become a Christian?" The third appearance is in First Peter 4:16: "Yet if any of you suffers as a Christian, do not consider it a disgrace, but glorify God because you bear this name."

Paul shows that the followers of Jesus were a community of Jews when he defends himself at a trial before the Roman governor. He calls his community "the Way" and says that they are faithful Jews:

> As you can find out, it is not more than twelve days since I went up to worship in Jerusalem. They did not find me disputing with anyone in the temple or stirring up a crowd either in the synagogues or throughout the city. . . . But this I admit to you, that according to the Way, which they call a sect, I worship the God of our ancestors, believing everything laid down according to the law or written in the prophets (Acts 24:11–14).

When Paul was tried by King Agrippa, he pointed out that before following Jesus, he had "belonged to the strictest sect of our religion and lived as a Pharisee" (Acts 26:5). If the Jewish authorities thought that Paul had rejected Judaism to start a new religion, they would have charged him with heresy or apostasy. But instead they "said to one another, 'This man is doing nothing to deserve death or imprisonment'" (Acts 26: 31).

Though at the time of Paul, in the fifties, Christians were a kind of Jew, by about 100, they were considered to be distinct from Jews. It was largely missionaries like Paul who had changed things. As they preached in non-Jewish places such as Greece, they didn't emphasize the Jewish aspects of their movement, but said that the promise of salvation was open to everyone. As more and more gentiles joined the group, the proportion of Jews got lower and lower. By about the year 90, Christians were no longer allowed to meet in synagogues. They had already been meeting in each other's homes sometimes. When Paul wrote to his followers in Rome, he said, "Greet Prisca and Aquila . . . Greet also the church in their house" (16:1, 5). After Christians were expelled from synagogues, their homes became their standard meeting places, and that continued until around 200, when the first permanent church buildings were constructed.

For further reading:

Acts of the Apostles.
John Dominic Crossan. *Jesus: A Revolutionary Biography.* New York: HarperCollins, 1994.
Julie Galambush. *The Reluctant Parting: How the New Testament's Jewish Writers Created a Christian Book.* San Francisco: HarperSanFrancisco, 2005.
Alan F. Segal. *Rebecca's Children: Judaism and Christianity in the Roman World.* Cambridge, MA: Harvard University Press, 1986.

B. DID JESUS START A CHURCH?

People sometimes describe Jesus as the founder of the "Christian church," but as we saw in Question A, he didn't use the word "Christian" and he didn't go to church. He was a Jew and he worshipped in the temple in Jerusalem. In the two verses of Matthew where he uses the word *ekklesia*, which is usually translated "church," he is talking about the community of Jews who follow him. If we want to say that Jesus started a church, then, we have to specify that *church* means a community and has nothing to do with church buildings, and that the community he started was Jewish.

After Jesus was gone, several communities formed around the apostles and Paul. Different groups had different ideas about what Jesus had done and how they should follow him. Many of those in Jerusalem emphasized their Jewish identity and required men joining them to be circumcised. Paul did not emphasize the distinction between Jews and gentiles, and so let noncircumcised men into the communities he started. Each of the communities founded by the apostles and Paul could be called an *ekklesia*, which is often translated as "church." The Book of Revelation, for example, is addressed from "John to the seven churches that are in Asia" (1:4).

These various churches came to be called "Christian," and Jesus was their inspiration, but from the beginning, there was never just one of them. There were only churches—communities—with different, often contrary ideas, such as about the need for circumcision. If Jesus had wanted to set up "a church"—a single community—it seems he would have spelled out the conditions for joining it. But there is no record of his doing that, which is why different churches—communities—had different ideas about who Jesus was and what he wanted of them.

A time-honored way to create an ongoing community—religious, political, or any other kind—is to write down what you believe, what your values are, what people have to do to join, how leaders will be chosen, how meetings and rituals will be conducted, and so on, and then pass down that information to the next generation. That's how, for instance, Rev. Sun Myung Moon started his Unification Church in South Korea in 1954, and how the followers of L. Ron Hubbard started the first local Church of Scientology in California in 1955.

It is also common for religious communities to establish themselves in particular places, centered in particular buildings. The Roman Catholic Church, for instance, is centered in Rome, with Saint Peter's Basilica as its main church. As far as we know, however, Jesus neither wrote anything nor told his followers to write anything. It was forty to seventy years after he was gone that people who didn't know him wrote the Gospels. Paul had written his letters in the fifties, but he never met Jesus, and so he approves of things that clash with Jesus' principles, such as slavery.

Besides not leaving written instructions, Jesus did not establish his movement in a particular place or build any buildings. Instead, he told his followers to travel from town to town, preaching, healing, and then moving on. When he sent out the twelve apostles to "proclaim the good news," he said, "Take no gold, or silver, or copper in your belts, no bag for your journey, or two tunics, or sandals, or a staff; for laborers deserve their food" (Matthew 10:7, 9–10). That is, they should travel light, letting the people they preach to feed them and give them lodging.

Eventually, various groups of Jesus' followers got organized, wrote down their ideas, and established themselves in particular places. A big impetus came from Emperor Constantine in the fourth century. He called bishops together in Nicaea and told them to write a creed. He commissioned buildings such as the Church of the Nativity in Bethlehem and the first Saint Peter's Basilica in Rome. All of this organizing and building, however, occurred long after Jesus was gone. That makes it questionable to say that Jesus started the church which Emperor Theodosius declared to be the state religion of the Roman Empire in 380.

Those who say that Jesus started a church usually refer to Matthew 16:18–19:

> You are Peter, and on this rock I will build my church, and the gates of Hades will not prevail against it. I will give you the keys of the kingdom of heaven, and whatever you bind on earth will be bound in heaven, and whatever you loose on earth will be loosed in heaven.

While this sounds like Jesus is saying that he will establish an institution and make Peter its leader, we should notice three things. First, there were no church buildings in the first century, so "build my church" can refer only to a community.

Secondly, Jesus is speaking in the future tense, about what he will do. But there is no record after that of his formally making Peter the leader of the entire community. Although the Roman Catholic Church claims that Jesus gave Peter the authority to govern all Christians, and that as first bishop of Rome Peter passed down that authority to all later popes, there is no record of Peter ever being in Rome, nor any record of his being a bishop. As Raymond Brown, past president of the Catholic Bible Association, has said, "Peter never served as the bishop or local administrator of any church, Antioch or Rome included."[1]

The third thing to notice is that two chapters later, in Matthew 18:18, Jesus says to his disciples, as a group, the same thing he says to Peter—"whatever you bind on earth will be bound in heaven, and whatever you loose on earth will be loosed in heaven." Right after that, he says, "Again, truly I tell you, if two of you agree on earth about anything you ask, it will be done for you by my Father in heaven. For where two or three are gathered in my name, I am there among them" (18: 19–20). So Jesus is not giving to Peter some special authority that he is not giving to his disciples as a group.

Succeeding generations of Jesus' followers organized themselves in different ways in different places, but not according to a master plan left by Jesus. Most early churches relied on a particular gospel rather than the four we have now. Some churches gave women prominent roles, some didn't. Some worshipped Jesus, some didn't. Some churches combined ideas from Jesus with Gnosticism—the belief that salvation can be gained through secret knowledge—while others opposed Gnosticism. After the Council of Nicaea declared Jesus Christ to be *homoousios* with God in 325, the majority of churches accepted that claim, but many did not. Later came the splits between the Roman church and the Greek churches, and then the Roman church and the Protestant churches.

If, then, "start a church" means something like "organize a religious institution and provide instructions on how to keep it going," it seems that Jesus did not start a church. What he did was preach about the Kingdom of God in a way that led to a new sect of Judaism. After he was gone, that sect came to be called "Christian," and it gradually separated from Judaism to become a number of churches.

For further reading:

Thomas Sheehan. *The First Coming: How the Kingdom of God Became Christianity*. New York: Random House, 1986.

C. DID JESUS WANT PEOPLE TO BE FORCED TO JOIN A CHURCH?

From the third century on, thousands of people were forced to join a church, in ways ranging from making it the official religion of the place where they lived to threatening to kill them if they refused. Edessa, now Urfa, in southeastern Turkey, was the first city-state to make Christianity its official religion. The first country to do that was Armenia. In 301, according to traditional accounts, most Armenians were Zoroastrians, but Saint Gregory the Illuminator convinced King Tiridates III to convert to Christianity and to have his people baptized.

In 380, as we have seen, Emperor Theodosius made Nicene Christianity the state religion of the Roman Empire, and after that, it was

illegal to follow any other religion. Around 540, Emperor Justinian ordered the forced baptism of seventy thousand people in Asia Minor.

In each case it was a particular form of Christianity that people were
forced into—the Armenian Apostolic Church, for instance, or the Roman Catholic Church. The practice of state churches has continued into
modern times. Article 1 of Pope Pius XI's 1929 Lateran Treaty with
Benito Mussolini, for instance, reaffirmed that "the Catholic, Apostolic
and Roman Religion is the only religion of the State." The Roman
Catholic Church is still the state religion of Argentina, Costa Rica, Mal-
ta, Monaco, and, of course, Vatican City. The Church of England, the
Anglican Church, has been the state religion of Britain since King Henry VIII, whom Parliament declared to be the head of that church. The
Greek Orthodox Church, the Russian Orthodox Church, and many others are also linked to states.

From the middle of the fifth century, the standard way to convert
large numbers of people to any church was to convert a king or other
leader and have him convert his community. Individuals were not asked
if they wanted to be baptized—they had to be if they wanted to continue living in their homelands. The entry for the year 498 in the *World
Christian Encyclopedia* (first edition), for example, says: "Christianity
spreading widely in Central Asia, with whole tribes converted." The
entry for 1266 notes this request from the Mongol ruler Kublai Khan to
Pope Clement IV: "Send me one hundred men skilled in your religion . . . and so I shall be baptized, and then all my barons and great
men, and then their subjects. And so there will be more Christians here
than there are in your parts." Because the pope sent only a handful of
preachers, Kublai Khan's plan failed, but if he had sent more, history
would have been quite different.

After Martin Luther split with the Roman Catholic Church in the
early 1500s, fighting broke out between Catholic and Lutheran groups.
To end it, the rulers of German-speaking states and Holy Roman Emperor Charles V worked out the Peace of Augsburg in 1555. Its main
principle was *Cuius regio, eius religio*, Latin for "Whose region, his
religion." If the prince was Lutheran, then everyone under him had to
be Lutheran. If the prince was Catholic, they had to be Catholic. No
other churches were permitted: Calvinists and Anabaptists were treated
as heretics and could be burned at the stake.

Even before the Peace of Augsburg, Sweden, Norway, Denmark, and Iceland had made their versions of Lutheranism their national religions. Today Sweden is widely considered the least religious country in the world, with just 18 percent of the population saying that they believe in God, and only 2 percent attending church regularly. Until 1996, however, newborn Swedes were automatically registered as members of the Church of Sweden as long as one of their parents was in the Church.

Forcing people to join a church was often more violent than simply declaring a state religion. In the late 700s, Frankish king Charlemagne fought for over thirty years against the Saxons in what is now Germany. When they were finally defeated, the Saxons were given a choice between baptism and death. The entry in the *World Christian Encyclopedia* for 780 is "Forced baptism of the Saxon race by Charlemagne; 4,500 executed in one day." Charlemagne exiled ten thousand of the Saxons and gave their land to the Abotrites, a group that had helped defeat them. Not surprisingly, the Saxons associated their new Christian religion with suffering. It was they who carved the oldest known crucifix, the Gero Cross, which is now in Cologne Cathedral.

In the late 1400s and early 1500s, the Catholic leaders of Spain announced that Jews and Muslims living within their borders must be baptized or get out of the country. Some 180,000 Jews had to leave. Of the 300,000 who converted and stayed, many were investigated by the Spanish Inquisition on suspicion of maintaining some Jewish practices, and 20,000 were burned at the stake as heretics. Earlier forced conversions of Jews had occurred in Spain in 1146 and 1391.

Catholics weren't the only Christians who forced people to convert. The *World Christian Encyclopedia* entry for 991 is "The whole population of Novgorod (Russia) baptized by bishop from Crimea."

All of this forced religion was quite inconsistent with Jesus' Love Ethic. He changed people's minds and hearts so that they *freely chose* to live in a new way—as brothers and sisters with God as their Father. And that is likely what he had in mind when he told his apostles, "Go therefore and make disciples of all nations, baptizing them." (Matthew 28:19). He did not mean that his followers should threaten people with exile or execution if they refused baptism.

For further reading:

Marina Caffiero. *Forced Baptisms: Histories of Jews, Christians, and Converts in Papal Rome*. Berkeley, CA: University of California Press, 2011.

D. DID JESUS WANT 34,000 CHURCHES?

We have seen how from the beginning of Christianity there was not one community but several. The splitting and the creation of new churches over the last nineteen centuries has left us with over 34,000. Figure 10.1 is a greatly simplified diagram of their development.

Among the church names that start with the letter A, you've probably heard of the Amish, the Anglicans, and the Assemblies of God. But how about the African Orthodox Autonomous Church South of the Sahara, the All-One-Faith-In-One-God-State, Inc., the Amanazarites, the American Carpatho-Russian Orthodox Greek Catholic Church, and the Apostolic Overcoming Holy Church of God? Among churches that no longer exist are the Abecedarians (pronounced "A-B-C-darians," taken from their contempt for knowledge, including learning the alphabet), the Acephalites (the Headless Ones), the Adiaphorists (the Indifferent Ones), the Agapemonites (the Love Dwellers), and the Angel Dancers. The number of churches continues to grow year by year. When the first edition of the *World Christian Encyclopedia* came out in 1982, it counted 20,800 denominations. Less than twenty years later, the second edition counted 33,820 "denominations and paradenominations." Could this ever-expanding diversity be what Jesus intended?

Churches aren't like restaurants. New York City, with its 4,200 restaurants, is an eater's paradise. It's great to be able to have French food on Monday, Japanese food on Wednesday, and Peruvian food on the weekend. The world's churches, however, are based on contrary beliefs, and it's simple logic that where two groups have contrary beliefs, they can't both be right. Fundamentalist Christians, for instance, insist that Genesis is literally true, and so everything was created in six days. Many nonfundamentalist Christians say that Genesis is not literal history, so animals may have evolved over millions of years. Either Genesis is literally true or it isn't, so one side in this debate believes something false. Similarly, most Western churches teach that Jesus' death on the cross was a sacrifice that atoned for human sin, while Eastern churches

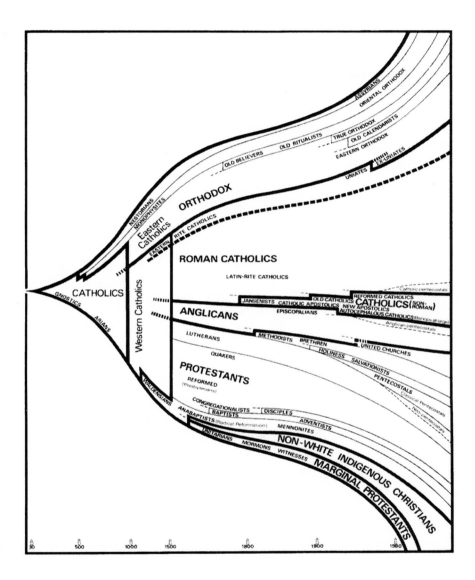

Figure 10.1. Development of New Churches (*World Christian Encyclopedia*, 1e. 1982. Figure "Fission and fusion in World Christian Traditions, AD 30–1985" from p. 35. By permission of Oxford University Press, U.S.)

deny that. The Roman Catholic Church says that Jesus created seven sacraments; most Protestant churches say there are only two sacraments. In the Eucharist, Catholics say, bread and wine are changed into the actual body and blood of Jesus Christ. Most Baptists say that the Eucharist only symbolizes the body and blood of Christ. Some Anglican churches ordain women as priests; the Roman Catholic Church insists that it's metaphysically impossible for a female to become a priest. Many churches say that homosexual activity is inherently sinful, while a growing number of churches deny that claim. On any of these issues, at least one side has to have a false belief, and Jesus would not agree with a false belief.

Making it even more dubious that Jesus wanted there to be thousands of churches is that they haven't just disagreed, but have killed each other over their beliefs. As Garry Wills says,

> The great scandal of Christians is the way they have persecuted fellow Christians, driving out heretics, shunning them, burning their books, burning them. Mary Tudor of England burned at the stake hundreds of Protestants. Elizabeth I of England had Jesuits physically chopped to pieces. Inquisitions executed all kinds of heretics. Popes preached crusades against Albigensians. New England Calvinists hanged Quakers. American Protestants burned convents.

All of this hatred and violence, of course, is utterly incompatible with Jesus' Love Ethic. "By this everyone will know that you are my disciples, if you have love for one another" (John 13:35). Jesus didn't teach or enforce doctrines, but where his beliefs or moral principles clashed with other people's, his response was not to kill them, but to talk with them to win them over. Killing is hardly a way to correct someone's error.

Paul writes to the Galatians, "My friends, if anyone is detected in a transgression, you who have received the Spirit should restore such a one in a spirit of gentleness" (6:1). Even if someone is clearly in the wrong, hostility is not the appropriate response. In his First Letter to the Thessalonians, Paul writes, "We urge you, beloved, to admonish the idlers, encourage the fainthearted, help the weak, be patient with all of them. See that none of you repays evil for evil, but always seek to do good to one another and to all" (5:14–15). Similarly, the Letter of James advises, "Let everyone be quick to listen, slow to speak, slow to anger" (1:19).

The first few centuries of Christians followed such advice, but then, as creeds became the test of being a Christian, violence was added to theological disagreements. In 380, Nicene Christianity became the state religion of the Roman Empire, and then disagreeing with the Nicene Creed was a crime punishable by death. Five years later, as we've seen, executions for heresy began. Between the Council of Nicaea in 325 and 550, as we've also mentioned, theological disagreements led to at least twenty-five thousand deaths. And since then, more than that number of Christians have been killed by other Christians in the name of correct belief.

Two of the major battle lines drawn between Christians have been, first, between the Western Roman Catholic Church and the Eastern Orthodox churches; and second, between the Roman Catholic Church and Protestant churches. Both conflicts are still alive today.

In the conflict between the Western and Eastern churches, one major issue is the authority of the pope. Starting with Leo I (440–461), popes claimed that they were not just bishops of Rome but the supreme rulers over all other bishops. They based that claim to supremacy on the idea that they were successors to the apostle Peter, the first bishop of Rome, whom Jesus made the first supreme leader of the church. The bishops of Constantinople, Jerusalem, Alexandria, Antioch, and other large cities rejected that argument and saw themselves as equals of the bishop of Rome, rather than his subjects.

Another major issue that split the Western and Eastern churches was a theological disagreement called the *Filioque* question. That's Latin for "and the Son." The Nicene Creed of 325 said of the Holy Spirit simply, "We believe in the Holy Spirit." In 381 at the First Council of Constantinople, that was expanded to "We believe in the Holy Spirit, the Lord, the giver of life, who proceeds from the Father. With the Father and the Son he is worshipped and glorified. He has spoken through the Prophets." In that longer creed, the Son is "begotten of" the Father, and the Holy Spirit "proceeds from" the Father. That makes it sound like the Father is superior to both of them. Theologians who championed the equality of the Son with the Father didn't like that implication. They wanted a creed in which the Son does something that the Father does, and producing the Holy Spirit seemed right for that purpose. So a number of theologians in the West began saying that the Holy Spirit "proceeds from the Father *and the Son*." That was eventually written into copies made of the 381 creed. Theologians and bishops in the East rejected that addition, pointing out that the creed said only that the Holy Spirit "proceeds from the Father."

These disagreements, along with other differences in theology, liturgy, and politics, created more and more animosity between Eastern and Western churches over the next five centuries, until in 1053 Michael Cerularius, patriarch of Constantinople, closed all the Latin churches in the city. The next year the pope sent a delegation to Constantinople to demand that Cerularius accept his supreme authority. When the patriarch refused, Cardinal Humbert, leader of the pope's delegation, excommunicated him—declared him to no longer be a Christian. In return, Cerularius excommunicated Humbert and the other delegates.

This splitting of the two churches is called the Great Schism, and it has never healed completely. A century and a half later, in 1204, in the Fourth Crusade, Western Christians invaded Constantinople and sacked the city. Some of the crusaders stayed on, establishing the Latin Empire (1204–1261) and other "Latin states" in the areas they conquered. Eventually, the crusaders were driven out, but the memory of their unprovoked invasion lingers on, as could be seen in 2000 when Pope John Paul II said he would like to visit Greece on a religious pilgrimage. Archbishop Kallinikos of the Greek Orthodox Church replied that the pope was welcome in Greece as the political head of Vatican City, but would not be allowed to make a religious visit as head of the Roman Catholic Church until that church "does penance" for the many indignities committed against the Eastern churches over the centuries.

The other great split, as we said, was between the Roman Catholic Church and the Protestant churches. What were at first disagreements about theological issues and church policies such as the sale of indulgences eventually grew into armed conflict. The century and a half of violence following the Protestant Reformation is often called the Wars of Religion. During the Thirty Years' War (1618–1648), fighting between Catholics and Protestants is estimated to have killed 15 to 30 percent of the people in the German states, including almost half the males. In France, a succession of kings and Catholic authorities persecuted the Protestant Huguenots: in 1547, seventy-two thousand were executed; in 1572, another seventy thousand. In Spain, Protestants were virtually eliminated by being burned at the stake.

Obviously, all of this violence between various churches clashes with the Love Ethic of Jesus in the most profound way. The division of his followers into warring factions cannot be what he had in mind.

For further reading:

David B. Barrett, George T. Kurian, and Todd M. Johnson, eds. *World Christian Encyclopedia*. 2nd ed. New York: Oxford University Press, 2000.

E. DO ANY CHURCHES TODAY EMBODY JESUS' KINGDOM OF GOD?

If Jesus did not plan the 34,000 denominations we have today, did he plan any of them? Are any churches what he meant by the Kingdom of God? Did any of them get it right? To answer these questions, we can go back to the Ten Tenets of Jesus in chapter 1, and compare churches against them:

1. Love Ethic: Love God and love all people.
2. God's Children: All human beings are brothers and sisters, with God as their Father.
3. Equality: Each person counts the same.
4. Socialism: From each according to their ability, to each according to their needs.
5. Servant Leadership: Leading people should not be dominating them, but serving them.
6. Festivity: Celebrate your loving relationships.
7. Antilegalism: Minimize the number of rules, and apply them flexibly to benefit people.
8. Divine Judgment: God alone is judge.
9. Forgiveness: Be ready to forgive anyone for anything.
10. Pacifism: "Do not resist an evildoer" (Matthew 5:39).

We cannot consider all 34,000 churches, but will look at five representative traditions: Roman Catholic, Orthodox, Lutheran, Calvinist, and Anabaptist. The points we make about them can be applied to most other churches.

ROMAN CATHOLIC AND ORTHODOX CHURCHES

In chapter 1, when we traced the development of Christianity over the first 350 years, we were talking about the early forms of these two groups, before they split. In that early period, as we saw, churches changed radically—from following Jesus' way of life to emulating the Roman Empire, which had made Christianity its state religion. Then in the Middle Ages and modern times, the disparity between what Jesus had preached and what the Roman Catholic and Orthodox churches did increased in several ways. Consider the Ten Tenets.

Tenet 1. Love Ethic

In the early churches, the emphasis was on caring for people—on preaching the Gospel to them and helping them live fulfilling lives. Christians who owned property sold it and gave the proceeds for distribution to those in need. There were no church buildings and Christians had no political power. Starting in the fourth century, however, bishops were given money, land, and buildings by emperors, and from then through the Middle Ages, they got more and more concerned with things other than the people they were supposed to serve. Modeling themselves on Roman governors, they worked to maintain and increase their own power. The pope adopted the title *Pontifex Maximus*—Greatest Bridge Builder—from the emperor. We still call the pope the "pontiff." Over the centuries, the concentration of the pope's power grew, as did the money and effort devoted to glorifying the papacy. If you've ever watched the election and inauguration of a pope on television, you've seen the display of wealth and status in Saint Peter's Basilica. Billions of dollars have been spent on architecture, sculptures, paintings, tapestries, vestments, ritual vessels, crucifixes, the Swiss Guard, and so on. The visual effect is to induce awe at the glory and splendor of the church's leaders. The pope is king of the church, and the cardinals are the "Princes of the Church" whom he addresses as "Lord Cardinals." You may have heard of the special red Prada shoes made for popes. Before the 1960s, they displayed their absolute power over the church and over the Vatican state by wearing a special tiara—three crowns nested into one large beehive shape. In Orthodox churches, bishops wear similar crowns, and there is great emphasis on rich finery even in ordinary rituals—expensive vestments and artwork, incense, and so on. All of this display shows a shift away from Jesus' criticisms of wealth and from his emphasis on caring for people.

Tenet 2. God's Children

In treating themselves as "holy father" and patriarch (father ruler), church leaders also strayed from Jesus' teaching that we are all God's children. "Call no one your father on earth," he said, "for you have one Father—the one in heaven" (Matthew 23:9). So no early Christian called another "father" in the way that priests, bishops, and popes were later called that. All Christians were God's children.

Tenet 3. Equality

Starting in the late second century, church leaders began thinking of Christians as consisting of two unequal classes—clergy and laity—with clergy being the higher, more religious class. There was no such division in the first century. The apostles were all "laypeople" and so was Jesus. In Paul's letters and in the Acts of the Apostles, at least twenty ministerial roles are mentioned, but none is "priest." Paul talks about thirteen roles in his first Letter to the Corinthians—emissaries, prophets, teachers, miracle workers, healers, assistants, guides, speakers in tongues, interpreters of speakers in tongues, wise men, interpreters of wisdom, spirit testers, and trainers. In Romans 12:6–8 he adds stewards, exhorters, distributors, patrons, and almsgivers; and in Ephesians 4:11 evangelists and shepherds. These are all functions, not job titles, and none is that of priest, bishop, or pope.

Early Christians did share Eucharistic meals, but there is no indication that anyone had an official role of presiding over those meals. As Hans Küng and Garry Wills show in books both titled *Why Priests?* there were no Christian priests in the first century.[2] All Christians were what were later called "laypeople."

The creation of the "higher" class of priests also fostered another kind of inequality, between women and men. Jesus treated women as equals. Paul describes many women as leaders in early Christian communities; he calls Junia "prominent among the apostles" (Romans 16:7). In a first-century fresco in the catacomb of Saint Priscilla in Rome, a woman is shown breaking the Eucharistic bread for six other women. But after Christianity became the religion of the Roman Empire, men reverted to the ancient pattern of dominating women and so banned them from leadership roles in the church. That ban has continued to this day in the Catholic and Orthodox churches. In 1994 Pope John Paul II wrote the apostolic letter *Ordinatio sacerdotalis*, in which he said, "I declare that the Church has no authority whatsoever to confer priestly ordination on women and that this judgment is to be definitively held by all the Church's faithful." Pope Benedict XVI reaffirmed the impossibility of ordaining women, and in 2008 decreed that any woman seeking ordination, and any bishop seeking to ordain a woman, would be immediately excommunicated. In 2010, the Vatican called such attempts *delicta graviora*—grave crimes against the church.

Late in the third century, the Catholic and Orthodox churches created yet another male class that was treated as higher and more religious than laypeople—hermits and monks. Men like Saint Anthony of Egypt withdrew from society to live austere lives alone, often in the desert. Saint Simon Stylites lived for thirty-seven years on a meter-square platform atop a pillar, forbidding any woman to come near. Eventually, some hermits formed communities and built monasteries. None of this withdrawal from society was based on Jesus' Kingdom of God. There were no hermits or monks among his disciples. Jesus didn't tell his followers to live apart from other people, or that doing so would make them better. His message was quite the opposite—feed the hungry, give drink to the thirsty, clothe the naked, welcome strangers, take care of the sick, and visit people in prison (Matthew 25:35–36).

In the Middle Ages, the supposedly superior "religious" classes of clergy and monks assumed more and more power and prestige, in further violation of Jesus' egalitarianism. They were the only classes, for example, who were taught to read and write.

Medieval society had three strata: those who pray on top, closest to God; those who fight (knights and soldiers); and those who work (serfs). Most bishops were noblemen from landowning families, further increasing their superiority to other classes of Christians. In parts of Europe, the church had vast land holdings and bishops commanded armies, sometimes leading them into battle.

At the bottom of the medieval social hierarchy were 90 percent of the population—the serfs, who lived and worked on manors owned by lords and who could not leave the manor or marry without the lord's permission. They tilled the fields; raised the livestock; and made the buildings, clothing, and other things needed for daily life. Though they did almost all the essential work, they were not treated as equals of the clergy and the lords. Instead, the clergy and lords were served by them and had almost complete power over their lives.

With all this inequality in medieval Christianity, it's not surprising that church leaders did not condemn the most unequal social arrangement of all—slavery. Popes, bishops, and monastic orders owned slaves, as did Orthodox leaders and monasteries. Pope Paul III, who reigned from 1534 to 1549 and called the Council of Trent to reform the Catholic Church, even sanctioned the enslavement of baptized Christians in Rome. While he did criticize cruel treatment of slaves, he also affirmed the right of clergy and laypeople to own them. That was the standard position of the Catholic Church and was reaffirmed as late as 1866 by Pope Pius IX. In a papal instruction of June 20 (number 1293), which some historians say was a rebuke to the Thirteenth Amendment in the United States, which prohibited slavery, Pius wrote:

> Slavery itself, considered as such in its essential nature, is not at all contrary to the natural and divine law, and there can be several just titles of slavery and these are referred to by approved theologians and commentators of the sacred canons. . . . It is not contrary to the natural and divine law for a slave to be sold, bought, exchanged, or given.

Tenet 4. Socialism

As the Catholic and Orthodox churches amassed land and wealth, the socialism of early Christians described in Acts 4:32–35 was largely forgotten. The resources of Christians were not pooled to distribute to those in need. Bishops and popes had more in common with landowners than with peasants, and so they tended to favor the rich. In the nineteenth century, when socialism became a political goal of revolutionary groups, Pope Leo XIII condemned it in his 1891 encyclical *Rerum Novarum*: "It is clear that the main tenet of Socialism, community of goods, must be utterly rejected, since it only injures those whom it would seem to benefit. . . . The first and most fundamental principle, if one undertakes to alleviate the condition of the masses, must be the inviolability of private property." This condemnation was reaffirmed by Pope Pius XI in his 1931 encyclical *Quadragesimo Anno*: "No one can be at the same time a good Catholic and a true socialist."

Tenet 5. Servant Leadership

Jesus' preaching about how "the greatest among you must become like the youngest, and the leader like one who serves" (Luke 22:26) was also forgotten, as bishops and popes became more concerned about enhancing their own positions than about the welfare of the people they led. Servant leaders would not bedeck and bejewel themselves in the expensive regalia worn by bishops, popes, and patriarchs. Church leaders did most of the things imperial leaders did—conduct large public rituals, acquire and lease land, tax people, and raise armies. In the Eastern Empire, the church was led by the emperor, following Constantine's claim to be "the bishop of bishops." After the Western Roman Empire collapsed in the late 400s, the pope was thought of as a substitute for the missing emperor in Rome, and in the early Middle Ages, he came to dominate the areas we now call Spain, France, and Germany.

Tenet 6. Festivity

As in early Christianity, the medieval and modern Catholic and Orthodox churches have set aside times for celebrations. The focus, however, has usually been not on the people involved, as at the marriage feast at Cana, but on something else, such as a saint's feast day or the visit of a church leader. Instead of being banquets of equals celebrating their community, church events have often been rituals at which laypeople were mere spectators.

Tenet 7. Antilegalism

While Jesus ignored most of the 613 biblical laws and reduced the applicable ones to loving God and loving people, the Roman Catholic and Orthodox churches developed complex systems of moral laws and their interpretation similar to those in rabbinic Judaism and made

Christian morality into a branch of doctrine. In managing church affairs, the Roman church developed a system of canon law complete with courts, lawyers, and judges that was modeled on the law code of Roman emperor Justinian. When published in 1983, the 1,752 canons filled seven books totaling 1,631 pages. The Orthodox Church also has a system of canon laws.

This legalistic approach to morality and church government is fundamentally different from Jesus' Love Ethic. "You shall love the Lord your God with all your heart, and with all your soul, and with all your mind" is not really a law, since it can't be enforced. You can be arrested for stealing a watch if you walk out of the store without paying for it. It's clear that the watch doesn't belong to you and yet you took it from the store. That offense took place on a particular date, at a particular time, in a particular place. But how would someone determine whether you had loved God "with all your heart, and with all your soul, and with all your mind"? When and where did that happen—or not happen—a critic might ask. How many times did it happen, or not happen? There's no sensible answer for such questions, because "You shall love the Lord your God with all your heart, and with all your soul, and with all your mind" is not a law but an ideal to strive for. In reality, probably no one has ever loved God totally, with all her heart, all her soul, and all her mind. It's obvious that Catholic and Orthodox Christians treat this as an ideal, not a law, in the way that, in confessing their sins, they don't say "I failed to love God with all my heart, all my soul, and all my mind."

Similarly, how would someone determine that you had not, or had, loved your neighbor as yourself? This, too, is not an enforceable law but an ideal to strive for. At our best, we will care as much about other people as we do about ourselves. But consider a day on which I ate three good meals but didn't contribute anything to the thirty-five thousand children who died of starvation around the world. Did I break a law that day? How many times? Did I break another law by not helping the millions suffering from cancer that day? And another law by not visiting prisoners? The whole law-based approach to morality that Christians adopted from Roman law just doesn't work with Jesus' Love Ethic.[3]

Tenet 8. Divine Judgment

Because human beings can't determine just what goes on in other people's minds and hearts, they are not very good at judging them morally.
Besides, Jesus said to leave such judgment to God. That's the point of
his parable of the wheat and the weeds (Matthew 13:24–30, 36–43).
The servants ask the master if they should dig up the weeds growing
along with the wheat, and he says, "Let both of them grow together
until the harvest; and at harvest time I will tell the reapers, 'Collect the
weeds first and bind them in bundles to be burned, but gather the
wheat into my barn.'" In chapter 1 we linked this idea that God alone is
judge to Jesus' preaching in Luke 6:37: "Do not judge, and you will not
be judged; do not condemn, and you will not be condemned. Forgive,
and you will be forgiven."

However much early Christians followed Jesus' teaching that God
alone is the one to judge and punish, churches since the fourth century
have engaged in the harshest kinds of judgment and punishment. Shortly after Christianity became the state religion of the Roman Empire, as
we've seen, Bishop Priscillian and six of his followers were beheaded for
heresy. Augustine judged the Donatists to be heretics for saying that
bishops who had renounced their faith should no longer serve as bishops, and he created his just war theory to legitimize waging war against
them. Between 325 and 550, Christians killed at least twenty-five thousand other Christians for having supposedly incorrect beliefs. From
1209 to 1220 Pope Innocent III conducted a crusade to wipe out the
Cathars, whom he judged to be heretics. In destroying the city of Béziers, the crusaders slaughtered twenty thousand Cathars.

The Catholic Church established the Inquisition in 1229 as a permanent investigation team to root out heretics. The thousands they tried,
judged, and punished over the centuries included converted Jews and
Muslims suspected of reverting to their old religions and women and
men suspected of witchcraft and devil worship. The Inquisition
changed its name to the Supreme Sacred Congregation of the Holy
Office in 1904, and then the Confraternity for the Doctrine of the Faith
in 1965. It was headed by Joseph Cardinal Ratzinger before he became
Pope Benedict XVI. One of the actions he took was ordering Father
Leonardo Boff, a leader of the liberation theology movement in Latin
America, to cease writing and speaking about liberation theology.[4]

Beyond judging some Catholics negatively, of course, the Roman Catholic Church has judged all non-Catholics negatively, especially for not having the true religion. According to Catholic doctrine, Protestants are heretics and Orthodox churches are schismatic.

The Orthodox churches have had far fewer heresy trials than the Catholic church, partly because the church in each area is self-governing—the Russian Orthodox Church, the Serbian Orthodox Church, the Romanian Orthodox Church, and so on. But they are not immune from judging outside groups. Orthodox churches, for example, judge all Roman Catholics and Protestants to be heretics. Jesus' principle that only God is to judge people, then, has long been forgotten in both of the two oldest Christian traditions.

Tenet 9. Forgiveness

Evaluating the Roman and Orthodox churches on this tenet is straightforward. When you judge and then kill a person, you haven't forgiven them. Both churches have the sacrament of penance, of course, to confer God's forgiveness for sins, but that is a different matter from humans forgiving each other, which is what Jesus was talking about. Even at the highest levels, church leaders have shown a reluctance to forgive. An old example is the animosity between the popes and the patriarchs of Constantinople. After their mutual excommunication in 1054, it was over nine centuries before they withdrew those hostile gestures—in 1965. In 1995 Pope John Paul II and Patriarch Bartholomew I of Constantinople again withdrew the excommunications, and in 1999 John Paul became the first pope since 1054 to visit an Eastern Orthodox country, Romania. Clearly, however, there had been no full mutual forgiveness. As mentioned in question D, in 2000 when Pope John Paul II asked to visit Greece on a religious pilgrimage, Archbishop of Athens and All Greece Kallinikos told him he was welcome as the ruler of Vatican City, but not as the ruler of the Roman Catholic Church.

Tenet 10. Pacifism

Since killing a person is the most serious action you can perform, the morality of killing is the most serious part of ethics. As we saw in chapter 9, Jesus preached nonviolence and pacifism, and so the first three centuries of Christians opposed all killing, including capital punishment and war. Once Christianity became the state religion of the Roman Empire in 380, however, Christians quickly overturned the central principle of Jesus, "Do not resist an evildoer" (Matthew 5:39). They now joined the army freely, and in 416 the empire *required* Roman soldiers to be Christians. On joining the army, their new oath was sworn "By God, Christ, and the Holy Spirit, and by the majesty of the emperor, which second to God is to be loved and worshipped by the human race."

The record of religiously sanctioned Christian violence from then to now is well known. Almost all the fighting in Europe between 500 and 1500 was done by Catholic and Orthodox soldiers, and their bishops, popes, and patriarchs did not dissuade them with Jesus' preaching about nonviolence. Indeed, bishops and popes often started the violence, as in the Crusades. Today, millions of Catholic and Orthodox Christians, like Christians generally, praise military service as noble, even as a sacred duty. The vast majority of the 65 million combatants in World War I were Christians, as were most of the 105 million in World War II. Tens of millions of them were Catholic and Orthodox, and their churches supported them with prayers and chaplains. The Catholic Church did not excommunicate or even publicly condemn Adolf Hitler, one of history's worst warmongers. Indeed, it made a treaty with him in 1933 that forced the only sizeable opposition he had in Germany, the Catholic Centre Party, to disband. That allowed him to assume absolute power in Germany and then launch World War II.

Of the Ten Tenets of Jesus, then, pacifism is the one most egregiously violated.

LUTHERAN AND CALVINIST CHURCHES

In the 1500s Martin Luther and John Calvin broke away from the Roman Catholic Church, and their followers formed several new churches that are now called Protestant. Churches inspired by Luther usually have "Lutheran" in their names, but most churches following Calvin do not include his name in theirs—the Netherlands Reformed Church, for instance, and the various Presbyterian churches.

Much of what Luther and Calvin were protesting, such as corruption in the Catholic hierarchy, stemmed from the division between priests and monks, on the one hand, and lay Christians on the other. In eliminating priests and monks from their groups, Luther and Calvin created greater equality—at least for men within their churches. Equality for women was centuries in the future, and men outside their communities—most notably, slaves—were not always thought of as equal, either.

Not dividing people into "religious" and "lay," the Lutheran and Calvinist churches also dropped a lot of the hierarchical organization and elaborate ritual of the Catholic Church. Together those changes brought Christians closer to Jesus' preaching about God's children— that all people are brothers and sisters, with only God as Father.

In Luther's and Calvin's new churches, tenet 5, Servant Leadership, was also better supported. As in Jesus' preaching, Paul's letters, and the Acts of the Apostles, Lutheran and Calvinist ministers were there to serve people. Tenet 6, Festivity, was reinforced, as socializing tended to focus on the people involved rather than things like saints' feast days. Reducing church hierarchy and the emphasis on tradition also helped somewhat with tenet 7, Antilegalism.

Tenet 4, Socialism, was not part of Luther's or Calvin's reforms. Tenets 8 and 9—Divine Judgment and Forgiveness—were little better served, as Lutherans and Calvinists also conducted heresy trials and punished rather than forgave. Churches descended from Luther and Calvin, too, have often judged other churches harshly. The *Westminster Confession of Faith*, for instance, says that the pope is the Antichrist (chapter 25) and that the Catholic Mass is a form of idolatry (chapter 29).

Tenet 10, Pacifism, was not a principle of Luther or Calvin. Overlooking the nonviolence in Jesus' preaching, their followers and Catholics fought for a century and a half. After that, too, support for wars of all kinds was just as strong among Lutherans and Calvinists as among Catholics. Most of the eighteen million who fought in Hitler's *Wehrmacht* (armed forces), for example, were Lutherans.

Nonetheless, on balance, if we use the Ten Tenets as a checklist, it looks like Luther's and Calvin's reforms should have created churches that were significantly closer to Jesus' worldview than Roman Catholicism and Orthodoxy had been. What greatly weakened that tendency, however, was Luther and Calvin's doctrine of the total depravity of human beings, which we examined in chapter 6. Also called "radical corruption" and "absolute inability," this teaching seems quite incompatible with Jesus' Love Ethic.

The Catholic Church, as we have seen, teaches original sin—that all humans inherit the sin of Adam along with his fallen nature. Nonetheless, it also teaches that human beings have retained a basic goodness and free will. In Luther's and Calvin's understanding of original sin, however, the corruption of human nature was so total that we have no good inclinations and no longer have free will.

Someone who accepts this utterly pessimistic description of human beings cannot consistently also accept the Love Ethic of Jesus. Jesus preached that we should love God and love other people. That assumes two things. First, we are able to love God and love people. It doesn't make sense to tell people they should do something they are unable to do. The second assumption is that there is something to love in people—something good, something worth caring about. But in Luther and Calvin's doctrine of total depravity, both of these assumptions are false.

First, according to Luther and Calvin, we are unable to love God or love people, because doing either would be doing something good, and it is not within our power to do anything good. That's why another name for this doctrine is "absolute inability." The human will, Calvin said, "cannot aspire after anything that is good."[5]

Second, according to Luther and Calvin, there isn't anything to love in people, anyway—nothing good for us to care about. All human beings are totally depraved, "defiled and polluted." I said above that to love other people would be good, but if people are totally depraved, then even that doesn't seem right. Wouldn't loving something that is totally depraved be itself depraved? If you told me you had a newfound love for Satan, I'd scratch my head in disbelief. How can you possibly love Satan, I'd ask, when Satan is "opposite to all good, and wholly inclined to all evil"? No Christian should love Satan.

Though the words above—"opposite to all good, and wholly inclined to all evil"—do apply to Satan, I got them from the *Westminster Confession of Faith*, chapter 6, sections 2 and 4, where they are applied to human beings. According to the doctrine of total depravity, people are "opposite to all good, and wholly inclined to all evil." But if that's true, then, just as we should not love Satan, we should not love people, because there is nothing good in either of them. If Luther and Calvin were right, how could we even love ourselves, when we are as totally depraved as everyone else?

To check Luther and Calvin's claims, we can turn to the Gospels. There we don't find anything about total depravity. Jesus doesn't teach that we inherit original sin from Adam, that we have no free will, or that we are unable to do anything good. On the contrary, he teaches that human beings are of such great worth that God loves us as his children. Why would God love us as his children if we are totally depraved? Jesus also says, "Love one another, as I have loved you" (John 15:12). If there is nothing to love in human beings, why would Jesus love us, or tell us to love each other?

And if it is not within our power to do good actions, why did Jesus preach so often about doing good actions? Why did he say in Matthew 25:31–46 that the criteria for entrance into heaven at the Last Judgment will be whether we fed the hungry, gave drink to the thirsty, welcomed strangers, clothed the naked, cared for the sick, and visited those in prison?

To illustrate what "Love your neighbor as yourself" means, Jesus tells the story of the Samaritan coming upon a man beaten by robbers and left for dead (Luke 10:30–37). The Samaritan

> bandaged his wounds, having poured oil and wine on them. Then he put him on his own animal, brought him to an inn, and took care of him. The next day he took out two denarii [two day's wages for a laborer], gave them to the innkeeper, and said, "Take care of him; and when I come back, I will repay you whatever more you spend."

If Luther and Calvin are right, however, there could not be a "good Samaritan"—because there are no good human beings at all. Jesus' preaching about caring for other people, then, is pointless. His Love Ethic makes sense only if people are able to care about each other, and if people are worthy of such care. Luther and Calvin's doctrine of total depravity is thus incompatible with Jesus' Love Ethic.

That's why love is seldom mentioned in the writings of consistent Lutherans and Calvinists. In chapter 6, section B, we mentioned Rev. R. C. Sproul, one of the best-known proponents of Calvinism. If you look for "love" in the index of his book *What Is Reformed Theology?*

you'll find nothing about love of people and just one page listed under "love of God." Turning to it, you'll find this:

> Love for God is not natural to us. Even in the redeemed state our souls grow cold and we experience feelings of indifference toward him. When we pray, our minds wander and we indulge in woolgathering. In the midst of corporate worship, we are bored and find ourselves taking peeks at our watches. . . . Our natural lack of love for God is confirmed by our natural lack of desire for him.[6]

Then Sproul cites Luther's answer to the question, "Do you love God?"

> Luther replied (prior to his conversion), "Love God? Sometimes I hate him." This is a rare admission among men. Even Luther's candid reply was less that totally honest. Had he spoke the full truth, he would have said that he hated God all the time.[7]

While Luther and Calvin emphasize human equality, then, it does us little good to be equal if we are equally depraved, unlovable, and worthy only of God's wrath.

ANABAPTIST CHURCHES

Luther and Calvin are the most famous early Protestant leaders, but there were dozens more. In the 1520s, in Zurich, Switzerland, Conrad Greibel started a group that came to be known as Anabaptists. Like "Christians," "Anabaptists" was at first a derogatory term used by their opponents. Also called the Radical Reformation, these people wanted to return to the Christianity described in the New Testament. One of their issues was whether infants should be baptized when they don't understand what baptism is and they can't make a faith commitment. Only adults who chose to follow Jesus were baptized in the first century, the Anabaptists said, and that is how it should still be. So if someone had been baptized as a child and wanted to join the Anabaptists, they were rebaptized. That's where "Ana-baptist" comes from: in Greek, *ana* means "again."

Anabaptists agreed with other Protestants that there should be no special class of ordained clergy, and they tended to give each congregation authority in self-governance and in matters of doctrine. They did not emphasize creeds.

Unlike Catholics, Orthodox, Lutherans, and Calvinists, they also argued that Christian churches should be kept separate from civil governments. In his book *Concerning Heretics and Those Who Burn Them* (1524), Anabaptist leader Balthasar Hubmaier condemned state-imposed churches and advocated freedom of religion, even for atheists.

Besides advocating political freedom, Anabaptists generally believed that human beings have free will, at least after they turn to Christ. They avoided using the term "original sin," since it's not in the Bible, and they did not believe that human beings are born depraved or inherit Adam's guilt. In Hubmaier's *Concerning Free Will* (1527), he quotes the prophet Ezekiel: "The son shall not bear the iniquities of the father nor shall the father bear the iniquities of the son" (Ezekiel 18:20).

From the Acts of the Apostles, some Anabaptists got the idea of common ownership of property. Following Jesus' preaching "Do not resist an evildoer" (Matthew 5:39), they were mostly pacifists and refused military service.

If we compare these Anabaptist beliefs with what Jesus said and did, they line up pretty well. Baptizing only believing adults is what the first Christians did. So is treating people as equals, with no special class of priests. A lack of emphasis on doctrine and a lack of legalism also match early Christianity. And while many Christian churches later got intertwined with governments, Jesus never advocated that, and it caused great harm. So keeping church and state separate seems like a good idea.

Here the contrast with Luther and Calvin is striking. Luther's *Augsburg Confession* (1630) is addressed to the holy Roman emperor: "Most Invincible Emperor, Caesar Augustus, most Clement Lord: Inasmuch as Your Imperial Majesty has summoned a Diet [assembly] of the Empire here at Augsburg . . . " Calvin was given supreme leadership of the city of Geneva, Switzerland, and in November 1552 the city council declared his *Institutes of the Christian Religion* to be a "holy doctrine which no man might speak against."

The Anabaptist understanding of human beings as having free will, not inheriting Adam's guilt, and not being totally depraved also contrasts with Luther and Calvin, and seems far more compatible with Jesus' Love Ethic. So do Anabaptist ideas about socialism and especially pacifism. Since killing people is the most serious action possible, a version of Christianity that gets the ethics of killing wrong is seriously mistaken. As we have seen, not just Lutheranism and Calvinism, but the Catholic and Orthodox traditions reject Jesus' pacifism.

Well aware of these and other differences, Lutheran, Calvinist, and Catholic authorities persecuted Anabaptists widely through the sixteenth and seventeenth centuries. Anabaptism was made a capital crime in many places. Even giving them food and shelter could be a crime. In 1527 the Duke of Bavaria ordered that the Anabaptists in his prisons be burned at the stake unless they recanted—in which case they were beheaded. Ferdinand I, Catholic king of Austria and holy Roman emperor (1503–1564), said that drowning them—"the third baptism," he mockingly called it—was "the best antidote to Anabaptism." Through all this persecution, Anabaptists stuck to their pacifism and didn't fight back.

Nonetheless, churches inspired by the Anabaptists gradually spread throughout Europe and—to escape persecution—to North America. With no stress on uniform doctrine, there was considerable variety among them, some advocating extreme chastity, for example, and others allowing sexual freedom.

Today, the largest group that counts the Anabaptists as spiritual ancestors are the Baptist churches. With forty-three million members worldwide and thirty-three million in the United States, they are the largest Protestant group of all. Scholars point out, however, that the first Baptist church sprang from a group splitting from the Church of England around 1606 and that there is little evidence of a strong influence of Anabaptism on them or on today's Baptists. In 1624, in fact, the five Baptist churches of London issued a condemnation of the Anabaptists.[8]

Of the thirty Baptist denominations in the United States, the largest by far is the Southern Baptist Convention, with fifteen million members. This group started in 1845 in a split with northern Baptists over slavery. It never had any formal or informal connections with Anabaptist groups. On issues like pacifism and refusing military service, most Southern Baptists have views contrary to the early Anabaptists. Many Southern Baptists, too, have Calvinist beliefs that are opposed to Anabaptist views on free will and total depravity. In surveys by LifeWay Christian Resources and the North American Mission Board, 30 percent of recent graduates of Southern Baptist seminaries described themselves as "five-point Calvinists."[9] That means they accept the five basic teachings of Calvin, the first of which is total depravity.

If we want to find churches today that are direct descendants of the Anabaptists, we have to look beyond large churches to small groups, primarily the Mennonites, Amish, and Hutterites. The total membership of all three around the world is less than two million. That's less than one-tenth of 1 percent of the world's 2,100,000,000 Christians.

The Mennonites were started by Menno Simons (1496–1561), a priest from Friesland (now in the Netherlands) who left the Catholic Church to lead Anabaptists in the Netherlands and northern Germany. He emphasized nonviolence and withdrawal from worldly pursuits. His followers today are noted for peacemaking, as by their Christian Peacemaker Teams; helping people in need, as by the Mennonite Disaster Service; and their commitment to social justice.

In 1693 there was a serious division among Mennonites in Switzerland when Jacob Ammann called for stricter discipline. His group then broke away to become the Amish. Today they are known for their simple dress, rural way of life, rejection of modern technology, and pacifism.

The Hutterites are an Anabaptist group started in 1533 by Jacob Hutter of Moravia. They emphasized the separation of church and state, pacifism, and the communal ownership of property. Suffering persecution in Europe and the Ukraine, they emigrated to the midwestern United States and then Canada in the late 1800s. Today they live in "colonies" of ten to twenty families each in rural areas. Land and property are owned by the community, and no one is paid for their labor. Unlike the Amish, the Hutterites use modern farm machinery.

What sets Anabaptists apart from many Christians is an understanding of Jesus Christ as not just their savior in whom they have faith, but as their teacher who shows them how to live. Instead of finding the importance of Jesus in his last hour on the cross, Anabaptists see his whole life as a lesson. Rather than their personal salvation, they stress serving God and other people. So instead of what they believe, they emphasize what they do.

In contrasting Anabaptists with mainline churches, I'm not denying, of course, that there have been many Christians in large churches who have taken Jesus' preaching to heart. In the Catholic tradition, there is

Francis of Assisi (1182–1226), famous for his pacifism, voluntary poverty, and service to the poor. In the last century, Dorothy Day (1897–1980) stood out with her Catholic Worker Movement, antiwar protests, and caring for people in need. In Latin America, the liberation theology movement has fought to overturn centuries of economic and political oppression for millions of poor people.

Among Lutherans, there is Albert Schweitzer (1875–1965), winner of the Nobel Peace Prize, who built and maintained a hospital in West Africa to serve thousands of indigenous people. Baptists have Rev. Martin Luther King Jr. (1929–1968), also a Nobel Peace Prize winner, with his nonviolent leadership of the American civil rights movement. King was inspired by an earlier Baptist minister, Walter Rauschenbusch (1861–1918), whose Social Gospel called for restoring Jesus' plan for the Kingdom of God as a world of peace and justice. "Because the Kingdom of God has been dropped as the primary and comprehensive aim of Christianity," Rauschenbusch wrote, "and personal salvation has been substituted for it, therefore men seek to save their own souls and are selfishly indifferent to the evangelization of the world."[10] In his Social Gospel, Rauschenbusch advocated replacing militarism with pacifism, individualism with collectivism, capitalism with socialism, and nationalism with internationalism.[11]

Today Presbyterian minister Mark Labberton preaches regularly about the social dimension of the Gospels and the Bible generally. The titles of his books show what he's up to: *The Dangerous Act of Loving Your Neighbor: Seeing Others through the Eyes of Jesus* and *The Dangerous Act of Worship: Living Out God's Call to Justice*. One congregation Labberton works with has started an annual "Do Justice" event, focusing on local projects.

Despite the commitment of individuals like these to what Jesus taught, however, the large churches have a long way to go to bring it back. Marrying Christianity to the Roman Empire 1,600 years ago overturned most of Jesus' Ten Tenets, and though the Protestant Reformation emphasized equality and servant leadership, it did not restore socialism, divine judgment, forgiveness, and pacifism. Luther and Calvin's emphasis on total depravity also undermined Jesus' Love Ethic by denying that human beings are good and worth caring about.

Still, Christianity has always been a religion of hope, and there are some encouraging signs. One is the recent election of Jorge Mario

Bergoglio as pope. Since the Roman Catholic church has come in for so many criticisms in this chapter, it's refreshing to find in its new leader so much promise of a return to the teachings of Jesus. The name he chose—Francis, after Francis of Assisi—bodes well, as does his work for social justice while he was archbishop of Buenos Aires.[12] He doubled the number of priests working in the slums there. He lived in a small apartment instead of the elegant archbishop's residence, cooking his own meals and taking the bus to work. The headline in the *New York Times* shortly after his election read "Francis Vows to Serve 'Poorest, Weakest' and Urges Leaders to Offer Hope." During his first Holy Week as pope, he broke with centuries of tradition to leave the Vatican for the ceremony that commemorates Jesus washing his apostles' feet on the night before he was crucified. Usually the pope washes the feet of twelve priests at the grand Basilica of Saint John Lateran, or at the more splendid Saint Peter's Basilica. But Francis went instead to a youth detention center near Rome, where many of the inmates are Gypsies and North African migrants. Kneeling on the stone floor with a pitcher of water, basin, and towels, he washed, dried, and kissed the feet of twelve of the prisoners, ages fourteen to twenty-one, including two young women, one a Serbian Muslim. "This is a symbol, it is a sign," Francis told them. "Washing your feet means I am at your service."[13]

Instead of moving into the splendid papal apartments in the Apostolic Palace, Francis chose the simple Vatican guest house, where he would be closer to ordinary people. In the months that followed, he visited a center for refugees and said that church properties should be used to shelter refugees. In walking among the crowds who come to see him, he has often hugged people with disabilities, along, of course, with countless children.

In a lengthy interview with fellow Jesuit Antonio Spadaro, published in September 2013 in *America* magazine, Francis criticized the authoritarian style of earlier popes—and himself in his early career as a Jesuit superior. He was given that authority at the "crazy" young age of thirty-six, he said, and "It was my authoritarian way of making decisions that created problems."[14] Now seventy-seven, Francis says that as pope he will lead by consulting people. To start, he appointed an advisory group of eight cardinals, and in November 2013 he sent the world's bishops a survey to give to laypeople with thirty-eight questions about controversial issues such as divorce and contraception.

In the interview with Spadaro, Pope Francis said that rather than repeating the church's condemnation of abortion, same-sex marriage, and contraception, he had chosen not to speak of those issues in the first six months of his papacy, in favor of presenting a bigger vision of the church based on concern for suffering people. "I see the church as a field hospital after a battle. It is useless to ask a seriously injured person if he has high cholesterol and about the level of his blood sugars. You have to heal his wounds. Then we can talk about everything else."

Some of Francis's most controversial comments in that interview were about homosexuals. "A person once asked me, in a provocative manner, if I approved of homosexuality. I replied with another question: 'Tell me: when God looks at a gay person, does he endorse the existence of this person with love, or reject and condemn this person? We must always consider the person.'" In July 2013, while returning to Rome on a plane, he was asked about homosexuals, and he answered, "Who am I to judge?" [15]

In November 2013, Pope Francis expressed his views about Christianity, modern society, and much else in a book-length "apostolic exhortation" titled *Evangelii Gaudium* (*The Joy of the Gospel*). [16] Like the original followers of Jesus, he said, we should joyfully spread the good news of Jesus Christ. "The Gospel, radiant with the glory of Christ's cross, constantly invites us to rejoice" (part 5). "I dream of a . . . missionary impulse capable of transforming everything, so that the Church's customs, ways of doing things, times and schedules, language and structures can be suitably channeled for the evangelization of today's world rather than for her self-preservation" (27). This ministry "seeks to abandon the complacent attitude that says: 'We have always done it this way.' I invite everyone to be bold and creative in this task of rethinking the goals, structures, style and methods of evangelization" (33).

In spreading the Gospel, Francis continues, Christians have

> to go forth to everyone without exception. But to whom should she go first? When we read the Gospel we find a clear indication: not so much our friends and wealthy neighbors, but above all the poor and the sick, those who are usually despised and overlooked, "those who cannot repay you" (Luke 14:14). . . . We have to state, without mincing words, that there is an inseparable bond between our faith and the poor. . . . I prefer a Church which is bruised, hurting and dirty because it has been out on the streets, rather than a Church which is

unhealthy from being confined and from clinging to its own security (48–49).

Throughout *The Joy of the Gospel*, Francis returns often to the centrality of the poor, not just in Christianity but in society in general.

> Just as the commandment "Thou shalt not kill" sets a clear limit in order to safeguard the value of human life, today we also have to say "thou shalt not" to an economy of exclusion and inequality. Such an economy kills. How can it be that it is not a news item when an elderly homeless person dies of exposure, but it is news when the stock market loses two points? (53).

Later he writes, "As long as the problems of the poor are not radically resolved by rejecting the absolute autonomy of markets and financial speculation and by attacking the structural causes of inequality, no solution will be found for the world's problems or, for that matter, to any problems. Inequality is the root of social ills" (202).

To bring the Gospel to the poor and to the whole world, Francis says in part 98—"No to warring among ourselves"—that Christians have to cooperate. Bemoaning centuries of sectarianism, he asks, "Whom are we going to evangelize if this is the way we act?"

Francis's comments about non-Christian religions are genial and complimentary. He speaks of an interreligious "dialogue, ever friendly and sincere," characterized by an "attitude of openness in truth and in love" (251).

> We hold the Jewish people in special regard because their covenant with God has never been revoked . . . The Church, which shares with Jews an important part of the sacred Scriptures, looks upon the people of the covenant and their faith as one of the sacred roots of her own Christian identity. . . . God continues to work among the people of the Old Covenant and to bring forth treasures of wisdom which flow from their encounter with his word. . . . We can also share many ethical convictions and a common concern for justice and the development of peoples (247, 249).

Of Muslims he says that they "hold the faith of Abraham, and together with us they adore the one, merciful God who will judge humanity on the last day. . . . They also acknowledge the need to respond to

God with an ethical commitment and with mercy towards those most in need" (252).

Francis has kind words even for nonreligious people with good intentions.

> As believers, we also feel close to those who do not consider themselves part of any religious tradition, yet sincerely seek the truth, goodness and beauty which we believe have their highest expression and source in God. We consider them as precious allies in the commitment to defending human dignity, in building peaceful coexistence between peoples and in protecting creation (257).

Reading Francis's words alongside those of Jesus, it's striking how similar they sound. His question "How can it be that it is not a news item when an elderly homeless person dies of exposure, but it is news when the stock market loses two points?" sounds like part of an updated Sermon on the Mount. Of the Ten Tenets, on which we gave a low score to the traditional Roman Catholic Church, the new pope advocates the Love Ethic, servant leadership, festivity, and forgiveness. Keeping in mind his position as the highest of Catholic clergy, he still leans heavily toward God's children, equality, antilegalism, and divine judgment. While he doesn't talk about socialism, his critique of market capitalism and his claim that the poor come first imply some form of socialism. Similarly, though he doesn't fully advocate the pacifism of Jesus, he has harsh words about wars and violence.

The *Joy of the Gospel* will lead to thousands of discussions in the months and years to come. Pope Francis is already the most talked about person on the Internet. Let's hope that in those interchanges, Christians of all kinds will raise some of the questions in this book, and that they will discuss them with the respect for alternative answers we have been emphasizing. In doing that, they might well reshape Christianity to be more like the Kingdom of God preached by Jesus.

For further reading:

Hans Kung. *Why Priests? A Proposal for a New Church Ministry*. Garden City, NY: Double-day, 1972.
Garry Wills. *Why Priests? A Failed Tradition*. New York: Viking, 2013.
William R. Estep. *The Anabaptist Story*. Grand Rapids, MI: Wm. B. Eeerdmans, 1995.
John Horsch. *Mennonites in Europe*. Scottdale, PA: Mennonite Publishing House, 1950.

Stuart Murray. *The Naked Anabaptist: The Bare Essentials of a Radical Faith*. Harrisonburg, VA: Herald Press, 2010.

Leonard Verduin. *The Reformers and Their Stepchildren*. Grand Rapids, MI: Wm. B. Eerdmans, 1964.

NOTES

I. WHY ASK QUESTIONS?

1. Irenaeus, *Adversus haereses* (*Against Heresies*), 1:9, 5.

2. Vincent of Lérin, *Commonitorium* (*Memorandum*), 2:6.

3. John Dominic Crossan, *Jesus: A Revolutionary Biography* (San Francisco: HarperSanFrancisco, 1989), 55.

4. Joseph Fletcher, *Situation Ethics: The New Morality* (Philadelphia: Westminster, 1966), 69, 70.

5. John Driver, *How Christians Made Peace with War: Early Christian Understandings of War* (Scottdale, PA: Herald Press, 1988), 14.

6. *Didache*, trans. Tim Sauder (Amberson, PA: Scroll Press, n. d.), 1, http://www.scrollpublishing.com/store/didache-annotated.html.

7. Augustine, *De moribus ecclesiae catholicae et de moribus Manicheorum* (*On the Morals of the Catholic Church and the Morals of the Manicheans*), 1:27.

8. Tertullian, *De praescriptione haereticorum* (*Prescription against Heretics*), 7.

9. Ramsay MacMullen, *Voting about God in Early Church Councils* (New Haven, CT: Yale University Press, 2006).

10. T. A. Burkhill, *The Evolution of Christian Thought* (Ithaca, NY: Cornell University Press, 1971), 78.

11. Gregory of Nyssa, *De deitate Filii et Spiritus Sancti* (*On the Deity of the Son and the Holy Spirit*).

12. *Codex Theodosianus* (*Code of Theodosius*), 16:10, 12.

13. *Codex Theodosianus*, 16:10, 12.

14. Tacitus, *Annales* (*Annals*), 15:44.

15. Eusebius, *Vita Constantini* (*Life of Constantine*), 1:4.

16. Hans Küng, *Why Priests? A Proposal for a New Church Ministry*, trans. Robert C. Collins (Garden City, NY: Doubleday, 1972), 54.

17. David B. Barrett, George T. Kurian, and Todd M. Johnson, eds., *World Encyclopedia*, 2nd edition (New York Oxford University Press, 2000), vi.

18. *Piers Morgan Tonight*, January 26, 2011.

19. Thomas Aquinas, *Summa Theologiae*, part 1, question 2, article 3.

20. See Elizabeth Achtemeier, "Metaphors," in *The Oxford Companion to the Bible*, ed. Bruce M. Metzger and Michael D. Coogan (Oxford: Oxford University Press, 1993), 515–17.

2. THOUGHTFUL FAITH

1. *World Christian Encyclopedia* (Oxford: Oxford University Press, 1982), 23.

2. John Chrysostom, *The Fathers of the Church*, vol. 68, *Discourses against Judaizing Christians*, trans. Paul W. Harkins (Washington, DC: Catholic University of America Press, 1979), 1:6, 25.

3. Martin Luther, *Luther's Works*, vol. 47, *On the Jews and Their Lies*, trans. Martin Bertram, (Philadelphia: Fortress, 1971), 306.

4. Luther, *On the Jews*, 172.

5. Luther, *On the Jews*, 268–92.

6. Martin Luther, *Luther's Works*, vol. 54, *Table Talk* (Philadelphia: Fortress, 1971), section 353.

7. Luther, *Luther's Works*, 51:126.

8. Luther, *Luther's Works*, 11:285.

9. See Bart D. Ehrman and Zlatko Plese, *The Apocryphal Gospels: Texts and Translations* (New York: Oxford University Press, 2011).

10. John Calvin, *Institutes of the Christian Religion*, trans. Henry Beveridge (Peabody, MA: Hendrickson, 2008), 360.

11. Martin Luther, *Large Catechism* (St. Louis, MO: Concordia, 1988), 1:1–3.

3. THE BIBLE

1. Michael D. Coogan, ed., *The New Oxford Annotated Bible*, 4th ed. (Oxford: Oxford University Press, 2010), 2195.

2. See *The New Oxford Annotated Bible*, 1823–25.

3. Wieland Willker, "A Textual Commentary on the Greek Gospels. Vol. 2b: The various endings of Mk," in *TCG 2006: An Online Textual Commentary on the Greek Gospels*, 4th ed., http://www-user.uni-bremen.de/~wie/TCG/TC-Mark-Ends.pdf.

4. *The New Oxford Annotated Bible*, 950.

5. Athanasius, *Contra gentes (Against the Heathen)*, 1:1.

6. "Billy Graham's *My Answer*," July 29, 2004, http://www.billygraham.org/articlepage.asp?articleid=3845.

7. Thomas Müntzer, *Expressed Exposure of False Faith in an Untrue World*, quoted in Gordon Rupp, *Patterns of Reformation* (Philadelphia: Fortress Press, 1969), 216.

8. Origen, *Contra Celsum (Against Celsus)*, 4:40.

9. Justin Martyr, *Dialogue with Trypho*, ch. 81.

10. Clement of Alexandria, *Stromateis (Miscellanies)*, 6:16.

11. Augustine, *De Genesi ad litteram (The Literal Meaning of Genesis)* .

12. Augustine, *De Genesi ad litteram*, 5:2.

13. Gordy Slack, "Inside the Creation Museum," *Salon*, May 31, 2007, http://www.salon.com/2007/05/31/creation_museum/.

14. Origen, *De principiis (The Fundamental Doctrines)*, 4:1, 16.

4. JESUS CHRIST

dei (The City of God), 10:20.
Sermons), 261.
, *Cur Deus Homo (Why the God-Man)*, 2:6.
ins, trans. Philip S. Watson (London: James

, *Protrepticus (Exhortation to the Greeks)*, 1:8, 4.
itione verbi dei (On the Incarnation), section 54.
t by the Blood of Jesus?," in *The Metaphor of*
estminster, 1993), 112–26.
ion *of the Epistle to the Romans*, in *The Library*
A *Scholastic Miscellany: Anselm to Ockham*, ed.
delphia: Westminster, 1956), 283.
on *of the Epistle to the Romans*, 282–83.
io?, ch. 11.
iting *about God in Early Church Councils* (New
ess, 2006), 56.
Beautiful," *New York Times*, May 9, 2010,

Travel, 8.

13. John Dominic Crossan, *Jesus: A Revolutionary Biography* (New York: HarperCollins, 2009), xii.

14. See Walter Ong, *Orality and Literacy: The Technologizing of the Word* (London: Taylor and Francis, 2002).

15. John Hick, *The Metaphor of God Incarnate* (Louisville, KY: Westminster, 1993); and Sallie McFague, *Metaphorical Theology: Models of God in Religious Language* (Philadelphia: Augsburg, 1982).

16. In *Readings in Christianity*, 2nd ed., ed. Robert E. Van Voorst (Belmont, CA: Wadsworth, 2001), 91–92.

5. THE TRINITY

1. Augustine, *De trinitate* (*On the Trinity*), 7:6, 11.

2. William C. Placher, *A History of Christian Theology: An Introduction* (Louisville, KY: Westminster Press, 1983), 74.

3. Placher, *A History of Christian Theology*, 75.

4. Robert Barr, *Main Currents in Early Christian Thought* (Glen Rock, NJ: Paulist Press, 1966), 67.

5. Alan Richardson, *Creeds in the Making: A Short Introduction to the History of Christian Doctrine* (Philadelphia: Fortress, 1981), 120.

6. Richardson, *Creeds in the Making*, 65.

7. Augustine, *De trinitate*, 5:12.

8. Alister E. McGrath, *Christian Theology: An Introduction*, 3rd ed. (Oxford: Blackwell, 2001), 321–22.

9. Placher, *A History of Christian Theology*, 78.

10. Basil of Caesarea, *Letter* 214, 4, in *The Letters*, Loeb Classical Series 190 (Cambridge, MA: Harvard University Press), 1926.

11. Gregory of Nyssa, "Ad Ablabium" ("On Not Three Gods").

12. McGrath, *Christian Theology*, 330.

13. McGrath, *Christian Theology*, 332.

14. Bernard Lohse, *A Short History of Christian Doctrine: From the First Century to the Present* (Philadelphia: Fortress, 1985), 68.

15. Augustine, *De Trinitate*, 6:7, 9; 7:6, 11; 8:1.

16. McGrath, *Christian Theology*, 333.

17. McGrath, *Christian Theology*, 335.

18. McGrath, *Christian Theology*, 336.

19. McGrath, *Christian Theology*, 337.

20. McGrath, *Christian Theology*, 339.

21. McGrath, *Christian Theology*, 339.

22. Gregory Nazianzus, *Third Theological Oration*, 8, in *Nicene and Post-Nicene Fathers*, second series, ed. Philip Schaff and Henry Wace (New York: Christian Literature Co., 1890–1900), 7:303.

6. THE FALL

1. Donald K. McKim, *Theological Turning Points: Major Issues in Christian Thought* (Atlanta: John Knox, 1988), 69.

2. John Chrysostom, *Sermon 10*, on Romans.

3. Augustine, *Contra Julianum* (*The Incomplete Work against Julian*), 5:1.

4. Augustine, *De peccatorum meritis et remissione* (*On Merits and Remission of Sins*), 1:11 (10); 3:14 (7).

5. Augustine, *De Nuptiis et concupiscentia* (*On Marriage and Concupiscence*), 2:15.

6. Augustine, *Contra Julianum*, 6:22.

7. Augustine, *Contra Julianum*, 5:1.

8. Martin Luther, *On the Bondage of the Will*, conclusion, in *The Library of Christian Classics*, vol. 17, *Luther and Erasmus: Free Will and Salvation* (Philadelphia: Westminster, 1969), 332.

9. John Calvin, *Compendium of the Institutes of the Christian Religion*, ed. Hugh Kerr (Philadelphia: Westminster, 1964), book 2, 2, 15.

10. *Westminster Confession of Faith* (1646), ch. 6, sections 2 and 4.

11. *Westminster Confession*, ch. 16, section 3.

12. *Westminster Confession*, ch. 6, section 6.

13. John Calvin, *Compendium*, book 2, 1, 6–7.

14. Quoted in Peter Brown, *Augustine of Hippo* (Berkeley: University of California Press, 1967), 391–92.

15. R. C. Sproul, Jr., "Comfort Ye My People—Justification by Youth Alone: When Does Comfort Become Confusion?" *World* 10, no. 7 (May 6, 1995), 26.

16. In *Readings in Christianity*, 2nd ed., ed. Robert E. Van Voorst (Belmont, CA: Wadsworth, 2001), 95.

17. John Calvin, *Institutes of the Christian Religion*, trans. Henry Beveridge (Peabody, MA: Hendrickson, 2008), 179.

18. Luther, *On the Bondage of the Will*, 332.

19. Calvin, *Institutes*, 185.

20. Calvin, *Institutes*, 185.

21. Clement of Alexandria, *Stromateis* (*Miscellanies*), 2, 14, 60; 2, 15, 66.

22. Luther, *On the Bondage of the Will*, 139.

23. Luther, *On the Bondage of the Will*, 315.

24. Luther, *On the Bondage of the Will*, 332.

25. Luther, *On the Bondage of the Will*, 121.
26. Calvin, *Institutes*, 198.
27. Calvin, *Institutes*, 199.

7. LIFE AFTER DEATH

1. "Pilgrim's Progress: An Interview with Rev. Billy Graham," *Newsweek*, August 14, 2006, 43.
2. Thomas Aquinas, *Summa Theologiae*, part 1, question 75, article 4.
3. Augustine, *De moribus ecclesiae catholicae et de moribus Manicheorum (On the Morals of the Catholic Church and the Morals of the Manicheans)*, 1:27.
4. Martin Luther, *D. Martin Luthers Werke* (Weimar, 1883–2009), 37:191.
5. William C. Placher, *A History of Christian Theology: An Introduction* (Louisville, KY: Westminster Press, 1983), 129–30.
6. Origen, *Homilies on Exodus*, 6:4.
7. In *Readings in Christianity*, ed. Robert E. Van Voorst, 2nd ed. (Belmont, CA: Wadsworth, 2001), 165.
8. In *Readings in Christianity*, 191.
9. John Morreall, "Perfect Happiness and the Resurrection of the Body," *Religious Studies* 16, no. 1 (1980): 29–35.

8. ANGELS AND DEMONS

1. Thomas Aquinas, *Summa Theologiae* part 1, question 51, article 1.
2. *New Catholic Encyclopedia*, s.v. "Angels" (New York: McGraw-Hill, 1967), 509.
3. *The New Oxford Annotated Bible*, 22, note for 18:1–5.
4. *New Catholic Encyclopedia*, s.v. "Angels," 510.
5. John Morreall, "Is God in Heaven?" *Journal of Higher Criticism* 9, no. 2 (2002): 217–33.
6. Justin Martyr, *Dialogue with Trypho*, ch. 127.
7. Theophilus of Antioch, *Ad Autolycum (Apology to Autolycus)*, 2:3.
8. Clement of Alexandria, *Stromateis (Miscellanies)*, 7, 6; 30, 1; 5, 11; 71, 5.
9. *New Catholic Encyclopedia*, s.v. "Angels," 515.
10. Rudolph M. Bell, *The Voices of Gemma Galgani: the Life and Afterlife of a Modern Saint* (Chicago: University of Chicago Press, 2003), 47, 185.

11. The Greek word here is *Tartaros*, which is not equivalent to *Gehenna* in Jesus' preaching. It seems to be a temporary state of darkness holding the evil angels until the judgment at the end of the world.

12. *New Catholic Encyclopedia*, s.v. "Demon" (New York: McGraw-Hill, 1967), 754.

9. THE GOOD LIFE

1. "Aseret ha-Dibrot: The 'Ten Commandments,'" *Judaism 101*, http://www.jewfaq.org/10.htm.

2. Don Hinkle, "Southern Baptists Commend Laura Schlessinger for Her Opposition to Homosexual Lifestyle," SBC Newsroom, June 14, 2000, http://www.sbcannualmeeting.org/sbc00/news.asp.

3. http://www.cyc-net.org/today2000/today000228.html.

4. "Statement by Dr. Laura Schlessinger," http://www.drlaura.com.

5. Kent Ashcraft, "Letter to Dr. Laura," *Seattle Weekly*, June 8, 2000, 4.

6. Virginia Code Ann. A7 20–57.

7. Scott v. State, 39 GA 321, 1869.

8. Loving v. Virginia, 1959.

9. "Iran Resorts to Hangings in Public to Cut Crime," *New York Times*, January 21, 2013.

10. Richard Nygaard, "'Vengeance is Mine' Says the Lord," *America*, October 8, 1994, 7.

11. Nygaard, "Vengeance is Mine," 8.

12. Tertullian, *De corona militis* (*Concerning the Military Crown*).

13. Leatherneck.com forums, "Bumper Sticker Slogans Seen on US Military Bases," http://www.leatherneck.com/forums/showthread.php?92307-Bumper-Sticker-slogans-seen-on-US-Military-Bases&s=a541b93e14485c16266079bd873e7065.

14. Kalle Lasn, *Culture Jam: How to Reverse America's Suicidal Consumer Binge—And Why We Must* (New York: Quill, 2000), 19.

10. CHURCHES

1. Raymond Brown, *Biblical Reflections on Crises Facing the Church* (Mahwah, NJ: Paulist Press, 1975), 70.

2. Hans Küng, *Why Priests? A Proposal for a New Church Ministry* (Garden City, NY: Doubleday, 1972). Garry Wills, *Why Priests? A Failed Tradition* (New York: Viking, 2013).

3. See Joseph Fletcher, *Situation Ethics: The New Morality* (Philadelphia: Westminster, 1966).

4. Harvey Cox, *The Silencing of Leonardo Boff: The Vatican and the Future of World Christianity* (New York: Harper Collins, 1989).

5. John Calvin, *Compendium of the Institutes of the Christian Religion*, ed. Hugh Kerr (Philadelphia: Westminster, 1964), book 2, 2, 15.

6. R.C. Sproul, *What Is Reformed Theology? Understanding the Basics* (Grand Rapids, MI: Baker, 1997), 127.

7. Sproul, *What Is Reformed Theology?*, 127.

8. J. Gordon Melton, "Baptists," in *Encyclopedia of American Religions*, 8th ed. (Farmington Hills, MI: Gale, 2009).

9. "The FAQs: Southern Baptists, Calvinism, and God's Plan of Salvation," the Gospel Coalition, http://thegospelcoalition.org/blogs/tgc/2012/06/06/the-faqs-southern-baptists-calvinism-and-gods-plan-of-salvation/.

10. Walter Rauschenbusch, "The Brotherhood of the Kingdom," *Record of Christian Work* 13, no. 7 (1894): 207.

11. Walter Rauschenbusch, *Theology for the Social Gospel* (New York: Abingdon, 1917).

12. See Hans Küng, "The Paradox of Pope Francis," *National Catholic Reporter*, May 21, 2013, http://ncronline.org/news/vatican/paradox-pope-francis.

13. "Pope Francis' Female Foot-Wash Outrages Traditionalists," *New York Daily News*, March 30, 2013.

14. "A Big Heart Open to God: The Exclusive Interview with Pope Francis," *America*, September 30, 2013.

15. "Pope on Homosexuals: 'Who Am I to Judge?'" *National Catholic Reporter* online, July 29, 2013, http://ncronline.org/blogs/ncr-today/pope-homosexuals-who-am-i-judge.

16. Francis, *Evangelii Gaudium* (Vatican City: Vatican Press, 2013), http://www.vatican.va/holy_father/francesco/apost_exhortations/documents/papa-francesco_esortazione-ap_20131124_evangelii-gaudium_en.pdf.

BIBLIOGRAPHY

Abelard, Peter. *Exposition of the Epistle to the Romans.* In *The Library of Christian Classics.* Vol. 10, *A Scholastic Miscellany: Anselm to Ockham,* edited by Eugene R. Fairweather, 276–87. Philadelphia: Westminster, 1956.

Achtemeier, Elizabeth. "Metaphors." In *The Oxford Companion to the Bible,* edited by Bruce M. Metzger and Michael D. Coogan, 515–17. Oxford: Oxford University Press, 1993.

Adler, Mortimer. *The Angels and Us.* New York: Macmillan, 1982.

Alexander, William M. *Demonic Possession in the New Testament: Its Historical, Medical, and Theological Aspects.* Eugene, OR: Wipf & Stock, 2001.

Allman, Mark J. *Who Would Jesus Kill? War, Peace, and the Christian Tradition.* Winona, MN: Anselm Academic, 2008.

"Angels." *New Catholic Encyclopedia,* 506–19. New York: McGraw-Hill, 1967.

Anselm of Canterbury. *Cur Deus Homo (Why the God-Man).*

Aquinas, Thomas. *Summa Theologiae.*

Athanasius. *Discourses Against the Arians.* In *The Nicene and Post-Nicene Fathers,* 2nd series, edited by Philip Schaff and Henry Wace, 4:100–48. Grand Rapids, MI: Wm. B. Eerdmans, 1957.

———. *Contra gentes (Against the Heathen).*

———. *De incarnatione verbi dei (On the Incarnation).*

Augustine. *Contra Julianum (The Incomplete Work against Julian).*

———. *De civitate dei (The City of God).*

———. *De Genesi ad litteram (The Literal Meaning of Genesis).*

———. *De moribus ecclesiae catholicae et de moribus Manicheorum (On the Morals of the Catholic Church and the Morals of the Manicheans).*

———. *De Nuptiis et concupiscentia (On Marriage and Concupiscence).*

———. *De peccatorum meritis et remissione (On Merits and Remission of Sins).*

———. *De trinitate (On the Trinity).*

———. *Sermones (Sermons).*

Aulén, Gustav. *Christus Victor: An Historical Study of the Three Main Types of the Idea of Atonement.* London: Macmillan, 1977.

Barr, Robert. *Main Currents in Early Christian Thought.* Glen Rock, NJ: Paulist Press, 1966.

Barrett, David, ed. *World Christian Encyclopedia.* New York: Oxford University Press, 1982.

Barrett, David, George Kurian, and Todd Johnson, eds. *World Christian Encyclopedia.* 2nd ed. New York Oxford University Press, 2001.

Basil of Caesarea. *The Letters.* Loeb Classical Series 190. Cambridge, MA: Harvard University Press, 1926.

Bell, Rudolph M., and Cristina Mazzoni. *The Voices of Gemma Galgani: The Life and Afterlife of a Modern Saint*. Chicago: University of Chicago Press, 2003.

Bendall, Kent, and Frederick Ferré. *Exploring the Logic of Faith: A Dialogue on the Relation of Modern Philosophy to Christian Faith*. New York: Association Press, 1962.

Boff, Leonardo. *Jesus Christ Liberator: A Critical Christology for Our Time*. Maryknoll, NY: Orbis, 1978.

Brown, Peter. *Augustine of Hippo*. Berkeley: University of California Press, 1967.

Brown, Raymond. *Biblical Reflections on Crises Facing the Church*. Mahwah, NJ: Paulist Press, 1975.

Bultmann, Rudolf. "The New Testament and Theology." In *The New Testament and Mythology and Other Basic Works*, edited by Schubert Ogden. Minneapolis: Augsburg Fortress, 1984.

Burkhill, T. A. *The Evolution of Christian Thought*. Ithaca, NY: Cornell University Press, 1971.

Caffiero, Marina. *Forced Baptisms: Histories of Jews, Christians, and Converts in Papal Rome*. Berkeley, CA: University of California Press, 2011.

Calvin, John. *Bondage and Liberation of the Will*. Grand Rapids, MI: Baker, 2002.

———. *Compendium of the Institutes of the Christian Religion*. Edited by Hugh Kerr. Philadelphia: Westminster, 1964.

———. *Institutes of the Christian Religion*. Translated by Henry Beveridge. Peabody, MA: Hendrickson, 2008.

Clement of Alexandria. *Protrepticus (Exhortation to the Greeks)*.

———. *Stromateis (Miscellanies)*.

Codex Theodosianus (Code of Theodosius).

Coogan, Michael D., ed. *The New Oxford Annotated Bible*. 4th ed. Oxford: Oxford University Press, 2010.

Cox, Harvey. *The Silencing of Leonardo Boff: The Vatican and the Future of World Christianity*. New York: Harper Collins, 1989.

Crockett, William, ed. *Four Views of Hell*. Grand Rapids, MI: Zondervan, 1992.

Crossan, John Dominic. *Jesus: A Revolutionary Biography*. San Francisco: HarperSanFrancisco, 1995.

Cullman, Oscar. *Immortality of the Soul or Resurrection of the Dead: The Witness of the New Testament*. Eugene, OR: Wipf & Stock, 2000.

Davidson, Gustave. *A Dictionary of Angels, Including the Fallen Angels*. New York: Free Press, 1967.

Dear, John. *The Questions of Jesus: Challenging Ourselves to Discover Life's Great Answers*. New York: Doubleday, 2004.

Delumeau, Jean. *History of Paradise: The Garden of Eden in Myth and Tradition*. Champaign, IL: University of Illinois Press, 2000.

"Demon (In the Bible)." *New Catholic Encyclopedia*, 4:752–54. New York: McGraw-Hill, 1967.

"Demon (Theology of)." *New Catholic Encyclopedia*, 4:754–56. New York: McGraw-Hill, 1967.

Didache. Translated by Tim Sauder. Amberson, PA: Scroll Press, n.d.

Douglas, Mary. *Purity and Danger: An Analysis of the Concepts of Pollution and Taboo*. London: Routledge, 1984.

Driver, John. *How Christians Made Peace with War: Early Christian Understandings of War*. Scottdale, PA: Herald Press, 1988.

Dulles, Avery. *The Assurance of Things Hoped for: A Theology of Christian Faith*. Oxford: Oxford University Press, 1994.

Dunn, James. *Did the First Christians Worship Jesus?* Louisville, KY: Westminster John Knox 2010.

Edersheim, Alfred. *The Life and Times of Jesus Messiah*. Rev. ed. Peabody, MA: Hendrickson, 1993.

Ehrman, Bart. *Misquoting Jesus: The Story behind Who Changed the Bible and Why*. New York: HarperCollins, 2007.

Ehrman, Bart D., and Zlatko Plese. *The Apocryphal Gospels: Texts and Translations.* New York: Oxford University Press, 2011.

Estep, William. *The Anabaptist Story.* Grand Rapids, MI: Wm. B. Eerdmans, 1995.

Eusebius. *Vita Constantini (Life of Constantine).*

Finley, Mitch. *Everybody Has a Guardian Angel . . . And Other Lasting Lessons I Learned in Catholic Schools.* New York: Crossroad, 1993.

Fletcher, Joseph. *Situation Ethics: The New Morality.* Philadelphia: Westminster, 1966.

Friedman, Richard. *Who Wrote the Bible?* San Francisco: HarperOne 1997.

Galambush, Julie. *The Reluctant Parting: How the New Testament's Jewish Writers Created a Christian Book.* San Francisco: HarperSanFrancisco, 2005.

Geisler, Norman. *From God to Us: How We Got Our Bible.* Chicago: Moody Press, 1974.

Good, Deirdre. *Jesus' Family Values.* New York: Church Publishing, 2006.

Gregory Nazianzus. *Third Theological Oration.* In *Nicene and Post-Nicene Fathers*, 2nd series. Edited by Philip Schaff and Henry Wace, vol. 7. New York: Christian Literature Co., 1890–1900.

Gregory of Nyssa. *Ad Ablabium (On Not Three Gods).*

———. *De deitate Filii et Spiritus Sancti (On the Deity of the Son and the Holy Spirit).*

———. *Sermo Catecheticus Magnus (Large Catechetical Sermon).*

Hendry, George. *The Holy Spirit in Christian Theology.* Rev. ed. Philadelphia: Westminster John Knox, 1965.

Harris, Sam. *The End of Faith: Religion, Terror, and the Future of Reason.* New York: W. W. Norton, 2005.

Hick, John. *The Metaphor of God Incarnate: Christology in a Pluralistic Age.* Louisville, KY: Westminster, 1993.

Horsch, John. *Mennonites in Europe.* Scottdale, PA: Mennonite Publishing House, 1950.

Laing, Jacqueline, and Wilcox, eds. *The Natural Law Reader.* Malden, MA: Wiley Blackwell, 2013.

Irenaeus. *Adversus haereses (Against Heresies).*

Jacobs, Alan. *Original Sin: A Cultural History.* New York: HarperCollins, 2009.

Jenkins, Philip. *Jesus Wars: How Four Patriarchs, Three Queens, and Two Emperors Decided What Christians Would Believe for the Next 1,500 Years.* New York: HarperOne, 2010.

The Jesus Seminar. *The Five Gospels: What Did Jesus Really Say?* New York: Macmillan, 1993.

John Chrysostom. *Discourses against Judaizing Christians.* The Fathers of the Church 68. Translated by Paul W. Harkins. Washington, DC: Catholic University of America Press, 1979.

———. *Sermon 10, on Romans.*

John of Damascus. *On the Orthodox Faith.*

John Paul II. *Fides et Ratio*, 1998.

Johnson, Luke Timothy. *The Creed: What Christians Believe and Why It Matters.* New York: Doubleday, 2005.

Justin Martyr. *Dialogue with Trypho.*

Küng, Hans. *Why Priests? A Proposal for a New Church Ministry.* Garden City, NY: Doubleday, 1972.

Lasn, Kalle. *Culture Jam: How to Reverse America's Suicidal Consumer Binge—And Why We Must.* New York: Quill, 2000.

Lohse, Bernard. *A Short History of Christian Doctrine: From the First Century to the Present.* Philadelphia: Fortress, 1985.

Luther, Martin. *Galatians.* Translated by Philip S. Watson. London: James Clarke, 1953.

———. *Large Catechism.* St. Louis, MO: Concordia, 1988.

———. *On the Bondage of the Will.* In *The Library of Christian Classics.* Vol. 17, *Luther and Erasmus: Free Will and Salvation.* Philadelphia: Westminster, 1969.

———. *Luther's Works.* Vol. 47, *On the Jews and Their Lies.* Translated by Martin Bertram. Philadelphia: Fortress, 1971.

———. *Luther's Works.* Vol. 54, *Table Talk.* Philadelphia: Fortress, 1971.

————. *Werke*. Weimar, 1883–2009.

MacMullen, Ramsay. *Voting about God in Early Church Councils*. New Haven, CT: Yale University Press, 2006.

Mattfeld, Walter. *The Garden of Eden Myth*. Raleigh, NC: Lulu, 2010.

McDaniel, Jay. "Christianity and the Pursuit of Wealth." *Anglican Theological Review* 69, no. 4 (1987): 349–61.

————. *Living from the Center: Spirituality in an Age of Consumerism*. St. Louis, MO: Chalice Press, 2000.

McFague, Sallie. *Metaphorical Theology: Models of God in Religious Language*. Philadelphia: Augsburg, 1982.

McGrath, Alister E. *Christian Theology: An Introduction*. 3rd ed. Oxford: Blackwell, 2001.

McKim, Donald K. *Theological Turning Points: Major Issues in Christian Thought*. Atlanta: John Knox, 1988.

McQuarrie, John. *Principles of Christian Theology*. 2nd ed. London: SCM PRESS, 1977.

Moreton, Bethany. *To Serve God and Wal-Mart: The Making of Christian Free Enterprise*. Cambridge, MA: Harvard University Press, 2009.

Morreall, John. "Can Theological Language Have Hidden Meaning?" *Religious Studies* 19 (1983): 43–56.

————. "Is God in Heaven?" *Journal of Higher Criticism* 9, no. 2 (2002): 217–33.

————. "Perfect Happiness and the Resurrection of the Body." *Religious Studies* 16, no. 1 (1980): 29–35.

————. "Serving God and Mammon? Consumerism and Religion in America." *Delta Epsilon Sigma Journal* 49 (2004): 100–12.

Murray, Stuart. *The Naked Anabaptist: The Bare Essentials of a Radical Faith*. Harrisonburg, VA: Herald Press, 2010.

Müller, Mogens. "Son of God." In *The Oxford Companion to the Bible*, edited by Bruce M. Metzger and Michael D. Coogan, 710–13. Oxford: Oxford University Press, 1993.

Nelson, James. *Body Theology*. Louisville, KY: Westminster John Knox, 1992.

The New Oxford Annotated Bible. 4th ed. Oxford: Oxford University Press, 2010.

Nygaard, Richard. "'Vengeance is Mine' Says the Lord." *America*, October 8, 1994, 6–8.

Ong, Walter. *Orality and Literacy: The Technologizing of the Word*. London: Taylor and Francis, 2002.

Origen. *Contra Celsum (Against Celsus)*.

————. *De principiis (The Fundamental Doctrines)*.

————. *Homilies on Exodus*.

Penelhum, Terence, ed. *Faith*. New York: Macmillan, 1989.

————. *Reason and Religious Faith*. Boulder, CO: Westview, 1995.

Rashdall, Hastings. *The Idea of Atonement in Christian Thought*. London: Macmillan, 1920.

Placher, William C. *A History of Christian Theology: An Introduction*. Louisville, KY: Westminster Press, 1983.

Prestige, G. L. *God in Patristic Thought*. Eugene, OR: Wipf & Stock, 2008.

Rahner, Karl. *The Trinity*. New York: Herder and Herder, 1970.

Rauschenbusch, Walter. "The Brotherhood of the Kingdom." *The Record of Christian Work* 13, no. 7 (1894).

————. *Theology for the Social Gospel*. New York: Abingdon, 1917.

Reimer, A. James. *Christians and War: A Brief History of the Church's Teachings and Practices*. Minneapolis: Augsburg Fortress, 2010.

Richardson, Alan. *Creeds in the Making: A Short Introduction to the History of Christian Doctrine*. Philadelphia: Fortress, 1981.

Roberts, Robert C. "Just a Little Bit More: Greed and the Malling of Our Souls." *Christianity Today*, April 8, 1996.

Rupp, Gordon. *Patterns of Reformation*. Philadelphia: Fortress Press, 1969.

Rupp, Gordon, and Philip Watson, eds. *Luther and Erasmus, Free Will and Salvation*. Atlanta, GA: Westminster John Knox, 1995.

Sauder, Tim, trans. *Didache*. Amberson, PA: Scroll Press, n. d.

Scroggs, Robin. *The New Testament and Homosexuality*. Minneapolis: Fortress, 1984.

Segal, Alan. *Rebecca's Children: Judaism and Christianity in the Roman World*. Cambridge, MA: Harvard University Press, 1986.

Sheehan, Thomas. *The First Coming: How the Kingdom of God Became Christianity*. New York: Random House, 1986.

Shermer, Michael. *The Science of Good and Evil: Why People Cheat, Gossip, Care, Share, and Follow the Golden Rule*. New York: Times Books, 2004.

Sproul, R. C. "Comfort Ye My People—Justification by Youth Alone: When Does Comfort Become Confusion?" *World* 10, no. 7 (May 6, 1995): 26.

———. *What Is Reformed Theology? Understanding the Basics*. Grand Rapids, MI: Baker, 1997.

———. *Willing to Believe: The Controversy over Free Will*. Grand Rapids, MI: Baker, 2002.

Steenberg, M. C. *A World Full of Arians: A Study of the Arian Debate and the Trinitarian Controversy from AD 360–380*. http://www.monachos.net/content/patristics/studies-themes/56-a-world-full-of-arians?title=A_World_Full_of_Arians.

Swinburne, Richard. *Faith and Reason*. Oxford: Oxford University Press, 1981.

———. "A Theodicy of Heaven and Hell." In *The Existence and Nature of God*, edited by Alfred Freddoso, 37–54. South Bend, IN: University of Notre Dame Press, 1983.

Tacitus. *Annales (Annals)*.

Taylor, Vincent. *The Atonement in New Testament Teaching*. London: Epworth, 1940.

Tertullian. *De corona militis (Concerning the Military Crown)*.

———. *De praescriptione haereticorum (Prescription against Heretics)*.

Theophilus of Antioch. *Ad Autolycum (Apology to Autolycus)*.

Twitchell, James. *Lead Us into Temptation: The Triumph of American Materialism*. New York: Columbia University Press, 1999.

Thomas Aquinas. *Summa Theologiae*.

Van Buren, Paul. *Christ in Our Place: The Substitutionary Character of Calvin's Doctrine of Reconciliation*. Edinburgh: Oliver and Boyd, 1957.

Van den Haag, Ernest. *Punishing Criminals: Concerning a Very Old and Painful Question*. Lanham, MD: University Press of America, 1991.

Van Inwagen, Peter. "The Possibility of Resurrection." *International Journal for Philosophy of Religion* 9 (1978): 114–21.

Van Voorst, Robert E., ed. *Readings in Christianity*. 2nd ed. Belmont, CA: Wadsworth, 2001.

Verduin, Leonard. *The Reformers and Their Stepchildren*. Grand Rapids, MI: Wm. B. Eerdmans, 1964.

Vincent of Lérin. *Commonitorium (Memorandum)*.

Westminster Confession of Faith (1646).

White, Richard. *Bibles, Science and Sanity*. Boulder, CO: Westview, 2007.

Willker, Wieland. "A Textual Commentary on the Greek Gospels. Vol. 2b: The Various Endings of Mk." *TCG 2006: An Online Textual Commentary on the Greek Gospels*. 4th ed. http://www-user.uni-bremen.de/~wie/TCG/TC-Mark-Ends.pdf.

Wills, Garry. *Why Priests? A Failed Tradition*. New York: Viking, 2013.

Wright, N. T. *Surprised by Hope: Rethinking Heaven, the Resurrection, and the Mission of the Church*. New York: HarperOne, 2008.

Zehr, Howard. *Changing Lenses: A New Focus for Crime and Justice*. Harrisonburg, VA: Herald Press, 1990.

INDEX

opposition to, 13–14; questionable views of, 34, 65; on resurrection, 153; on "spirit," 107, 108

pederasty, 192

Pelagius, 133

penal substitution theory of atonement, 83, 86, 87

person, 100, 102, 110; Holy Spirit as, 106–108, 108, 109; in theory of Trinity, 99–100, 100, 104–105, 105, 106–108, 109

Peter, Saint, 18, 144, 210, 214, 221

Pharisees, 33, 46, 142, 153, 185, 194, 211

philosophy, Greek, 3, 11–14, 16, 26, 27, 95, 142, 146

Pius IX (pope), 227

Placher, William, 104

Plato, 12, 13, 102, 142, 146

Platonism, 12, 27, 95

Plotinus, 12, 13

polygamy, in Bible, 63, 188

polytheism, 99, 103, 114, 115, 116, 119

Pontifex Maximus, 20, 224

possession, demonic, 177–181

Priscillian, 17, 18, 97, 196, 230

Psalms, 57–58

punishment, 8, 15, 17, 123, 128, 146, 154, 170, 184; in atonement theory, 83, 88; capital, 193–198; by churches, 230, 233; eternal, 42, 157–162; and the Fall, 121, 123, 128; and free will, 139; theories of, 160–162, 197–198; Yahweh, 88, 200

purgatory, 24, 150, 151–152, 152

Qur'an, 56–57, 92, 99

Rahner, Karl, 117

Ratzinger, Joseph, 230

Rauschenbusch, Walter, 240

reason, opposed to faith, 36–40

redundancy, in Bible, 26

reformation, punishment as, 161, 197

reincarnation, 25

replica, 155–157

restraint, punishment as, 161, 161–162, 197, 197–198

resurrection, 148, 150, 152; Jesus on, 13, 96, 142, 144, 145, 146, 147, 148, 149, 152; of Jesus as model for human resurrection, 153–157; Old Testament prophecies of, 146–147

retaliation. *See* retribution

retribution, punishment as, 160, 161, 197, 198

revelation, 37, 58, 59, 60, 117

Roman Catholicism. *See* Catholicism

Roman Empire, 14, 15, 16, 17, 18, 20, 21, 93, 220, 225

Sabbath, 8, 32, 185, 193, 205–206

sacrifice, 82, 83–84, 86, 88, 89

Sadducees, 142, 146, 153, 210

saints, 20, 24, 47, 149–150, 164, 171, 233

salvation, 2, 68, 81–85

Satan, 163, 164, 234; as angel who rebelled, 174–175; death of Jesus as payment to, 2, 33–34, 45, 82; in hell, 169, 170; humans under control of, 133; images of, 167–168; in Job, 59, 91

savior. *See* salvation

Saxons, 217

Schism, Great, 22, 222

Schweitzer, Albert, 240

Servant Leadership, as tenet of Jesus, 6–7, 223, 228, 233, 240, 244

simile, 26

Simon Stylites, 24, 226

Simons, Menno, 239

sin, original: Anabaptists, 237; Augustine, 123, 127–128, 133, 137; and the Fall, 121; Jesus, not in, 121, 235; Luther and Calvin, 83, 86, 88, 126–127, 127, 133, 138; Paul of Tarsus, 122; Sproul, R. C., 129

slavery, 21, 34, 63–64, 65, 67, 82, 181, 188, 191–192, 213, 227, 238

Smith, William Robertson, 71

Snow, Samuel, 45

Social Gospel, 240

Socialism, as tenet of Jesus, 207, 223, 227, 233, 237, 240, 244

sola scriptura, 66, 68

son of David, 77, 90

son of God: Jesus as, 14, 27, 54, 77, 89–92, 95, 96, 101, 112; Satan as, 175

son of man, 41, 64, 77, 89, 148, 176

Song of Solomon, 52, 58

ABOUT THE AUTHOR

John Morreall is professor and chair of the Department of Religious Studies at the College of William & Mary in Virginia. His books on religion are *Analogy and Talking about God*; *Comedy, Tragedy, and Religion*; *The Religion Toolkit: A Complete Guide to Religious Studies*; and *50 Myths about Religions*. A member of the Fellowship of Merry Christians, he is also an expert on the nature and value of humor, with his books *Taking Laughter Seriously*; *The Philosophy of Laughter and Humor*; *Humor Works*; and *Comic Relief: A Comprehensive Philosophy of Humor*. He is currently at work on his second book on humor in religion: *Divine Comedy*.

CPSIA information can be obtained at www.ICGtesting.com
Printed in the USA
BVOW07*0905100614

355926BV00002B/2/P